Single-chip Microcomputers

Single-chip Microcomputers

Edited by
PAUL F. LISTER

McGRAW-HILL BOOK COMPANY
New York   St. Louis   San Francisco   Montreal   Toronto

Library of Congress Cataloging in Publication Data
Main entry under title:
Single-chip microcomputers.

Includes index.
1. Microcomputers. 2. Microprocessors. I. Lister,
Paul F. II. Title: Single-chip micro-computers.
QA76.5.S5538 1984 001.64 84-19444
ISBN 0-07-038030-9

First published in Great Britain by
Granada Publishing 1984

1234567890 DOC/DOC 8987654

ISBN 0-07-038030-9

Printed and bound by R. R. Donnelley & Sons Company.

Contents

*Reprinted with permission from *Electronic Design*, vol. 31, No. 11; copyright Hayden
Publishing Company, Inc., 1983.
[†]No longer at Mostek.

Preface

Single-chip microcomputers, or microcontrollers as they are sometimes called, are of major significance to applications engineers. These more dedicated devices significantly outstrip general-purpose microprocessors in terms of dollar volume. Shipments of single-chip microcomputers have been predicted to grow at a compound rate of 77% per annum to a level of nearly 3 billion dollars in 1985 (source: Creative Strategies International). This rate is faster than for other integrated components.

Semiconductor manufacturers produce a variety of single-chip microcomputers ranging from simple, cheap, 4-bit microcontrollers to comparatively powerful devices with capabilities rivalling the most powerful general-purpose processor chips. The major impact of microelectronics on products is coming from single-chip microcomputers. These devices are used in products as diverse as hand-held games, washing machines, cars, televisions and computer peripherals.

The central objective of this book is to provide engineers, technicians and engineering managers with a broad view of the types of device available, their characteristics and some insight into the sorts of applications that different devices have been used in. Applications material is important because while the detail may be specifically directed to one device, central issues such as interfacing strategies are generally applicable. Many potential users of single-chip microcomputers have little electronics experience (a typical use of these devices is as timer/controllers to replace electromechanical components). It is hoped that the material presented here will go some way to raise the level of confidence of these potential users.

Chapter 1 provides an introduction to the world of single-chip microcomputers. Relatively little prior knowledge is assumed; a reader with some elementary familiarity with the architecture of popular microprocessors such as the Intel 8080, Zilog Z80 or Rockwell 6502 found in many personal computers and single-board educational systems, will have little difficulty with this chapter. A historical overview is followed by an overview of the structure of microcomputers. A section on special architecture microcomputers is included since devices of this type are of growing importance. The rest of this chapter is a discussion of the major issues that arise in designing a microcomputer into a product.

Chapters 2 to 6 are manufacturer specific chapters, each discussing one manufacturer's microcomputers. Each chapter presents an introduction to the major family members and discusses applications. Most include detailed application material that will prove valuable to applications engineers who will be designing microcomputer based products. This material along with much of the discussions of architecture, peripheral devices and programming issues, provides a broad background of insight and experience that will be valuable regardless of the specific micro-computer context in which an applications engineer is working.

Chapter 2 discusses the Motorola M6801 and M6805 families. The comprehensive presentation of the instruction set and hardware features provides a good general introduction for the reader who has little background in these areas. The case study of a speedometer/tachometer/odometer is presented in sufficient detail to be a valuable introductory example of applications engineering.

Chapter 3 presents an overview of the Texas Instruments TMS1000 and TMS7000 series. The TMS1000 is currently the most pervasive device, widely used in high volume low-cost applications.

Chapter 4 presents the relatively advanced Zilog Z8 in some detail along with variants such as the Z8671 with a BASIC interpreter in ROM and various Z8 family peripheral devices.

Chapter 5 presents the National Semiconductor COPS 400 micro-controllers. These devices are biased towards high volume, low-cost applications. A case study of a digital TV tuning system is discussed.

Chapter 6 presents an overview of the Mostek MK68200, an advanced 16-bit microcomputer based on the powerful architecture of the MK68000 microprocessor. The capabilities of this device in the context of robotic control systems is discussed.

A book such as this is only possible through the efforts of the contributing authors, Graham Livey, Chris Moller, Brian Jasper, Reinhold Hohol, Alan Gant, Patrick McGehearty, Denise Burrows and Peter Vinson.

I wish to thank the microcomputer manufacturers, Motorola, Texas Instruments, Zilog, Intel, National Semiconductor and Mostek for their co-operation and permission to reproduce various figures. Dr Livey would like to thank M. Ritchie, M. Catherwood, R. Bettelheim and J. R. Livey for their help with Chapter 2. Thanks are also due to Bernard Watson of Granada for his assistance and to my wife, Muriel Lister, for typing and secretarial services.

Paul F. Lister
University of Sussex

CHAPTER 1

Microcomputer Fundamentals

By Paul F. Lister

1.1 EVOLUTION OF THE MICROCOMPUTER

The single-chip microcomputer is the culmination of both the development of the digital computer and the integrated circuit, arguably the two most significant inventions of the century.

Digital computers have developed from a historical background of calculating machine evolution spanning several hundred years. It is generally accepted that the major milestone in the development of the first computer was the Analytical Engine designed by Charles Babbage in around 1837. This mechanical design, although never fully implemented, had all the major characteristics of a modern computer. It was, however, some hundred years later that the developments that led directly to the modern digital computer took place.

Howard Aiken pioneered the development of a calculating machine based on relays, the Mark 1 built for IBM in 1944, at Harvard. The first electronic computer ENIAC (Electronic Numerical Integrator and Calculator) followed in 1946 developed by John Mauchly. This slow, primitive machine was based on some 18,000 valves (vacuum tubes) and weighed 30 tons. At this time a computer called EDVAC (Electronic Discrete Variable Automatic Computer) was being developed by John von Neumann and others at Princeton; it was completed in 1951. The major concept introduced by von Neumann was that of combining the separate program and data stores of the Aiken machine and hence storing both program and data in the same format so that machine instructions could be processed by the machine itself. This ability for the machine to manipulate its own instructions has facilitated the development of higher-level languages for computer programming.

These two types of architecture are found in single-chip microcomputers. Some employ the split program/data memory of the Harvard architecture, shown in Fig. 1.1, others follow the philosophy, widely adopted for general-purpose computers and microprocessors, of making no logical distinction between program and data memory as in the Princeton architecture, shown in Fig. 1.2.

The second generation of computers followed the development of the transistor in 1948. As larger machines evolved through the 1960s with more sophisticated operating systems, the third generation evolved.

1

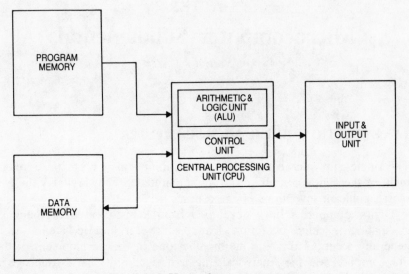

Fig. 1.1 A Harvard type computer.

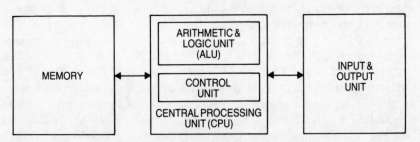

Fig. 1.2 A conventional Princeton computer.

The integrated circuit, involving the placing of more than one transistor on a piece of semiconductor, was the cornerstone of this development. These early integrated circuits had only a few (~20) transistors connected to form a module. However, as fabrication techniques developed it was possible to place more and more components in an integrated circuit. Small-scale integrated (SSI) circuits led to medium-scale integrated (MSI) devices (a few hundred transistors) and then around 1970 to large-scale integrated (LSI) circuits with a few thousand transistors in a circuit. The application of LSI devices to computer design has given rise to a fourth generation of computers. The next generation, the fifth, based on genuine very-large-scale integrated (VLSI) circuits and artificial intelligence methods, is currently the subject of intense worldwide development stimulated by a Japanese initiative.

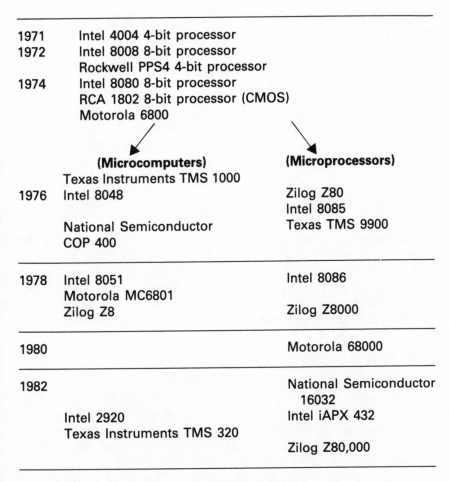

Fig. 1.3 Microcomputer evolution.

The LSI technology of the early 1970s enabled a small computer to be built using just a few integrated circuits. This was recognised by Marcian E 'Ted' Hoff Jr. who was working at Intel on a programmable calculator project and who is generally credited as being the inventor of the microprocessor. This led to the development of the Intel 4004 CPU – a 4-bit processor implemented using about 2,300 transistors. This and the development of the EPROM (erasable programmable read only memory) were the pivotal developments in the microprocessor revolution.

The Intel 8008, an 8-bit processor followed in 1972. In 1974 Intel introduced the 8080 which, along with the Zilog Z80 (introduced in 1976), has been widely adopted in personal computers. Around this time Texas Instruments introduced their 4-bit single-chip microcomputer, the

TMS 1000, which has become widely used in consumer products such as toys and games; devices such as this that are widely used as logic replacement are often called microcontrollers. This type of device reflects the beginning of the dichotomy that separates single-chip microcomputers from microprocessors. A manufacturer of large integrated circuits is faced with the problem of how best to use the circuit complexity available. At a given state of fabrication technology it is possible to design a relatively powerful processor or a less powerful processor and include the other functional units necessary to provide a complete microcomputer. Figure 1.3 illustrates this with some approximately contemporary examples.

1.2 STRUCTURE OF A MICROCOMPUTER

In general terms a single-chip microcomputer is characterised by the incorporation of all the units of a computer, as shown in Figs 1.1 or 1.2, into a single device. Figure 1.4 illustrates the principal features found in many microcomputers. The characteristics of these features are discussed in outline in the following sections as a general introduction to the aspects of particular facilities that are discussed in subsequent chapters.

1.2.1 Read only memory (ROM)

ROM is usually for the permanent, non-volatile storage of an applications program. Many microcomputers and microcontrollers are intended for high-volume applications and hence the economical manufacture of the devices requires that the contents of the program memory be committed permanently during the manufacture of the chips. Clearly, this implies a rigorous approach to ROM code development (see section 1.5.5) since changes cannot be made after manufacture. This development process may involve emulation using a sophisticated development system with a hardware emulation capability as well as the use of powerful software tools.

Some manufacturers provide additional ROM options by including in their range devices with (or intended for use with) user programmable memory. The simplest of these is usually a device which can operate in a microprocessor mode by using some of the input/output lines as an address and data bus for accessing external memory. This type of device can behave functionally as the single-chip microcomputer from which it is derived albeit with restricted I/O and a modified external circuit. The use of these ROMless devices is common even in production circuits where the volume does not justify the development costs of custom on-chip ROM; there can still be a significant saving in I/O and other chips compared to a conventional microprocessor based circuit. More exact

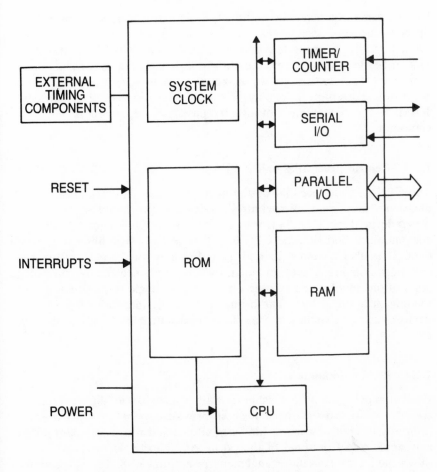

Fig. 1.4 Principal features of a microcomputer.

replacements for ROM devices can be obtained in the form of variants with 'piggy-back' EPROM (Erasable Programmable ROM) sockets or devices with EPROM instead of ROM. These devices are naturally more expensive than the equivalent ROM device, but do provide complete circuit equivalents. EPROM based devices are also extremely attractive for low-volume applications where they provide the advantages of a single-chip device, in terms of on-chip I/O, etc., with the convenience of flexible user programmability.

1.2.2 Read/write memory (RAM)

RAM is for the storage of working variables and data used during program execution. The size of this memory varies with device type but it has the same characteristic width (4, 8, 16 bits, etc.) as the processor. Special function registers, such as a stack pointer or timer register are often logically incorporated into the RAM area. It is also common in Harvard type microcomputers to treat the RAM area as a collection of registers; it is unnecessary to make a distinction between RAM and processor registers as is done in the case of a microprocessor system since RAM and registers are not usually physically separated in a micro-computer.

1.2.3 Central processing unit (CPU)

The CPU is much like that of any microprocessor. Many applications of microcomputers and microcontrollers involve the handling of binary-coded decimal (BCD) data (for numerical displays, for example), hence it is common to find that the CPU is well adapted to handling this type of data. It is also common to find good facilities for testing, setting and resetting individual bits of memory or I/O since many controller applications involve the turning on and off of single output lines or the reading of a single line. These lines are readily interfaced to two-state devices such as switches, thermostats, solid-state relays, valves, motors, etc.

1.2.4 Parallel input/output

Parallel input and output schemes vary somewhat in different micro-computers; in most a mechanism is provided to at least allow some flexibility of choosing which pins are outputs and which are inputs. This may apply to all or some of the ports. As an example of this, Fig. 1.5 shows the internal circuit arrangement for an Intel 8048/8051 bidirectional I/O pin. Writing a '1' to the pin causes Q2 to turn on for a short time providing fast totem-pole TTL compatible pull-up of the output. However, the pin is held up by R1 which is about 50 kilohms; large enough to allow an external output connected to the pin to pull it down if the pin is an input. Hence to use a pin as an input simply requires that a '1' be written out to it to ensure that Q1 is off.

Some I/O lines are suitable for direct interfacing to, for example, fluorescent displays, or can provide sufficient current to make interfacing to other components straightforward.

Some devices allow an I/O port to be configured as a system bus to allow off-chip memory and I/O expansion. This facility is potentially useful as a product range develops, since successive enhancements may become too big for on-chip memory and it is undesirable not to build on the existing software base.

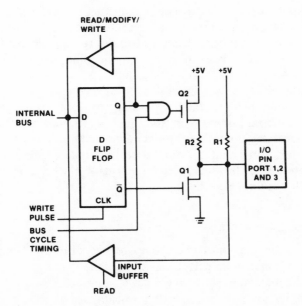

Fig. 1.5 Intel pseudo-bidirectional I/O port circuitry (Source: Intel Corp.).

1.2.5 Serial input/output

Serial communication with terminal devices is a common means of providing a link using a small number of lines. This sort of communication can also be exploited for interfacing special function chips or linking several microcomputers together. Both the common asynchronous and synchronous communication schemes require protocols that provide framing (start and stop) information. This can be implemented as a hardware facility or U(S)ART (Universal (synchronous) asynchronous receiver/transmitter) relieving the processor (and the applications programmer) of this low-level, time-consuming, detail. It is merely necessary to select a baud-rate and possibly other options (number of stop bits, parity, etc.) and load (or read from) the serial transmitter (or receiver) buffer. Serialisation of the data in the appropriate format is then handled by the hardware circuit.

1.2.6 Timer/counter facilities

Many applications of single-chip microcomputers require accurate evaluation of elapsed real time. This can be determined by careful assessment of the execution time of each branch in a program but this rapidly becomes inefficient for all but the simplest programs. The preferred approach is to use a timer circuit that can independently count precise time increments and generate an interrupt after a preset time has elapsed. This type of timer is usually arranged to be preloadable with the required count. The timer then decrements this value producing an interrupt or setting a flag when the counter reaches zero. Better timers then have the ability to automatically reload the initial count value. This relieves the programmer of the responsibility of reloading the counter and assessing the elapsed time before the timer is restarted, which otherwise would be necessary if continuous precisely timed interrupts were required (as in a clock, for example). Sometimes associated with a timer is an event counter. With this facility there is usually a special input pin, that can drive the counter directly.

1.2.7 Timing components

The clock circuitry of most microcomputers requires only simple timing components. If maximum performance is required, a crystal must be used to ensure the maximum clock frequency is approached but not exceeded. Many clock circuits also work with a resistor and capacitor as low-cost timing components or can be driven from an external source. This latter arrangement is useful if external synchronisation of the microcomputer is required.

1.3 4-, 8- AND 16-BIT DEVICES

Microcomputers and computers in general are usually classified in terms of the characteristic width of the internal data paths. This width, 4, 8, 16 or 32 bits, has a great bearing on the performance of the device in specific applications. There are currently no 32-bit single-chip microcomputers, but this is perhaps only a matter of time; such devices would form the heart of high-performance, low-cost personal and small business computers.

The data path width inside a microcomputer implies that there is circuitry to manipulate that number of bits in parallel during an operation. Circuit complexity is therefore virtually a linear function of this width. It is usually more economical in chip area and hence yield and production costs to produce 4-bit devices rather than 8 or 16-bit ones. However, 4-bit devices, for example, are not suited to all types of application.

It is a feature of practically all reasonable general-purpose computer architectures that, regardless of data path width, any computational problem can be solved, in a logical sense, by any processor. The crucial issue is the time it takes and, to a lesser extent, the ease of programming it.

Four-bit devices are widely used in calculators and small controllers. This type of device can handle binary coded decimal (BCD) data one decimal digit at a time. Information involving more than one decimal digit must be processed in a digit serial manner. Individual bits can be manipulated readily for I/O purposes, but address processing with only 4-bits is difficult. These devices are therefore suited to low end applications involving relatively small amounts of data driven by modest scale programs operating within a comparatively relaxed time scale. Devices such as these satisfy many application requirements and they represent the largest single category of microprocessor type components. Texas Instruments claim to have shipped in excess of sixty million of their TMS1000 family 4-bit microcomputers.

Eight-bit microcomputers represent, for many more demanding applications, a sensible compromise in terms of performance and on-chip circuit utilisation. With 8 bits, two BCD characters can be manipulated simultaneously. Eight bits is necessary for the convenient handling of alphanumeric data in the ASCII code widely used in terminals, displays and character handling in general. Reasonable precision arithmetic is possible with 16-bit data which is not too onerous with an 8-bit processor.

This is also a convenient size for instruction op-codes and addresses can be specified with only one or two 8-bit words. Hence it is feasible to modify the strictly Harvard architecture to allow a measure of flexible interaction between program and data memories.

Sixteen-bit devices can offer the general-purpose computing capabilities of a small minicomputer and the regularity of architecture and instruction set found in microprocessors such as the Zilog Z8000, Motorola 68,000 or the National Semiconductor 16032. This size of data path permits alphanumerical data in ASCII, etc., to be packed at two characters per word or BCD packed at four digits per word.

Sixteen bits is much more appropriate for signal derived data. Digital representations of signals correspond (if properly scaled) to a signal-to-noise power ratio of approximately 6 dB per bit of representation. This means that 8 bits allows a maximum of around 50 dB signal-to-noise ratio. This is not very good in analogue circuit terms and there is no room for adding the signal samples together, for example, without continuously having to rescale. Twelve bits is more appropriate for most applications (~70 dB) and a 16-bit processor can handle this data directly with some headroom. Clearly, 12- or 16-bit data can be manipulated with an 8/bit (or 4-bit) processor, but with a time penalty. It should be borne in mind that double word length operations often involve more than just the required operation applied to each half of the data in turn. Intermediate carries have to be managed and appropriately different sign management undertaken for each part of the data. This can mean that double word length operations take significantly more than twice the execution time of a single length operation.

Thirty-two-bit processors offer the capability of handling a good resolution floating-point number as a single datum as well as the vast addressing and comprehensive processing capabilities normally associated with these microprocessors.

1.4 SPECIAL PURPOSE MICROCOMPUTERS

Some applications demand performance that is not available with a general-purpose architecture; this has given rise to a group of micro-computers with architectures adapted to a particular type of task. Signal processing is one such area and devices suited to this are finding application in telecommunications and instrumentation systems.

The digital processing of analogue signals is about performing operations on digital representations of analogue data. This invariably requires real-time processing involving operations that general-purpose architectures are not particularly optimised for. Specifically, multiplication is often central to the processing required.

For example, digital filters are usually implemented as a summation of previous stored values each weighted by a coefficient. Hence in the time interval between one input sample and the next many multiplications may be required.

1.4.1 Intel 2920

The Intel 2920 is a radical departure in the development of single-chip microcomputers. It is the first major deviation for a device of this type from a general-purpose architecture. As such it is surely the first of many such devices to come. The 2920 has an architecture specifically arranged to permit the fast, real-time, handling of analogue signals.

A block diagram of the 2920 is shown in Fig. 1.6 and Fig. 1.7 shows the analogue section in more detail. Four analogue inputs and eight analogue outputs are provided, all are multiplexed from a single 9-bit digital to analogue converter. Figure 1.8 illustrates the arithmetic unit and data memory organisation. This area bears a close resemblance to the ALU and scratchpad memory arrangement of a bit-slice processor such as the Advanced Micro Devices Am2901. Note, however, that data words are 25 bits long.

Control of the RAM, shifter, ALU and analogue sections is managed in parallel at the microprogram level. In fact the basic instructions of the 2920 are microinstructions and they do not decode to sequences of lower level steps. All arithmetic operations are performed in two's complement representation as are shifts (the sign-bit is brought down).

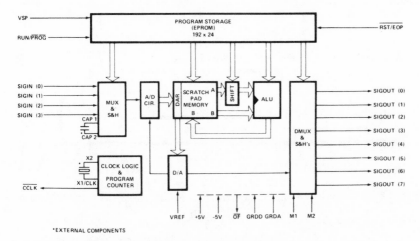

Fig. 1.6 Block diagram of the Intel 2920 (Source: Intel Corp.).

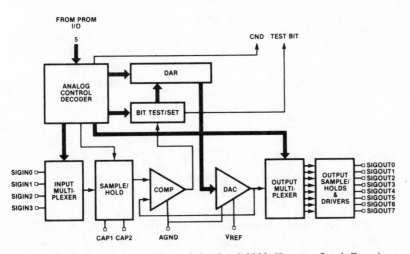

Fig. 1.7 The analogue section of the Intel 2920 (Source: Intel Corp.).

Although no multiplication hardware is included, multiplication, particularly by a constant, can readily be implemented by successive additions of shifted operands. A single shift operation allows an operand to be moved any amount from up two places to down thirteen places. No conditional branching is allowed (this is usually unnecessary in signal processing) although conditional arithmetic is; hence a sample period typically consists of the sequential execution of all 192 instructions each requiring around 400 nanoseconds; the sampling rate is then approximately 13 kHz.

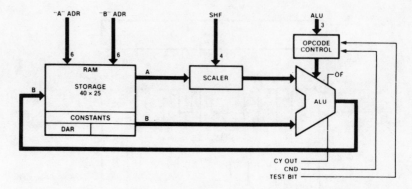

Fig. 1.8 Arithmetic unit and data memory organisation of the Intel 2920 (Source: Intel Corp.).

Some application areas for the 2920 are:

1. *Filtering* – around 40 poles (20 complex pairs) are possible.
2. *Waveform generation* – arbitrary functions with external control.
3. *Low frequency modulation and demodulation* – AM, FM or PM.
4. *Non-linear functions* – rectifiers, limiters, multipliers, etc.
5. *Other functions* – phase-locked loops, adaptive filters, linearisation.

1.4.2 Texas Instruments TMS320

The TMS 320 is another device with an architecture adapted for real-time signal processing. The main features are a 16-bit parallel hardware multiplier and a 32-bit accumulator (Fig. 1.9). A barrel shifter is also provided with capabilities similar to that in the Intel 2920 for performing multiple place shifts in a single operation. The TMS320 does not incorporate an analogue interface but does have a flexible and powerful instruction set which makes it suitable for application areas such as digital filtering, Fourier analysis, speech analysis and synthesis and image processing.

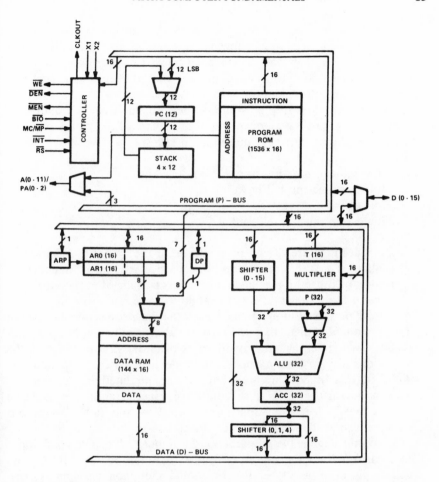

Fig. 1.9 TMS320 architecture (Source: Texas Instruments).

1.5 MICROCOMPUTER SYSTEM DESIGN ISSUES (with Chris Moller[†] and Peter Vinson[*])

1.5.1 Writing a functional specification

The advice 'Start by thinking out what you want it to do' may seem rather obvious, but the temptation in microcomputer product design is to take a rather woolly idea along to the microcomputer manufacturer and let him do the product definition on your behalf. Clearly, the manufacturer

[†]See Chapter Three.
[*]Peter Vinson is with Texas Instruments Ltd.

knows best what the chip can do. However, this awareness of the potential of the device, while allowing the customer to more fully exploit the device chosen, may lead the customer away from his original concept, which was orientated towards a market that the customer probably understands far better than the manufacturer.

Therefore, the first step must always be to define what is required, in layman's terms. Little understanding of the technical realities is required at this stage. Some pertinent questions to ask are:

How will the user interact with the machine?
How portable must it be?
How durable must it be?
How much must it sell for?

These questions are driven by inputs from the customer's marketing organisation. The user interaction issue particularly, is of fundamental importance, as it can be the single most important factor in the success or otherwise of the product. It is worthwhile to write out, quite informally, scripts for typical user interactions. Check that keypress sequences cannot get unreasonably long; that the system can only be in one (or just possibly, two) states, when a given series of outputs is presented to the user. In this way an ideal machine can be defined. Later, the parameters defined at this stage may well have to be modified in the light of engineering constraints, but this initial product definition provides a yardstick by which it is possible to measure how fully initial aspirations have been achieved, when the final design is assessed.

The second stage is the preparation of a complete functional definition. This is driven from the user specification outlined above, but must be much more rigorous. It is the functional definition that the system engineer will work to, and it is the engineer's job to interpret it completely literally. This is especially true when the engineer is outside the organisation. Again, there may be changes to the functional specification during the engineering work, but these should be minor changes of detail, and should be put down in writing and appended to the functional specification. Following is a check-list of items a functional specification for a microcomputer project should include:

Environmental conditions:
 Operating temperature*;
 Storage temperature;
 Humidity and Corrosion;
 Vibration;
 User abuse.
Necessary safety standards*.

Repairability/modularity.
Complete functional description of user interface to software.
Definition of any hardware interfaces used.
Display size, colour, brightness.
Keyboard size.
Size and Weight*.
Battery life/power consumption*.
Failure modes.
Prototype requirements:
    Form;
    Function;
    Form and function.
Maximum component cost.
Any information which is available about future directions for the product (this may influence decisions taken at the outset).

The points marked * are particularly important 'make-or-break' factors, where it is unlikely that a compromise could be reached at a late stage in the design cycle to fulfil an undeclared constraint. For example, a requirement for the system to operate at temperatures up to 100°C might well rule out all members of a microcomputer family! A feasibility study may well be considered desirable where the microcomputer manufacturer will be doing the design work. The purpose of this study is to show that the manufactuer's product will indeed perform the required function. (The manufacturer would be most unhappy to spend a large amount of engineer time on the project, only to find that it was required by the specification to design with a competitor's part!!) Provided that at the conclusion of the feasibility study the functional specification is firm, acceptance of the project by the engineer represents a high degree of confidence that it can be met. For this reason, concessions may be sought at that stage, for anything which might materially affect the viability of the project. Incidentally, the semiconductor manufacturer runs a design service with the ultimate objective of selling silicon, and so it is in the manufacturer's interest to ensure that reasonable values are taken for any parameters not given in the specification.

1.5.2 Is a custom part the answer?

The reason for considering a custom masked part is almost invariably cost. It is very easy to be seduced by extremely low unit costs quoted by the manufacturer, combined with a circuit diagram which only has a handful of components. However, in many cases, the total cost of production has not changed; what has happened is that the costs have become less visible. How does one assess these hidden costs, to confirm that a custom-masked part really is the way to go?

All electronic design requires an initial marketing input, in addition to the technical specifications discussed above, namely, the quantity of product at which the total project cost divided by the quantity to be sold is a minimum. To give an extreme example, consider a heating controller. If only one of this type is going to be built, the development costs will exceed the cost of the components, almost no matter how it is built. Therefore, the optimum solution is probably to buy boards off-the-shelf, and program them in a high-level language. However, if hundreds of thousands are to be built, the development cost will be insignificant, when amortised across all the products, and the cost of the individual components in each unit becomes the most significant factor. It is in this field that the single-chip microcomputer can really excel. If the initial assumption is that the development costs will be paid off over, say, the first 20,000, then additional sales will be very profitable. However, there are inevitably pitfalls with custom parts which deserve discussion.

1.5.2.1 CASH FLOW

Looked at in the broadest sense, the choice of a mask-ROMed part is an initial investment of money, to ultimately save money when large volumes of the final product are produced. Most of this money has to be invested before the first sample parts appear. Costs are incurred both by the customer, getting his code developed, emulated, and completely debugged, and by the manufacturer, who, in putting this code on to a special mask, incurs material and labour costs. He will usually ask the customer to pay these costs on receipt of the first samples, regardless of whether he ultimately orders a quantity or not.

1.5.2.2 MINIMUM QUANTITIES

On receipt of the code, the manufacturer produces a sample batch of parts. From this, several thousand silicon chips are obtained, and so the manufacturer must charge the cost of all of this material to the customer. Fortunately a significant part of the cost of an integrated circuit is in the packaging, so he will normally only package as many parts as are needed for evaluation samples, prior to getting an order for a production quantity. Once that approval is received, the manufacturer can package the remainder of the batch relatively easily. Only at this point does it start to become cost-effective, and that is why a manufacturer will insist on an order for a minimum quantity.

1.5.2.3 PROTOTYPING

One of the motives for specifying a custom part is to lower the component count. In general, re-programmable (EPROM) parts will either require more components (e.g. separate EPROMs) or an expensive 'piggy-back' package, where the EPROM sits on top of the microcomputer package. In either case, significant additional cost will be incurred for units which are required to emulate the final product both in form and function. Also, it is likely that a reprogrammable solution will drain more current than the custom part, and this may entail unsightly battery packs for prototypes (or a cable under the table!). All of this tends to mean that it is difficult (but probably not impossible, in most cases) to produce a small batch of units, for example to test market acceptability, and then either migrate to a masked product, or go back and iterate the design.

1.5.2.4 INFLEXIBILITY

As indicated above, iterative design, with successive market trials, is difficult from a product engineering point of view. It also tends to lead to lots of good ideas which come in as the program is going to mask. This is dangerous, because it means that the most recent good ideas will have been implemented, but not fully tested. A serious software bug is potentially disastrous, when it has been cast into silicon. The only way round it is to remask, or devise a hardware fix (only sometimes possible, and almost always adding something to the cost of every unit). Given the total inflexibility of ROM-based code, considerable care must be taken by the software author to write rigorous code (often difficult in the restricted machine-code of lower-cost microcomputers), and by the product engineers designing the hardware of the product. Typically, timescales are short, and only a short time allowed for emulation of the hardware (it may even still be in design when the software goes to mask!) and the later any mistake is spotted, the more expensive it will be to get around it.

Perhaps this sounds a little daunting to the newcomer, and so a reminder of what the objective is, is probably in order. A custom-masked microcomputer represents a completely general-purpose device, with the capacity of tens of thousands of transistors, for less than the cost of half a dozen TTL packages. In a really cost-effective design, the microcomputer may well perform ALL the necessary electronic functions, and surely for electronics per penny, the single-chip microcomputer must remain unbeatable for a long while to come.

1.5.3 Could a microcomputer cope?

Having established that a microcomputer is the way to go, the next task is to choose a particular type, preferably the cheapest that will fulfil all the design requirements. Not only does the design engineer have to assess rival manufacturers' claims, but he has to use yardsticks that are appreciably different from those used to assess microprocessor performance. Although processing power may be a factor (as outlined below), it is not usually the main one. These are the factors to consider when assessing a particular product's suitability.

1.5.3.1 INPUT AND OUTPUT

One of the first areas to cut down on when attempting to reduce the cost of producing a part is the Input and Output. Extensive I/O costs the manufacturer money due both to the more expensive packaging required as the pin-count increases, and the additional testing required. Hence, parts with few I/O pins will be much less expensive than those with more. Judging the minimum I/O requirements should be one of the first areas for attention in producing a minimum cost design. As suggested elsewhere in this book, individual contact-closures do not require their own input pins on the microcomputer, unless they are changing very rapidly. Similarly, outputs can be multiplexed to displays, to take advantage of persistence of vision. Though many input events may be tested by a polling routine, input events which require rapid response (say less than 500 microseconds), even when the microcomputer is busy doing other things, may necessitate an interrupt input, not provided in some parts.

If additional microprocessor peripheral chips are needed to complete the system function, a bus interface will be needed, and as this requires quite a number of pins to implement completely, many single-chip microcomputers do not provide one. Those that do usually do so as an option, at the expense of a number of regular I/O pins. However, even the apparent need for a bus can sometimes be eliminated by clever design. For example, a PMOS microcomputer may require a small (say 128 bits) non-volatile memory (not normally available on-chip). Were this to be implemented using a conventional CMOS 128 × 1 RAM, seven address lines, plus data in and out, and a Read/Write line would be required; a total of ten lines. Use of a shift-register instead, while not providing true random-access, would only require data in/out and a clock signal – a total of three lines.

1.5.3.2 CODE SIZE

Microcomputers usually come in various sizes within a product family, with differing amounts of I/O, RAM and ROM. Of course, the cost increases correspondingly. As the program specification expands and more features are added, it may well be that the program size goes just over the planned 1024 bytes (or equivalent), necessitating the next larger part, and possibly increasing the cost by 50%. In this case, the extra bells and whistles will have proved very expensive. On the other hand, if the basic function really does need just a little over a kilobyte, any additional features that the designer can fit into the remainder of the 2 Kbytes comes for free! As RAM is much more expensive to implement than ROM, in terms of silicon 'real-estate', far fewer bytes of RAM are usually provided. As additional features tend also to need additional variables, RAM space may also become a decisive factor in assessing the necessary microcomputer size. A sense of perspective is therefore needed about the real cost of additional features.

1.5.3.3 PROCESSING POWER

Usually, the rate at which input information can be handled, and output information generated, is not a limitation in microcontroller applications.

Real-world processes happen far slower than the microcomputer executes code. However, there are a couple of danger areas to check out. The first of these concerns the 'divide-by-n' problem. Suppose that it is required to produce a musical scale square-wave output. The usual way to do this is to have a fast counter which counts (normally down) a predetermined amount, toggles the output, and then repeats the process. Notes that are a semitone apart have frequencies in the ratio 100:106 approximately (= 50:53), meaning that for a given frequency, and one a semitone lower, the fast loop must be going about 100 times faster (to go round the loop twice per cycle). For a 1 kHz tone, the decrement-and-jump sequence must therefore execute in less than 10 microseconds – too fast for most low-cost microcomputers. In practice, this means that at higher frequencies, liberties may have to be taken with the musical scale.

The second problem arises when something must not be interrupted while something else is attended to. For example, it is irritating if the multiplexed display flickers while the measurements are being taken. (The irritation, incidentally, depends both on the duration of the flicker, and its frequency.) If the measurements have to be taken every time the display is multiplexed, it becomes important to keep measurement time to a minimum, or the display will not spend a sufficient percentage of the time on, and will appear dim to the user. This becomes more acute with, for example, light-emitting diode displays, as the number of digits to be multiplexed increases, and beyond about twelve digits, this becomes insoluble, without driving the displays with very large peak currents, (via correspondingly expensive driver transistors), in order to keep the average current at a reasonable level.

1.5.3.4 REAL-TIME PROGRAMMING

A frequent system requirement is for the microcomputer to keep track of the time of day, or otherwise do something at a precisely defined time interval. This may present something of a problem. Microcomputers, when executing code, will typically execute different branches of the code in different circumstances. For example, a heating controller will execute one branch if the room is already warm enough, and another if it needs heating. As normally written, these two branches will take slightly different amounts of time to execute. If it is arranged that the program update a 'time-of-day' clock every second, one of these branches will cause the clock to lose or gain. Over weeks or months, the error may become quite significant. One solution is to pad out the shorter branch with delays, so that both are the same. In practice, though, there are usually so many different possible branches that writing code this way is extremely difficult. It also causes another requirement, namely that the speed of the microcomputer remains constant with variations in temperature, battery life, etc. This means that a crystal or ceramic resonator must be used as the timing element for the chip, rather than a less expensive resistor-capacitor network.

A better solution is to make the program run faster than necessary, and then wait for an externally driven event to increment the time-of-day. Mains-driven equipment is often designed this way, using the mains waveform as the timing source. If an internal timer is used, accuracy will usually demand a crystal clock source for the microcomputer.

1.5.3.5 POWER DRAIN

Some microcomputer applications require very low power drain, either because they must operate for long periods without access to mains power, or because the equipment into which they are being put is small (as in the case of hand-held instruments). As discussed previously, these considerations lead naturally to CMOS parts. However, even these have a significant power drain while operating (though not as high as PMOS), and so they are usually provided with a 'power-down' mode. This turns off the bulk of the chip, leaving only the RAM containing the program variables powered-up, and also the real-time clock, if present. Typically, the microcomputer wakes up either on an external stimulus (such as a keypress), or on an interrupt from the timer (i.e. after a preset amount of time). To keep the average power consumption low, it continues to be important that the periodic processing on 'wake-up' is kept short. Another important factor for CMOS is that the power consumption is roughly proportional to the system clock frequency, and so for the lowest possible current drain, the chip should be run at the lowest frequency consistent with reliable operation and getting everything done in time. CMOS parts will also operate over a wider voltage range than competing technologies, and power consumption is again very roughly proportional to supply voltage. Where current drain and battery size are both at a premium, for example in digital watches, operating voltages as low as 1.5 volts are found. However, special manufacturing techniques are required to achieve this, and few microcomputers will work much below 3 volts.

1.5.4 Choosing the most appropriate technology

PMOS technology is nearly twenty years old as a production technology. However, this does not mean that it is obsolete even if the 'glamour' of NMOS and more recently CMOS have overtaken it in pure performance. It remains the simplest process leading to the lowest costs and highest yields and is particularly suitable for 4-bit microcomputers and applications such as speech synthesis where raw speed is unimportant. PMOS devices now use modern processing techniques and can be manufactured to run over a wide voltage range at a fairly low current to allow operation directly from a 9-volt battery. High voltage outputs can also be readily added enabling direct drive to Vacuum Fluorescent displays.

NMOS technology became a production technology a decade ago when processing technology had improved to the stage that n-channel transistors could be reliably formed; since the mobility of electrons in n-channel transistors is higher than that of holes in p-channel transistors, higher speeds were possible since speed is limited by the charging and discharging of on-chip 'wiring' and gate capacitance; however, this performance is at the cost of higher power consumption. Most of the 8-bit microprocessors were designed in NMOS as this gave the 5-volt TTL compatibility needed for the memory and support logic required by a microprocessor. The 8-bit microcomputers are often an extension of these devices as improvements in technology allowed the ROM, RAM and I/O to be moved onto the 'chip', so these, too, have the advantage of speed but again pay the penalty of high power consumption making battery operation difficult.

CMOS was the first mos technology described theoretically. However, it did not become a viable production process until NMOS was producible. Even then the much larger 'chip' area needed for early CMOS processes restricted its application to small scale integration logic (i.e. RCA 4000 CMOS logic). Improvements to CMOS implementation together with general improvements to mask quality and process yields has enabled complete microcomputers to be built using CMOS technology for the past few years. Generally these have been extensions to existing families of 4- or 8-bit microcomputers to minimise the cost of development for both the manufacturer and the user. The advantages of CMOS are the wide operating voltage range and the very low power consumption. The wide operating voltage range is largely due to the 'symmetrical' nature of the circuitry, which tends to make input threshold voltages a percentage of the supply voltage rather than an absolute value. The low power consumption is due to there being two complementary transistors in the path between the power supply lines with only one being on at a time (except possibly during switching from one state to the other), which contrasts with PMOS and NMOS where in one of the logic states there is a current path as both transistors are conducting. Even in mains powered applications CMOS can be useful, as CMOS micro-computers usually have power-down or halt modes where the contents of at least the RAM can be preserved until the next time power is available. Table 1.1. gives a comparison of the major features of these three fabrication technologies.

	PMOS (Metal gate)	NMOS (Silicon gate) (Depletion loads)	CMOS
Relative number of process steps	1	1.2	1.8
Relative clock speed	1	10	(2 metal gate)
Relative power drain	10	50	1
Relative cost	1	1.3	2.0
Operating voltage range ((Vmax-Vmin)/Vav)	Good 30%	Poor 10% to 20%	Very good 75%
Directly display drive	Light Emitting Diode Vacuum Fluorescent	possibly Light Emitting Diode	Liquid Crystal Displays

Table 1.1 Fabrication technologies.

1.5.5 ROM code development and approval cycles

The first, and perhaps the most important, step that takes place when final customer approval of the software for a masked ROM part has taken place is that a copy of the software is archived. This ensures that if it is ever necessary to re-tool the device, for example if a different front-end (manufacturing line) is chosen or different mask size is required, then the data exists to do this.

The object code version of the software is then converted to a 'Gate Placement Deck', which is a standardised format for representing the patterns to be programmed into the ROM of the final device and is largely device independent. This is used as the input data to the 'Gate Placement' program which calculates the positions of the gates required by the software and generates the geometry data for these gates. This geometry data is later merged with the fixed geometries in the non-programmable parts of the device in order to make the final mask.

Most commonly the actual programming takes place by the geometries on the 'Gate' mask defining those transistors (MOSFETS) where the oxide will be thin, which allows the transistor to be turned on by appropriate logic signals; transistors not defined will have thick ('Field') oxide and cannot be turned on under any normal circumstances. In low-threshold technologies this thick oxide alone may be insufficient and these 'unwanted' transistors are ion-implanted by another masking step to guarantee they cannot conduct. Of course, this extra mask is also automatically generated; unfortunately it also adds to the cost, as this mask is also unique to the software.

Contrary to common belief the masking steps unique to the software in a microcomputer are relatively early in the manufacture of the slices (discs of silicon commonly about 100 mm diameter). This contrasts with the masking of, for example, bipolar ROM's, which commonly occurs at the 'Contacts' stage of the processing and which is near the end of the manufacturing process, and this means it is impractical to stockpile part complete slices to speed delivery of prototypes.

To optimise the delivery of the first prototypes, slices can be started in the front-end at the same time as the pattern generator tapes are delivered to the mask manufacturer. This should mean that the finished masks reach the front-end at the stage when they are needed to program the device. Usually only a few slices are processed in a prototype batch to speed production; however, even this small number is usually processed in two halves to ensure that equipment malfunction or operator error does not damage all the prototype material.

While the slices are being processed the 'Automatic Test Generator' program is run, using the original gate placement deck to generate a test program to probe test the slices when they reach the end of the slice manufacturing process and to final test the devices after assembly. Both these tests are carried out on 100% of the devices, and a quality assurance sample will be re-tested at both probe and final test to ensure the appropriate quality level is being met.

Next, the finished slices are assembled to provide the customer samples. Usually the samples will be made using ceramic packages, as although these are more expensive they are more convenient in the small quantities needed for prototype verification; the high degree of automation used in current plastic assembly means that it is very inefficient to consider the assembly of less than 1000 devices at a time.

Finally, the packaged devices are final tested and delivered to the customer for approval. Due to the high degree of automation used in the conversion of the original software to the actual device, the device should function immediately in the application, with perhaps some minor adjustment of some component values from the original emulation (hardware used to 'emulate' the function of the microcomputer during software development).

1.6 FUTURE TRENDS

Microprocessors and microcomputers have evolved rapidly in the last decade from limited, 4-bit, calculator-like circuits employing around a thousand devices, through 8-bit microprocessors such as the Intel 8080 employing around 8000 transistors and the 8048, to the present time where integrated circuits employing around 75,000 transistors, the Motorola 68,000 and the Intel iAPX432 using some 200,000 devices are in production. Many manufacturers are discussing the potential of circuits employing one million devices, expected around 1986. As far as microcomputers are concerned, such devices are likely to be powerful, possibly 32-bit, with a wide range of input and output facilities and large on-chip memories. New features of these circuits are likely to be on-chip speech input-output and high-level language programming. The latter is hinted at by Zilog's Z8671, a mask programmed version of the Z8 with an on-chip BASIC interpreter (see Chapter 4). Also in this direction are several devices (e.g. the Rockwell RF611-12 and Zilog's Z800) which include or are adapted for a threaded-code language such as FORTH. This language has the advantage over interpreted BASIC of generally having a much faster execution speed, making it suitable for real-time control (for which it was developed).

Much of the circuitry of these powerful single-chip microcomputers will be concerned with providing easy-to-use input/output facilities such as analogue I/O and display drivers. Increased customisation will permit the tailoring of I/O to an application by the use of a gate array approach to the I/O area.

It may be possible soon to incorporate sensors on the silicon alongside processing capability. Integrated transducers under development cover temperature, pressure, dew-point, acceleration and hall-effect devices. VLSI technology opens up a wide range of possibilities for the architecture of systems; multiple processor arrangements on a single-chip for either enhanced throughput or fault tolerance; on-chip communication facilities for distributed systems. The Restructurable Integrated Circuit (RIC) from Texas Instruments is an example of such developments. The transputer from Inmos is a single-chip microcomputer specifically organised to be corrected into large processing arrays and pipelines.

Emerging VLSI design methodologies are encouraging chip designers to adopt a much more structured approach than hitherto. Chip topologies are becoming much more regular and regionally defined which makes it easier for a manufacturer to customise the functional units provided on a chip to suit a particular application. This is the next logical step on the path between uncommitted logic arrays and fully custom-designed circuits.

SUMMARY

Microcomputers have evolved from the mainstream developments in computer and integrated circuit technologies. Their structure has much in common with microprocessors and associated devices but with many features, particularly related to input/output, that are adapted to the types of applications that microcomputers are directed at.

Four-bit microcomputers are widely used; 8-bit devices are also very popular since they satisfy many application requirements. Sixteen or more bit architectures are suitable for high-performance systems or applications such as signal, image or speech processing where this data path width, combined with adapted architecture, can yield devices with the necessary speed for these application areas. Some of the system design issues in choosing a microcomputer are examined, highlighting some of the problems that can arise when using a masked-ROM device. The basic issues in assessing the performance of a single-chip micro-computer for a particular application are discussed.

CHAPTER 2

The Motorola M6801 and M6805 Families

By Dr Graham J. Livey

2.1 HISTORICAL BACKGROUND

Although Motorola's first home-grown 8-bit single-chip microcomputer, the MC6801, appeared on the market in 1978, we had, for some time, been producing and testing the MC3870 under a second-sourcing agreement with MOSTEK. The MC3870 allowed us to experience, at first hand, many of the manufacturing and testing problems which are unique to mask programmed single-chip devices. It also gave the opportunity to examine the application areas open to the microcomputer at that time, and to assess the microcomputing power and features needed to open up a wide range of exciting new consumer and industrial markets.

Almost every electrical or electro-mechanical control application existing in the world today could be replaced by a microprocessor controlled system. However, to make the silicon solution acceptable, it must be better or cheaper, and preferably both, than the existing solution. The processing power of the microprocessor makes the first point easy to achieve: in fairly complex, low production volume, control systems, the cost of a microprocessor and its attendant RAM, ROM and peripheral interface circuitry can be far outweighed by the improvement in performance and reliability over its electromechanical equivalent. However, for less complex mass production applications, such as in the automotive and consumer electronics industries, the microcomputer can provide sufficient processing power and interface circuitry on one silicon chip to produce a cost-effective solution to many control problems.

The MC6801 was designed, with all these considerations in mind, around the central processing unit (CPU) of the MC6800 microprocessor, improved and optimised for control applications rather than computing operations. Integral on the silicon chip are several input/output ports to allow the CPU to interface with external circuitry and sensors, a sophisticated multi-function timer, a serial communications interface, and areas of program memory (ROM) and temporary storage (RAM). The MC6801 is a very versatile device, capable of operating not only as a true single-chip microcomputer under the control of the program fixed in its on-board ROM, but also in a number of expanded modes using up to 64 Kbytes of external RAM or ROM. Consequently it is suited to a very wide range of simple and complex control applications.

The MC6801 was designed in NMOS (Negative-channel Metal Oxide on Silicon) with a gate length of 5.1 μm, and contains approximately 25,000 transistors. This resulted in a large die size, and in 1979 the design was converted to HMOS technology (High-density NMOS) with a 3.9 μm geometry. Since the manufacturing costs are directly related to the die size this allowed the MC6801 to be sold at a much lower price.

As prices continue to fall, more and more markets open up to the use of microcomputer controlled applications. Semiconductor manufacturers are able to tap these markets by introducing families of relatively unsophisticated, inexpensive microcomputers. In 1979, Motorola introduced the MC6805P2, in HMOS, which was to be the first member of a rapidly expanding family of devices. It was developed from the MC6801 by removing many of the computer-orientated features and augmenting its control features. Because simpler applications require simpler programs to control them, one of the accumulators was removed and the RAM and ROM and a number of internal registers were reduced in size. The 16-bit timer was replaced with a simpler, less silicon-intensive, 8-bit timer, and the serial interface was removed completely. Removal of some of the I/O capability allowed the devices to be produced in a 28-pin package. A new software tool, bit manipulation, was added to allow input/output pins to be monitored and controlled individually.

The modular structure of the layout of the MC6805P2 allows new M6805 family members to be created without resorting to a complete redesign. The CPU is surrounded by a number of well defined blocks containing the RAM and ROM and the hardware associated with the timer and the I/O ports. These blocks can be removed and new blocks added without affecting the other tried and tested parts of the device. New M6805 family devices can, therefore, be developed and introduced with a minimum of effort. This design concept allowed the MC6805U2 (additional ROM and I/O capability) and the MC6805R2 (additional ROM and A/D Conversion circuitry) to follow close on the heels of the MC6805P2. The HMOS family has grown rapidly over the last few years through the addition of a number of variants based on these three devices and through the introduction of the MC6805T2 which contains phase locked loop circuitry for television and radio applications.

The modular design concept was carried through to the MC146805E2, F2 and G2. Implemented in Silicon-gate CMOS (Complementary Metal Oxide on Silicon) these devices exploit the very low power consumption of this semiconductor technology, making them ideal for use in battery operated equipment and in applications where current drain is a major constraint.

Continuing the trend towards cheaper microcomputers set by the M6805 family, in 1982 Motorola introduced the MC6804P2 which exploits the savings in silicon made possible by adopting a serial architecture.

The MC6801, having eight different operating modes, is really a whole family of devices in one chip and was not intended to be the first member of a family like the M6805. However, the needs of the market place have resulted in the introduction of a number of devices based on this microcomputer. The MC68120, developed from the MC6801 by adding a dual-ported RAM and system bus, was introduced as an intelligent peripheral controller for use with Motorola's M68000 series 16-bit microprocessors, but can be used in many other applications. The MC6801U4, introduced in 1982, is an enhanced version of the MC6801 featuring extra on-board RAM and ROM and additional timer functions.

Single-chip microcomputers present a number of problems, to both the user and the manufacturer, which do not exist with normal non-customised parts. The user's software is programmed into the on-board ROM at a early stage of the wafer fabrication process and cannot be changed once this stage has been completed. Consequently, the user has to be confident that the application software is correct and that the finished microcomputer will function as expected in the application system, before committing it to ROM. To help the user do this, Motorola, in common with other manufacturers, has developed a number of in-circuit emulator systems. These replace the microcomputer on the user's circuit board and provide not only real-time emulation of the microcomputer's hardware and software characteristics but also a number of sophisticated debugging tools.

As a final test, the user can program the debugged software into an erasable programmable version of the microcomputer. Motorola produces pin-compatible EPROM versions of the MC6801 and a number of HMOS and CMOS M6805 family members. They are also ideally suited to microcomputer applications where the production volumes are lower than Motorola's minimum order quantity of mask programmed parts, or where the software may have to be periodically updated.

The first stage in the manufacturing process is to convert the customer's software and any user selectable options into a matrix of rectangles on a high resolution mask. This program layer mask becomes one of a set of similar masks which are used in turn to build up the integrated circuit using photographic and etching techniques. Obviously, once a silicon wafer has been exposed to this mask, it is committed to the customer's software and cannot be altered in any way or sold to other customers. Small prototype batches of wafers are rushed through the manufacturing process and a few sample parts are delivered to the customer for his approval. When the customer has verified that the samples are acceptable, the dice remaining from the prototype batches are assembled and tested and production batches are started to meet the balance of the customer's order. Motorola has had to develop new production control techniques to monitor and control the simultaneous processing of large numbers of customised wafer batches.

Microcomputers are difficult devices to test, not only because of the wide variety and complexity of the on-board hardware but also because access to the internal data and address busses from the outside world is sometimes very limited. This is particularly true for the M6805 and M146805 families but fortunately these have a special test mode of operation which makes the busses available via the I/O ports. They also contain a special self-test software routine which allows the CPU to perform a simple functional test of the on-board circuitry.

From a technical point of view it may be more appropriate to examine Motorola's M6805 family first, as these devices are, in general, less complex and appear, at first glance, to be much easier to understand than the M6801. However, the basic principles involved are the same for both families and the apparent complexity of the M6801 devices is due mainly to the larger number of on-board functions and the number of registers required to monitor and control these functions. In view of this and the fact that the M6805 family has now grown into a very complex and versatile range of simple and not-so-simple devices, the M6801 family will be examined first.

2.2   THE M6801 FAMILY

All devices in this family have been derived from the MC6801 microcomputer by adding different hardware features to meet the needs of the marketplace. A complete list of these devices is given in Table 2.1 along with their main features.

The MC6801 may be configured to operate in three different modes: Single-Chip, Expanded Multiplexed, and Expanded Non-Multiplexed, which provide different hardware features. These basic modes are further subdivided to make eight different configurations available to the user. It is up to the user to decide which mode of operation is best suited to a specific application. Figure 2.1 shows a basic block diagram of the MC6801.

2.2.1   The Single-Chip Mode of Operation

The major functions available in this mode are as follows:

Enhanced 6800-type CPU.
3 8-bit I/O Ports.
1 5-bit I/O Port.
16-bit Timer.
Serial Communications Interface.

30

Table 2.1 M6801 microcomputer family.

MCU	Process	Pins	ROM	RAM	I/O	Special Features
MC6801	HMOS	40	2.0 K	128	29	3-Function Timer, Serial Port
MC6803	HMOS	40	NONE	128	13	3-Function Timer, Serial Port
MC6801U4	HMOS	40	4.0 K	192	29	6-Function Timer, Serial Port
MC6803U4	HMOS	40	NONE	192	29	6-Function Timer, Serial Port
MC68120	HMOS	48	2.0 K	128	21	Dual-Ported RAM, 6 Semaphores
MC68121	HMOS	48	NONE	128	5	Dual-Ported RAM, 6 Semaphores
MC68122	MOTOROLA Programmed Cluster Terminal Controller					
MC68701	HMOS	40	2.0 K	128	29	3-Function Timer, UV EPROM
MC68701U4	HMOS	40	4.0 K	192	29	6-Function Timer, UV EPROM

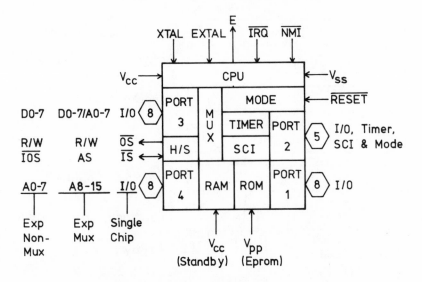

Fig. 2.1 The MC6801 microcomputer.

128 bytes of RAM.
2048 bytes of ROM.
8-bit Data Bus.
16-bit Address Bus.
Mode Select Circuitry.

The Address/Data Multiplexer connected to port 3 is not used in the Single-Chip Mode. Each block is examined in more detail following.

2.2.2 The Central Processing Unit (CPU)

The CPU is the heart of the microcomputer and is responsible for fetching the instructions from the program stored in ROM, interpreting these instructions and taking the appropriate action. It has to control the operation of the ports, the timer and the serial interface, perform logical and arithmetic operations on data obtained from these and from ROM and RAM, and make decisions on the results of these operations. To help it perform these duties quickly and efficiently it is equipped with a number of special dedicated registers as shown in the programming model in Fig. 2.2. These will be examined in detail when discussing the programming aspects of the MC6801.

An on-board oscillator supplies the CPU with the basic clock signal which it uses to generate the control signals needed to synchronise all communications to the on-board circuitry via the data and address busses.

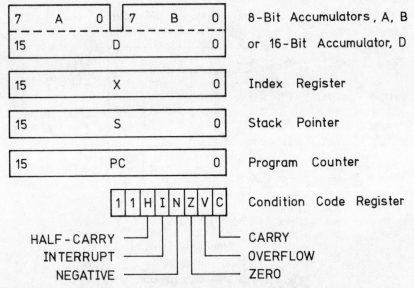

Fig. 2.2 The MC6801 programming model.

This oscillator can be driven by applying a TTL clock signal to the EXTAL pin or by connecting a quartz crystal across the XTAL and EXTAL inputs. This basic input frequency is usually around about 4 MHz and is divided by four by internal circuitry to supply a basic clock frequency (the E clock) of 1 MHz on which all internal timing is based. This E clock signal is also made available to the outside world for synchronisation purposes when communicating with other microprocessors and peripheral devices.

Three other inputs to the CPU may be considered interrupt functions of differing degrees of priority. When the CPU recognises one of these interrupts, it suspends normal processing and proceeds to service the requirements of the acting interrupt.

The lowest priority of these three is $\overline{\text{IRQ}}$ which is a level sensitive, active low, maskable interrupt. It is recognised by a logic zero applied to the pin, but will be ignored if a special mask bit has been set either by software or by another interrupt service routine in progress. Provided this input is held low, the IRQ request will be serviced as soon as the mask bit is cleared. This interrupt feature is normally used to service peripheral devices which do not require an immediate response from the CPU. $\overline{\text{NMI}}$ is a negative edge triggered, Non-Maskable Interrupt and would be used by a peripheral device which requires the immediate attention of the MC6801. The interrupt request signal is latched by the first negative edge of the E clock after the application of a logic zero and will be acted upon immediately by the CPU even if it is currently servicing a lower priority interrupt request.

When the CPU recognises an $\overline{\text{IRQ}}$ or $\overline{\text{NMI}}$, it completes the instruction being executed, increments the Program Counter (PC) to point to the address of the next instruction, and then stores the contents of its special purpose registers in an area of RAM known as the stack. It then fetches, from a special area of ROM known as the vector space, the address of the start of the appropriate interrupt handling procedure which it loads into the PC and continues processing from that address. On completion of the interrupt service routine, the registers are reloaded from the stack, and processing continues with the instruction addressed by the PC, i.e. the instruction immediately following the break from normal processing. $\overline{\text{RESET}}$ is a special form of interrupt which takes priority over all others. When this pin is held low all processing is suspended and all registers, ports and on-board functions are set to a predetermined state. When the $\overline{\text{RESET}}$ input is taken high, the start address of the program is fetched from the vector space and loaded into the PC. Before starting to execute instructions, the CPU reads in the logic states applied to three pins on Port 2 which define the operating mode required, and the internal architecture of the device is configured accordingly. On-board circuitry ensures that this reset sequence also occurs when the device is powered-up initially.

2.2.3 I/O Ports

In the single-chip mode of operation these ports are the only means of communication between the CPU and the outside world. Associated with each port are two registers, a Data Register (DR) and a Data Direction Register (DDR). Each port pin can be configured individually as an input or an output by setting the corresponding bit in the DDR to a 0 or a 1 respectively. Data written by the CPU to the Data Register will appear on the pins configured as outputs, and data read from the Data Register will reflect the logic state applied to the input pins.

Although Port 2 will operate as described above the pins all serve other functions. P20, P21 and P22 are used by the CPU to determine the operating mode when the device is brought out of the $\overline{\text{RESET}}$ state. During the first few machine cycles after $\overline{\text{RESET}}$ reaches a logic 1 level, the logic states applied externally to these pins are read into the lowest three bits of the Port 2 Data Register and then latched into the top three bits of this register. The pins then become available for I/O or other functions as required. P20 and P21 also serve the on-board timer and P22, P23 and P24 serve the on-board serial communications interface. Enabling either of these devices automatically supersedes the I/O function of the corresponding port lines.

Port 3 can be used in conjunction with two handshake lines, OS (Output Strobe) and IS (Input Strobe), to provide an asynchronous parallel interface for data transfer between the MC6801 and another intelligent processor or peripheral. Four bits in another register, the Port 3 Control and Status Register are available to configure and control this interface. Data input to Port 3 by another device can be latched by this device applying a negative-going edge to the IS line. If required, this can also be used to interrupt the MC6801 CPU so that the incoming data can be quickly processed and the port freed up for new data. The output strobe can be configured to go low either when the MC6801 reads data from or writes data to the Port, thus extending the handshaking protocol back to the other processor.

2.2.4   The 16-bit Timer

It would be difficult to conceive of an industrial or commercial application for a microcomputer that would not have a requirement for even a simple timing function. It is possible to write software in such a manner that simple timing functions can be performed at the same time as performing other tasks without an independent on-board timer. However, such software (see Section 1.2.6) is difficult to write and to modify as it uses the microcomputer machine cycle as its basic unit of time and involves calculation of loop and subroutine cycle times and software somersaults to ensure that all timings are equal for different program paths. Fortunately, most single-chip microcomputers are supplied with a multifunctional on-board timer.

A block diagram of the MC6801 timer is shown in Fig. 2.3. The key element is a 16-bit free-running counter, the Counter Register, which is incremented during each negative half cycle of the microcomputer E clock. Software can read the contents of this register at any time without affecting its value but any write to this register will load it with the value $FFF8_{16}$. As this register is 16 bits wide (2 bytes) and the MC6801 data bus is only 8 bits wide, the upper byte of the register must always be read first. The process of reading the upper byte automatically causes the lower byte to be shifted into a buffer which can then be read by the CPU, ensuring that a false reading is not obtained due to the finite time taken by the two read instructions. To clarify this, imagine that the counter register is read when the contents are $00FF_{16}$. 00_{16} would be read on the first read and FF_{16} would be stored in the buffer. The second read would read the lower byte as FF_{16}. If the buffer were not present, the counter register would be incremented by the E clock by several counts and may be 0107_{16}, say, by the time the second read is performed. This would read the low byte as 07_{16} and the overall result would be 0007_{16} which would obviously be incorrect.

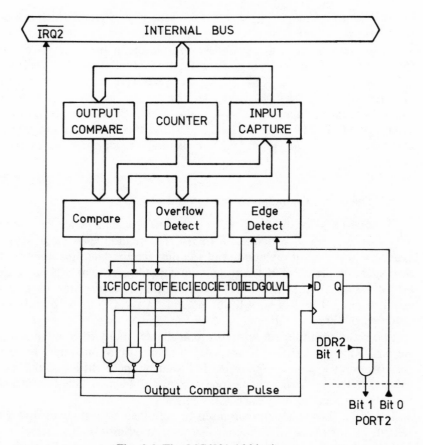

Fig. 2.3 The MC6801 16-bit timer.

Overflow detect circuitry sets the Timer Overflow Flag (TOF) in the Timer Control and Status Register (TCSR), and software can permit or inhibit the generation of an internal IRQ signal when this overflow occurs.

The Output Compare Register is a 16-bit read/write register which can be used for a number of different functions. When the value in the Counter Register is the same as the value set in the Output Compare Register, the Output Compare Flag (OCF) in the TCSR is set and again an IRQ signal may or may not be allowed to interrupt the CPU. Also when this condition occurs, the value stored in the Output Level bit (OLVL) in the TCSR is automatically clocked out to P21, and this level will appear on the pin provided this bit is configured as an output in the Port 2 DDR. This function can be used to generate output waveforms and to indicate when periods of time have elapsed.

The Input Capture Register is a 16-bit read-only register which can be used to time external events. Edge detect circuitry monitors P20 and when an appropriate transition occurs on this input the contents of the Counter Register are shifted into the Input Capture Register. The Input Edge bit (IEDG) in the TCSR can be set by software to specify whether a negative- or positive-going edge causes the capture. At the same time an Inpute Capture Flag (ICF) is set and if the Enable Input Capture Interrupt bit (EICI) is set an IRQ signal is generated. This function is particularly useful for timing and measuring the duration of external events.

2.2.5   The Serial Communications Interface (SCI)

As discussed previously, Port 3 can be used to provide a means of passing data very quickly in a parallel format. This method, however, is very expensive in terms of the number of I/O pins required and the amount of time spent by the CPU in controlling the data transfer. The SCI on board the MC6801 provides a means of transmitting and receiving data in a serial format. It makes very little demand on the CPU's time and uses only two or three I/O lines.

Two serial transmission formats are available, standard Non-Return to Zero (NRZ), or Mark-to-Space, and Biphase, or Manchester, format. Both transmit a start bit (a 'zero') followed by the eight bit of the data byte, followed by a stop bit (a 'one'). Figure 2.4 shows how 'zeros' and 'ones' are represented by each format.

The NRZ format is normally used by terminals and modems and can tolerate a variation in frequency between transmitter and receiver of 3.75%. In applications where this tolerance cannot be met, the Biphase format would be more useful as it can tolerate a 25% difference in frequency between the transmitter and the receiver.

Figure 2.5 shows a simplified block diagram of the SCI. The user has access, via software, to four 8-bit registers; the write-only Transmit Data Register (TDR), the read-only Receive Data Register (RDR), the Transmit/Receive Control and Status Register (TRCS) and the Rate and Mode Control Register (RMCR). The data byte to be transmitted is loaded by software into the TDR. The SCI logic then transfers it into the Transmit Shift Register from where it is clocked out bit by bit on Port 2 bit 4 (TX). Similarly, data is received in a serial fashion by the Receive Shift Register via Port 2, bit 3 (RX) and then moved into the RDR. The RMCR contains four bits which allow the user to select either Biphase or NRZ format and one of four transmission rates. The SCI normally derives its basic baud rate (bit transmission rate) from the on-board E clock and uses only the TX and RX lines for communication. However, this demands that the transmitter and receiver on the MC6801 and on the

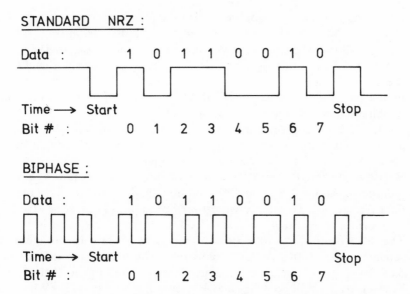

Fig. 2.4 Serial data transmission formats of the MC6801.

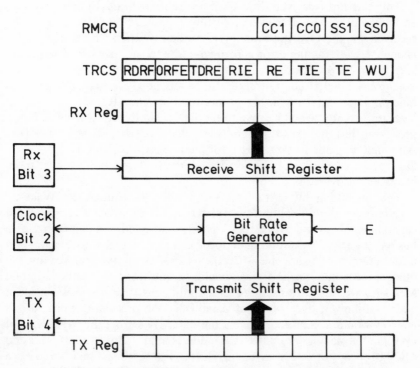

Fig. 2.5 The MC6801 serial communications interface.

other device are in synchronism, within the tolerance of the transmission format. In NRZ format, which can tolerate a difference in baud rate of only 3.75% between the two, the user may input an external clock to generate the baud rate of the SCI or he may output a clock signal from the SCI to be used by the other device. Port 2, bit 2 is used to input or output this clock signal. The RMCR is normally set up by software during an initialisation routine shortly after reset.

The TRCS register contains three flag bits and five control bits which allow the user to control the operation of the SCI and to monitor its status. Whenever the SCI moves a byte of data from the Transmit Data Register into the Transmit Data Shift Register, a flag (TDRE) is set to indicate to the CPU that the TDR is empty and ready for a new byte of data. Setting the Transmitter Interrupt Enable bit (TIE) causes the SCI to generate an internal interrupt (IRQ2) whenever the TDR is empty. This allows the CPU to continue processing while the transmitter is sending out data at a relatively slow rate. The transmitter and receiver may be switched on or off independently by setting or clearing the Transmitter Enable bit (TE) and Receiver Enable bit (RE). When the Receive Data Shift Register has received a complete byte, the data is transferred into the RDR.

This sets the Receiver Data Register Full flag (RDRF) and generates an interrupt if the Receiver Interrupt Enable bit (RIE) is set. The receiver sets the Overrun/Framing Error flag (ORFE) whenever an error is detected. A framing error is recognised by the occurrence of an invalid stop bit in the data stream and usually happens when the receiver loses synchronism with the transmitter or when noise occurs on the transmission line. An overrun error occurs when the Receive Data Shift Register is ready to send a byte to the RDR, but the RDR is full, i.e. the processor has not read the previous byte of data from the RDR. Although only one flag bit is used for the two error conditions, the RDRF flag will be clear if a framing error has occurred and will be set if there has been an overrun.

The remaining bit in this register is used to control the Wake-up feature. Consider an application which requires the processing power and capabilities of several MC6801s which are connected to a common 2-wire bus via their SCI transmit and receive lines. In order to ensure that information sent from one MC6801 to another is not received by the other processors, each device would be allocated a unique address. Messages would be transmitted in a continuous stream consisting of an address followed by a block of data. Only the processor allocated this address would accept and process the data. By setting the Wake-Up bit (WU) after having examined the address information, a disinterested MC6801 can put its receiver to sleep. The CPU is relieved of the responsibility of servicing the Receiver Data Register Full interrupt requests and can concentrate on other processing tasks. At the end of the message the line goes idle (continuous 'ones'), and after ten bit times the receiver wakes up ready to receive the address information preceding the next block of data.

The transmitter in the MC6801 transmits nine consecutive 'ones' when it is turned on before it transmits the first byte of data. These 'ones', combined with the last stop bit of the previous message, ensure that there is always at least ten consecutive 'ones' before each message, which is sufficient to wake-up all the receivers.

2.2.6 The On-Board RAM

The on-board Random Access Memory provides 128 8-bit bytes of temporary storage space.

This is used by the CPU to store any variable data which may be referred to and modified during processing. The CPU can read data from a RAM location directly onto one of its own dedicated registers, modify or perform some logical or arithmetic operation on the data and restore the result in the RAM. However, it is not always necessary for the software to use this READ/MODIFY/WRITE sequence as the CPU can perform many operations directly on the contents of RAM without involving another register.

Random Access Memory usually loses its data when the power supply to the microcomputer is switched off. In many applications it is useful to switch off the devices from time to time to conserve power, particularly in the automotive industry where the power is supplied from the car battery when the engine is not running. However, it may be necessary to retain some of the temporary information stored in the RAM while the car is not in use, and to retrieve this information when the engine is next started. For this purpose, sixty-four bytes of the on-board RAM have a standby capability. An extra supply pin is provided on the device which supplies power to these bytes only. The rest of the device can be switched off and the data in the Standby RAM will be retained, using very little power, provided the power supply to the Standby Supply pin is not removed. One bit in the RAM/EPROM Control Register is used to control the Standby RAM. This bit can be set by software but can only be cleared by the Standby Voltage being removed or reduced below a certain level. Before the main power supply to the device is removed, the software should set this bit to a 'one'. On being powered up sometime later, the software should check the state of this bit. If it is still a 'one', then the data in the Standby RAM is still valid, but if it is a 'zero', then it is likely that the data has been corrupted during the time when the main power supply was off. A second bit in this control register, the RAM Enable Bit, allows the user to disable the RAM completely. This feature is useful in some of the other operating modes where external RAM is used.

2.2.7   The On-Board ROM/EPROM

Like any other computer, the MC6801 requires software to run it. This is generally written by the programmer, in a mnemonic assembly language which is converted by an assembler, to the hexadecimal bytes of machine code understood by the CPU. This consists of instruction bytes and fixed data bytes which can then be programmed into the 2048-byte on-board ROM space. Sixteen bytes of this ROM are reserved as a vector space, where the programmer must store the start addresses of the Reset and interrupt service routines.

The program is stored in the ROM by Motorola during manufacture. The process is long and complex and the resulting devices cannot be modified in any way by the user. However, many software and hardware tools and techniques are available to the user to ensure that his program is fully debugged before it is committed to production.

Motorola supplies a version of the MC6801, the MC68701, which has an Erasable Programmable Read Only Memory on board instead of the mask-programmed ROM. The 2 K ROM on this device can be erased – by exposing it to U.V. light – and reprogrammed by the user, and is ideal for use in developing software and in specialist low-volume applications which do not warrant the expense of having the software built in during manufacture. Two bits in the RAM/EPROM Control Register allow software, residing outside the MC68701, to program the on-board EPROM using the device's own CPU.

2.2.8   The Address and Data Busses

The on-board functions available to the CPU have been examined at some length. The following section discusses how the CPU communicates with them.

All Motorola microprocessors and microcomputers have an internal architecture based on the principle of memory-mapped I/O. This means that every RAM and ROM location and every register associated with the on-board hardware functions has a unique address and can be treated simply as a memory location. This makes life simpler for the programmer as he does not have to learn and remember one set of instructions to talk to the RAM, another to talk to the timer, yet another to talk to the Serial Communications Interface, and so on. A 16-bit wide address bus provides the CPU with the capability to address 2^{16} (65536 or 64 K) memory locations and an 8-bit wide data bus provides the means of transferring data to and from these locations. Figure 2.6 shows how the address space is organised. The first 32 bytes, from 0000_{16} to $001F_{16}$, are reserved for all the internal registers. The 128 bytes of on-board RAM are located from 0080_{16} to $00FF_{16}$, the bytes between 0080_{16} and $00BF_{16}$ having the standby power capability described earlier. The address space from 0000_{16} to $00FF_{16}$ is known as page zero and the internal registers and RAM are located in this area for a particular reason. Many instructions in the MC6801 instruction set take the form of an instruction followed by an address. This is converted by the assembly into one instruction byte followed by one or two address bytes. If there is only one address byte, the CPU assumes that the address lies in page zero, i.e. the first byte of the address is 00_{16}. Because the CPU spends most of its time manipulating data in the RAM and talking to the on-board facilities via the internal registers, most of the instructions in the program can use this one byte address form. The program is, therefore, more byte efficient and the CPU spends less time decoding instructions.

The on-board ROM is located right at the top of the address map, from $F800_{16}$ to $FFFF_{16}$. The last 16 bytes of this area, from $FFF0_{16}$ to $FFFF_{16}$ are reserved for the interrupt and reset vectors. The programmer may use the interrupt vector space for part of his program, provided that

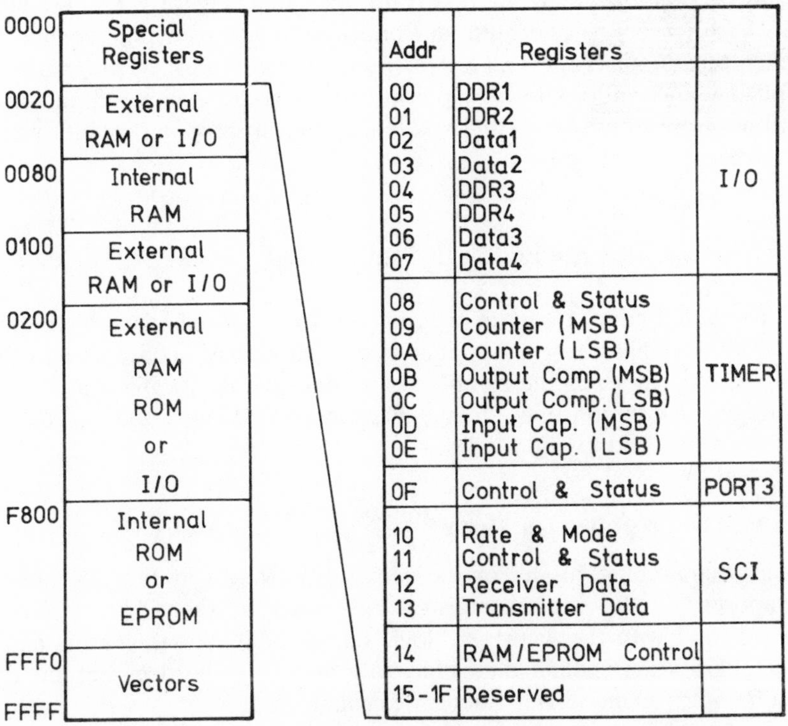

Addr	Registers	
00	DDR1	
01	DDR2	
02	Data1	
03	Data2	I/O
04	DDR3	
05	DDR4	
06	Data3	
07	Data4	
08	Control & Status	
09	Counter (MSB)	
0A	Counter (LSB)	
0B	Output Comp.(MSB)	TIMER
0C	Output Comp.(LSB)	
0D	Input Cap. (MSB)	
0E	Input Cap. (LSB)	
0F	Control & Status	PORT3
10	Rate & Mode	
11	Control & Status	SCI
12	Receiver Data	
13	Transmitter Data	
14	RAM/EPROM Control	
15-1F	Reserved	

Memory map (left):
- 0000 Special Registers
- 0020 External RAM or I/O
- 0080 Internal RAM
- 0100 External RAM or I/O
- 0200 External RAM ROM or I/O
- F800 Internal ROM or EPROM
- FFF0 Vectors
- FFFF

Fig. 2.6 The MC6801 memory map and special function registers.

| PRIORITY | VECTOR | | DESCRIPTION |
	MS	LS	
Highest	FFFE	FFFF	Reset
	FFFC	FFFD	Non-maskable Interrupt
	FFFA	FFFB	Software Interrupt
	FFF8	FFF9	Interrupt Strobe 3
	FFF6	FFF7	Input Capture IRQ2
	FFF4	FFF5	Output Compare IRQ2
	FFF2	FFF3	Timer Overflow IRQ2
Lowest	FFF0	FFF1	Serial I/O IRQ2

Fig. 2.7 The MC6801 vector space.

no interrupt can occur, but the Reset Vector at $FFFE_{16}$, $FFFF_{16}$ must always contain the start address of the program. Figure 2.7 shows how this vector space is allocated and prioritised. Each function capable of generating an interrupt is allocated two bytes which must be programmed with the start address of the appropriate interrupt service routine. This address is fetched by the CPU and loaded into its program counter when an interrupt is recognised.

2.3 SOFTWARE ASPECTS OF THE MC6801

Before attempting to write a program for any microcomputer, the aspiring user has to become familiar with three basic concepts and the specific ways in which these apply to the particular device it is intended to program. These concepts are the Programming Model, the Instruction Set, and the Addressing Modes.

2.3.1 The Programming Model

The Programming Model of the MC6801 is shown in Fig. 2.2 and is composed of the special registers dedicated to the CPU. Used in conjunction with the arithmetic logic unit (ALU), these registers allow the CPU to manipulate data efficiently and to make decisions on the results of arithemetic and Boolean calculations.

The Accumulators, A and B, are two 8-bit general purpose registers for performing arithmetic calculations and data manipulation. The programmer can consider these two registers as a double-length Accumulator D, and a number of instructions are available which operate on this 16-bit register directly.

The Index Register, X, is intended mainly for use in the indexed modes of addressing, which will be described later. Being 16-bits wide, it may be loaded with any address in the MC6801's memory map. This register can also be used for temporary storage or as a limited function accumulator when the indexed addressing mode is not being used. The Program Counter, PC, is incremented every time a byte of the program is fetched from ROM by the CPU. It always contains the address of the next instruction or data byte to be processed.

The Stack Pointer, S, always contains the address of the next available or 'empty' byte in an area of RAM known as the Stack. This stack is used by the CPU, when it jumps out of the main program to a subroutine or to an interrupt service routine, to store the contents of some of the registers. When the CPU encounters a jump-to-subroutine (JSR) instruction it 'pushes' the contents of the PC onto the stack. This ensures that the program will be able to return to the correct address at the end of the subroutine. The sequence is as follows: the low order byte of the PC is stored in the RAM location addressed by the Stack Pointer; the Stack Pointer is decremented; the high order byte of the return address is stored in the new location addressed by the stack pointer; finally, the stack pointer is decremented again to point to the next empty byte on the stack. The last instruction in a subroutine is always a return-from-subroutine instruction (RTS). On encountering this, the CPU 'pops' the return address back off the stack in the reverse order, this time incrementing the Stack Pointer before each byte, and continues processing at the instruction immediately following the JSR. There are, at the programmer's disposal, a number of instructions which operate on the stack, and the Stack Pointer and data may be pushed and popped at any time.

This gives a remarkable amount of programming flexibility and allows some wonderful software somersaults to be performed, but must be used with caution: a 'push' without a 'pop' during a subroutine causes an invalid return address to be loaded into the PC, resulting in the CPU losing its place in its program. The programmer may set the stack anywhere in available RAM but must ensure that it does not grow down to the point where it clashes with the RAM locations used for normal data storage. This can occur when multiple levels of subroutine nesting are possible.

An interrupt is a special form of subroutine. When it is recognised, the CPU stores not only the PC but also the contents of the Index Register, the Accumulators, and the Condition Code Register. This ensures that when the interrupt service routine is complete, the registers and the

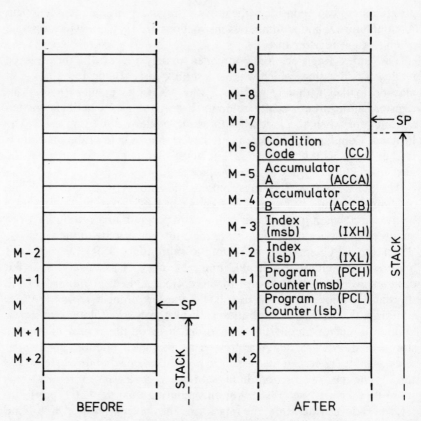

Fig. 2.8 Stack Pointer operation in the MC6801.

processor can be returned to their original state, if required. Fig. 2.8 shows the operation of the Stack Pointer and the contents of the stack when an interrupt occurs during a subroutine.

The last register in the Programming Model, the Condition Code Register, contains six flag bits each of which can be individually set or cleared by software. The I-bit is the interrupt mask bit and may be set to a 1 (interrupts inhibited) by using the Set Interrupt Mask (SEI) instruction, or cleared to 0 using the Clear Interrupt Mask (CLI) instruction. This bit is also set to a 1 automatically by the CPU when an interrupt is received, and cleared when the Return-from-Interrupt instruction is executed. The remaining five flags are set, cleared, or left unchanged, depending on the results of various arithmetic operations performed by the Arithmetic Logic Unit (ALU). To understand fully the significance of these bits, the user must be familiar with the concepts of 1's complement and 2's complement arithmetic. Basically, the former uses the eight bits of each byte to represent an unsigned number between

0 and 255 (FF_{16}), whereas the latter considers a byte with bit 7 set as a negative number and a byte with bit 7 clear as a positive number. The remaining seven bits represent the magnitude. This system provides a number range from -128 ($1000\ 0000_2$ or 80_{16}) through 0 to $+127$ (0111 1111 or $7F_{16}$). Let us look at a simple example of an arithmetic operation which illustrates the use of the flags in the Condition Code Register.

Assume that the two accumulators, A and B, each contain the hexadecimal value 88_{16} and that we add B to A using the instruction ABA:

```
A  =          1000   1000
B  =          1000   1000
_____

A + B  =  1   0001   0000    C=1, H=1, V=1, N=0, Z=0
          C    H
```

The highest order bits of A and B are both ones and their addition results in a zero in bit 7 with a carry of 1. The Carry bit, C, which is used in 1's complement arithmetic to indicate a carry from or a borrow to bit 7 would, in this case, be set to 1. The Half-Carry bit, H, serves the same function for carries from bit 3 to bit 4, and in this case would also be set to 1. This flag is very useful in binary coded decimal (BCD) arithmetic applications. From a 2's complement point of view, we have added two negative numbers and ended up with a positive result. In other words we have exceeded the maximum negative number allowed (-128) and 'rolled over' into the positive number range. The Overflow flag, V, is used to indicate when such a 2's complement overflow has occurred, and in our example would be set to a 1. The Negative flag, N, is set if bit 7 of the result is a 1, and cleared if bit 7 is a zero, and therefore indicates whether a result is negative or positive. The remaining flag, Z, is set if the result is zero, and is cleared if the result is any other value. In the example shown, using ABA, it is fairly easy to see why each of the flag bits was set to a 1 or a 0. However, the effect of an instruction on the CCR flags is not always so easy to determine. The user should consult the programming manual for a detailed description of each instruction and its effect on the flags.

2.3.2 The Instruction Set of the MC6801

The MC6801 CPU understands instructions in the form of hexadecimal bytes, known as Opcodes. These opcodes tell the processor to perform certain actions such as Add, Branch, Jump, Test, Decrement, etc., and in many cases are followed by either one or two bytes of data or address information.

The instructions can be grouped together according to the type of operations performed.

2.3.2.1 CONDITION CODE REGISTER INSTRUCTIONS

These instructions are all inherent instructions, i.e. they do not require a one or two byte operand to specify data or an address. They allow the programmer to set and clear the Carry and Overflow Flags and the Interrupt Mask Bit. Two instructions allow the accumulator A to read from or write to the Condition Code Register.

2.3.2.2 ARITHMETIC INSTRUCTIONS

This group includes all the instructions which allow data in RAM and accumulators A, B and D to be added, subtracted, multiplied, and negated (i.e. 2's complement). Some of them allow the carry bit to be used in calculations, and a Decimal Adjust (DAA) instruction simplifies BCD arithmetic by allowing the contents of the Accumulator A to be adjusted, after another arithmetic operation, to the BCD value. The Multiply instruction multiplies the unsigned values in A and B and stores the result in D.

2.3.2.3 LOGIC INSTRUCTIONS

These instructions allow Boolean arithmetic to be performed. The logical AND, and inclusive and exclusive OR, can be performed on the A and B accumulators, with data from ROM or RAM. The 1's complement instruction operates directly on RAM locations as well as on A and B.

2.3.2.4 DATA TEST INSTRUCTIONS

These differ from the Logic instructions because they do not overwrite data in either the accumulators or the memory with the result. They only affect the flags in the condition code register and can be used to test selected bits in A or B, to compare A and B with memory or with each other, and to test whether the contents of A, B or memory are equal to zero or negative.

2.3.2.5 DATA HANDLING INSTRUCTIONS

These are used to manipulate data within the accumulators and memory and to move the data from place to place. Data may be cleared to zero, decremented or incremented by one bit, and rotated or shifted left or right in a number of different ways depending on how the Carry bit is used. Load and Store instructions can be used to transfer data between the accumulators and memory, and transfer instructions allow data to be transferred from A to B and B to A. The contents of A and B can also be pushed to and pulled from the stack.

2.3.2.6 INDEX REGISTER INSTRUCTIONS

The index register instructions are specifically designed to make the best use of this register for addressing purposes. Its contents can be loaded, stored, incremented, decremented, pushed, pulled and compared with contents of memory locations. The 16-bit address in X can be transferred to and from the stack pointer. The ABX instruction adds B to X and allows a dynamic offset, calculated in B to be added to a base address in X to produce an effective address. This facility is useful in table look-up routines.

2.3.2.7 STACK POINTER INSTRUCTIONS

Six instructions allow the contents of the stack pointer to be loaded and stored, incremented and decremented and transferred to and from the index register. As mentioned before, great care must be used when modifying this register to ensure return addresses are not lost or corrupted.

2.3.2.8 BRANCH AND JUMP INSTRUCTIONS

We have already seen how the six flags in the condition code register are set or reset during execution of the program. The Branch instructions allow the CPU to use the status of these flags to control the flow of the program. They consist of an opcode followed by a one-byte address offset which the CPU adds to the present value of its program counter to produce the effective address of the next instruction, if the branch test result is true. This offset is a 2's complement value so the CPU can branch forward 127 bytes or back 128 bytes from the instruction immediately following the branch instruction. Some of the branch instructions test only one flag bit, e.g. BCC (Branch if Carry Clear) will be true only if the Carry bit is clear, and BEQ (Branch if the result equals zero) will be true only if the Zero bit is set. Others test a combination of flags, e.g. BGT (Branch if the result is greater than zero) will be true if either the Zero bit is clear, the Negative bit is set and Overflow is set. A close examination of the branch instructions will show that each instruction, except one, has a logical complement, e.g. Branch if Equal to Zero (BEQ), Branch if not Equal to Zero (BNE), and Branch if Plus (BPL), Branch if Minus (BMI).

Consequently, Branch Always (BRA) has its complement, Branch Never (BRN). Neither of these two instructions test the condition code register flags but they do have their uses in certain software situations. Branch to Subroutine (BSR) does not have a logical complement and again does not test the status of the flags.

Whereas the branch instructions use a one-byte address offset, the Jump and Jump-to-Subroutine instructions use a one- or two-byte address to control the program flow. Software Interrupt (SWI) sends an IRQ signal to the CPU which suspends normal processing while executing a software interrupt handling routine. The Wait for Interrupt instruction (WAI) causes the CPU to suspend processing until an interrupt is received.

2.3.3 The Addressing Modes

Instructions which use the Inherent Addressing Mode consist of a one-byte opcode and no operand as the address is inherent in the instruction itself. For example, INCA causes the contents of accumulator A to be incremented by one. The other addressing modes result in an internally generated double byte effective address. The concepts of these addressing modes can be explained using a simple example, e.g. loading data into accumulator A.

86FB	LDAA	$\neq$$FB	IMMEDIATE ACC A	= FB
96FB	LDAA	$FB	DIRECT	'' = Contents of FB.
B6F800	LDAA	$F800	EXTENDED	'' = Contents of F800.
A602	LDAA	2,X	INDEXED	'' = Contents of Address in index register + 2.

2.3.3.1 IMMEDIATE ADDRESSING
In this mode the opcode is immediately followed by the byte of data to be loaded. The effective address generated is, therefore, the address in ROM of the LDAA opcode plus 1, and in our example the accumulator would be loaded with the value FB_{16}. The Assembler program recognises that the immediate mode is being used by the presence of the $\neq$ sign in the instruction and it selects the appropriate opcode 86_{16}.

2.3.3.2 DIRECT ADDRESSING
In this mode, one byte of data follows the opcode. This byte is the low order byte of the address of the location containing the data. The high order byte is assumed to be zero and the effective address in the example would, therefore, be $00FB_{16}$. The accumulator would be loaded with the contents of location $00FB_{16}$. The assembler distinguishes this mode from the immediate mode by the absence of the $\neq$ sign and would generate a different opcode, 96_{16}, followed by the operand FB_{16}. Since the I/O and RAM, which are usually addressed more frequently than ROM, are located in Page Zero, the programmer can economise on ROM space and execution time by using direct addressing.

2.3.3.3 EXTENDED ADDRESSING
This mode is similar to the Direct Addressing Mode but uses two bytes instead of one to specify the address. The assembler differentiates this

from the direct mode by the presence of the two bytes of information following the instruction and would generate the opcode, $B6_{16}$, followed by those two bytes. In our example the effective address is $F800_{16}$, and the accumulator would be loaded with the contents of this ROM location.

2.3.3.4 INDEXED ADDRESSING

In this mode, the opcode is followed by one byte which the CPU adds to the contents of the index register to create the effective address. In our example, if the index register contained, say, $F1E3_{16}$, the CPU would add 2 to create an effective address of $F1E5_{16}$ and would load the contents of that address into A. Typically, this mode is used in table look-up routines where the index register is loaded with the start address of the table and the accumulator loaded with the appropriate entry number in the table.

2.4   THE MC6801 IN THE EXPANDED MODE

The MC6801 has been examined in some detail in its role as a true single-chip microcomputer, and it is obvious that it is suited to a wide variety of applications in this mode. However, as users become more familiar with such devices and appreciate their processing powers, they also become more adept at finding ways of enhancing their own end product by making more and more use of this processing power. Very complex applications may require more program memory or more I/O capability than is available in the MC6801's Single-Chip Mode and a user may wish to operate the device in an expanded mode. In the single-chip mode, the data and address busses are confined within the device and are not accessible from the outside. The expanded modes make these busses available to the outside world and allows interfacing to external RAM, and standard 8-bit bus-compatible peripheral devices, at the expense of the on-board I/O capability, as shown in Figs. 2.9 and 2.10.

2.4.1   The Expanded Non-Multiplexed Mode

When the MC6801 is brought out of the $\overline{\text{RESET}}$ state in this mode, it configures Port 3 as an 8-bit bidirectional data bus and Port 4 as an 8-bit input port. However, any of the internal low order address lines (A0 to A7) may be brought out on these pins by reconfiguring the Port 4 DDR bits to make them outputs. This allows the user to access a maximum of 256 external read/write memory locations. These locations reside in the memory map from 100_{16} to $1FF_{16}$, internal logic decoding the high order address lines, A8 to A15, and outputting a signal on $\overline{\text{IOS}}$ when the address is in this range. The $\overline{\text{IOS}}$ signal can be used to enable devices connected to the external bus. The CPU's internal read/write signal

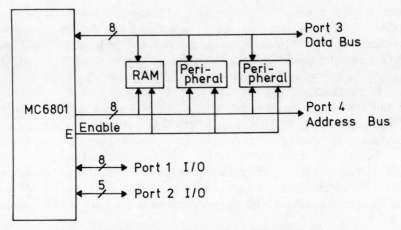

Fig. 2.9 The MC6801 in expanded non-multiplexed mode

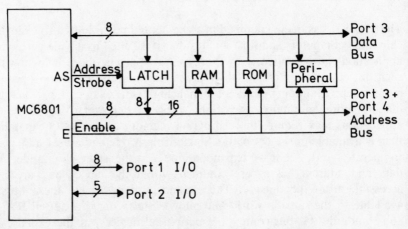

Fig. 2.10 The MC6801 in expanded multiplexed mode

(R/$\overline{W}$) is also brought out to control the direction of data flow. The user can retain any Port 4 pins as input pins if they are not required for off-chip addressing functions.

2.4.2 The Expanded Multiplexed Mode

There are five variations of this mode and a detailed description of each can be obtained from the MC6801 data sheet and User's Manual.

In this mode, all sixteen address lines are made available to the outside world giving access to almost 64K of external read/write memory locations. This is achieved by time-multiplexing the data bus information with the eight low order address lines on Port 3 and bringing out the high order address lines on Port 4. As in the non-multiplexed mode, if the full range of external memory addresses is not required, any unused pins on Port 4 may be used as inputs. The processor generates an address strobe (AS) signal which is always high when address information is present on the multiplexed bus, and this is brought out instead of the $\overline{IOS}$ signal in the non-multiplexed mode. The falling edge of this signal can be used to control an external latch which traps the address information and keeps it asserted on the external memory or I/O device while data is being transferred. As in the expanded non-multiplexed mode, the R/$\overline{W}$ signal controls the direction of data transfer.

2.5   OTHER M6801 FAMILY MEMBERS

Table 2.1 (see p. 30) lists all the members of the MC6801 family.

2.5.1   MC6803

This device cannot be considered a true single-chip microcomputer as there is no on-board ROM available. Consequently, the device can only operate in an expanded mode with the user's program in external memory. In every other way the MC6803 is hardware and software identical to the MC6801.

2.5.2   MC6801U4

This is basically an MC6801, upgraded in a number of key areas. The on-board ROM has been doubled to 4096 (4 K) bytes, running from $F000_{16}$ to $FFFF_{16}$ in the memory map. The RAM has been increased to 192 bytes (40_{16} to FF_{16}) although the number of bytes capable of standby operation has been reduced to 32 ($40_{16}-5F_{16}$). The CPU has been slightly modified to prevent response to an $\overline{NMI}$ interrupt until the stack pointer has been loaded by software. This ensures that a valid area of RAM is allocated for storing the return address.

The MC6801 timer has been enhanced significantly by adding two extra Output Compare functions, one extra Input Capture function and a Counter Alternate Address feature. The extra input capture and output compare functions utilise three pins of Port 1 to input and output signals in the same way as the MC6801. These functions operate independently and are controlled by two new 8-bit Timer Control registers and monitored by one new 8-bit Timer Status Register. On the MC6801 timer, in order to clear a flag in the TCSR, the program has to read that register and then read or write to the appropriate 16-bit register. Since reads of the Counter Register tend to occur frequently during processing, it is possible to clear the Timer Overflow flag inadvertently. In the MC6801U4 the 16-bit Counter Alternate Address allows the software to read the counter register without clearing this flag, even if the TCSR has been read earlier.

Like the MC6801, the MC6801U4 is available with 4 K bytes of U.V. erasable PROM on board.

2.5.3 MC68120

The MC68120 is a general purpose, single chip, intelligent peripheral controller (IPC) based on the MC6801. It can be used to provide an interface between a microprocessor and the final peripheral devices via a System Bus Interface and control lines. The major difference between the MC68120 and the MC6801 is that the 128 bytes of on-board RAM on the former are dual-ported. This means that the RAM can be shared between the MC68120's own CPU and another external CPU. To support this function, the I/O capability of Port 1 has been sacrificed and eight pins have been added to provide an 8-bit Systems Data Bus and an 8-bit Systems Address Bus. There is no standby power capability on the dual-ported RAM.

Because the RAM can be accessed by two different CPUs, there has to be some way of ensuring that both CPUs do not access the RAM at the same time. Simultaneous accesses of the same RAM location, particularly those involving a write operation, produce undefined results. Six semaphore registers, each containing a semaphore bit and an ownership bit, can be assigned individually to different areas of the RAM. They do not physically control the shared RAM but are used by software in both CPUs to establish which may or may not access the RAM. The semaphore bit (SEM) indicates whether the resource is available (SEM=0) for access or not (SEM=1), and the ownership bit indicates which processor last accessed the resource, i.e. last set the SEM bit. If the resource is available, i.e. SEM = 0, and one of the CPUs reads this register, the SEM bit is automatically set and the OWN bit is set to indicate that this CPU has control. When the CPU has finished using the shared resource, it should write to the Semaphore Register. This operation clears the SEM bit to zero again, indicating that the resource is again available. If, for example, one CPU loads the RAM with data for the attention of the other CPU, the OWN bit can be monitored to find out if the data has been processed and the RAM available for new data. If both CPUs access the semaphore register simultaneously, arbitration logic ensures that only one of them is granted access.

To provide the basic timing for the MC68120 an externally generated enable signal must be applied to the E input pin, as there is no on-board oscillator. The three pins of the MC6801 which are allocated to crystal inputs and standby RAM power supply are used on the MC68120 for signals controlling the transfer of data on the System Bus. System Chip Select ($\overline{CS}$) is generated by the external processor and is used to activate the System Data Bus Interface. System Read/Write (SR/$\overline{W}$) is generated by the external processor and controls the direction of data transfer between it and the dual-ported RAM. Data transfer to and from the RAM can be synchronous or asynchronous. Data Transfer Acknowledge ($\overline{DTACK}$) is a bidirectional control line which is used to determine synchronous or asynchronous system bus access and to provide a data transfer acknowledge signal to the external CPU during asynchronous transfers.

The $\overline{HALT}/\overline{BA}/\overline{NMI}$ pin provides two basis functions which are software selectable by controlling a Halt Control (HC) bit in the MC6812's Function Control Register. When configured as an $\overline{NMI}$ input it behaves in the same way as the $\overline{NMI}$ input on the MC6801. When configured as a bidirectional HALT-Bus Available line this pin allows peripheral devices to access the local bus. External circuitry is required to decode the information on this line.

When a peripheral device wants to access the local data and address busses (Ports 3 and 4 on the MC68120), it applies a logic zero ($\overline{HALT}$) to this pin. The MC68120 CPU completes its present instruction, suspends processing and outputs a logic zero ($\overline{BA}$) to indicate that it has finished processing and that the bus is available. This output signal can be used to control tri-stating buffers which disconnect Ports 3 and 4 from the bus on the user's circuit board. The MC68120 will not continue processing until the $\overline{HALT}$ signal has been removed and the local bus reconnected via the tri-state buffers to the main bus again. This function can be used when debugging software, as it allows the user to step through his program instruction by instruction. To do this the $\overline{HALT}$ signal must go high for one E clock cycle and then return low.

The MC68120 instruction set and programming model are identical to those of the MC6801, as is the operation of the Timer, the Serial Interface, the Parallel Handshaking Interface and the Mode Selection.

The MC68121 is to the MC68120 what the MC6803 is to the MC6801, i.e. it has no on-board ROM available for the user's software. There is no Eprom version of the MC68120.

The MC68122 Cluster Terminal Controller is an MC68120 with the ROM preprogrammed by Motorola. This device is intended to relieve a host microprocessor of the time-consuming tasks related to communicating with peripherals such as terminals and line printers. It performs the tasks necessary to handle strings of characters and the proper control functions for communicating with asynchronous, communications compatible components and provides the host microprocessor with a wide range of features.

2.6 THE M6805 FAMILY

A rapidly expanding portion of the available market for the single-chip microcomputer does not require the power and sophistication of devices like the members of the 6801 family. This area includes the vast consumer goods market, for example, washing machines, television, central heating controllers, etc., and the automotive market, where the requirement is for relatively cheap, less sophisticated devices tailored to suit particular control applications. The M6805 family, born out of a desire to meet the needs of this section of the market, has developed as the market has grown and developed. The first member of the family, the MC6805P2, was evolved from the MC6801 by reducing and simplifying many of the computer-orientated aspects and developing and improving the control-orientated capabilities. The other major concept used in the design was that the layout on the silicon chip should be very modular to allow future additions to the family to be designed simply by adding more silicon and without involving a complete redesign.

Table 2.2 lists all the current members of the family along with some of their most important hardware features. The prospective user has a choice of technology, HMOS or CMOS package sizes, 28- or 40-pin, varying amounts of on-board ROM, RAM and I/O and a number of special I/O features. As these devices are intended for use in control rather than computer orientated applications, there is generally no requirement to access large areas of external RAM or ROM. Consequently, only one member of the family has an external data and address bus. We will examine the attributes that are common to all family members and then look at some of the special I/O functions that are available.

2.6.1 The MC6805P2 CPU

A basic block diagram of the MC6805P2 is shown in Fig. 2.11. The basic timing required by the CPU is obtained from an on-board oscillator driven by an external crystal or clock connected to the Xtal and EXtal pins. If very accurate timing is not required, the oscillator may be configured to operate as an RC relaxation type; a resistor or short-circuit link can be connected between Xtal and EXtal and will determine the frequency of oscillation. The $\overline{INT}$ input operates as a maskable interrupt input, similar to $\overline{IRQ}$ on the MC6801 but it also has the ability to detect the zero cross-over point of a sinusoidal AC waveform. This allows applications such as servicing time of day routines and controlling AC

Table 2.2 M6805 microcomputer family.

MCU	Process	Pins	ROM	RAM	I/O	Special Features
MC6805P2	HMOS	28	1.0 K	64	20	Self-check
MC6805P4	HMOS	28	1.0 K	112	20	Self-check, Standby RAM
MC6805P6	HMOS	28	1.8 K	64	20	Self-check,
MC6805R2	HMOS	40	2.0 K	64	24*	4-Channel A/D
MC6805R3	HMOS	40	3.8 K	112	24*	4-Channel A/D
MC6805T2	HMOS	28	2.5 K	64	19	Phase Lock Loop
MC6805U2	HMOS	40	2.0 K	64	24*	Self-check
MC6805U3	HMOS	40	3.8 K	112	24*	Self-check
MC68HC05C4	CMOS	40	4.1 K	176	24	2 Serial Ports, 16-bit Timer
MC146805F2	CMOS	28	1.0 K	64	16	Self-check, STOP & WAIT Modes
MC146805G2	CMOS	40	2.0 K	112	32	Self-check, STOP & WAIT Modes
MC68705P3	NMOS	28	1.8 K	112	20	Bootstrap ROM, UV EPROM
MC68705P5	NMOS	28	1.8 K	112	20	As P3 + EPROM Security Bit
MC68705R3	HMOS	40	3.8 K	112	24*	Bootstrap ROM, A/D, UV EPROM
MC668705U3	HMOS	40	3.8 K	112	24*	Bootstrap ROM, UV EPROM
MC1468705G2	CMOS	40	2.0 K	112	32	Bootstrap, STOP & WAIT Modes, UV EPROM

*Plus 8 INPUT ONLY lines.

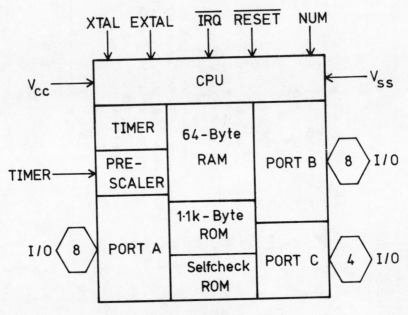

Fig. 2.11 The MC6805P2 microcomputer.

power control devices. The NUM pin is used by the manufacture for testing purposes and should always be connected to ground by the user. $\overline{RESET}$ performs the same function as in the MC6801.

Fig. 2.12 shows the programming model of the MC6805P2, and helps to illustrate how the MC6805P2 was derived from the MC6801 by reducing some of the silicon-intensive functions without detracting greatly from the performance. Only one 8-bit accumulator has been provided, but the index register, X, which has been reduced to 8-bits, can be used as an auxiliary accumulator.

The stack pointer in the MC6805P2 serves the same purpose as in the M6801. The $\overline{RESET}$ pin and the Reset Stack Pointer (RSP) instruction, which reset the stack pointer to its maximum value ($7F_{16}$) are the only means available to the user to control this register. Bits 5-10 are fixed in hardware so the address range of the stack pointer is from 60_{16} to $7F_{16}$, i.e. 32 bytes. The length of the stack pointer and the address range differ on other M6805 family members according to the Memory Map and the RAM size. The program counter also varies from device to device according to the memory map, and on current members may be 11, 12 or 13 bits long.

The Condition Code Register in all M6805 devices contains only five flags, the two's complement overflow flag, V, having been considered of little value in controller applications.

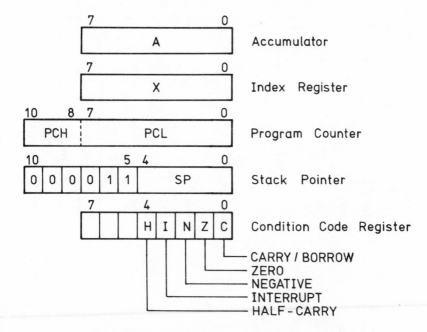

Fig. 2.12 The MC6805P2 programming model.

The MC6805P2 memory map in Fig. 2.13 again illustrates the concept of memory-mapped I/O, where all ROM and RAM locations and all the registers associated with on-board hardware can be treated as memory locations. At the bottom of the address range, in page zero, are located the special function registers and the RAM.

At the top of the address range are the vectors for Reset and for hardware and software interrupts. Between these two extremes are located different areas of on-board ROM. All M6805 family members contain an additional area of on-board ROM which can be programmed during manufacture with a special self-test or bootstrap program. The simple circuit in Fig. 2.14 allows the MC6805P2 self-test program to exercise the on-board RAM, ROM, Timer, Ports and interrupt. Applying 9 volts to the Timer input pin causes the CPU to begin processing at the start of the self-test program instead of the user's program in the main ROM. A flashing code on four LEDs indicates the results of this self-test routine. Alternatively, a bootstrap program in this area allows short test programs to be loaded into RAM via one of the I/O Ports. These features allow the user to perform relatively simple and efficient goods-inward and field testing on devices which, by their nature, are difficult to test.

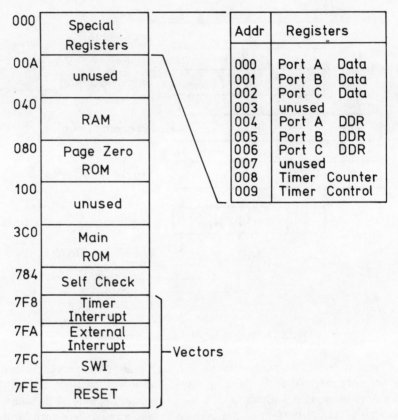

Fig. 2.13 The MC6805P2 memory map and special function registers.

2.6.2 The M6805 Instruction Set

Strictly speaking, the M6805 family instruction set is neither source or object code compatible with the M6801, but it is very similar, and the user should find little difficulty in adapting from one to the other. All M6801 instructions which operate on the B-accumulator and on the V flag in the Condition Code Register have been removed. Stack pointer control has been reduced to only one instruction (Reset Stack Pointer, (RSP), and the decimal adjust accumulator (DAA) instruction has been removed although the half carry has been retained. These reductions in the instruction set have created space in the op-code map needed to include a set of Bit Manipulation instructions. Bit manipulation is extremely useful in low-end control applications and two different classes have been included in the M6805 instruction set.

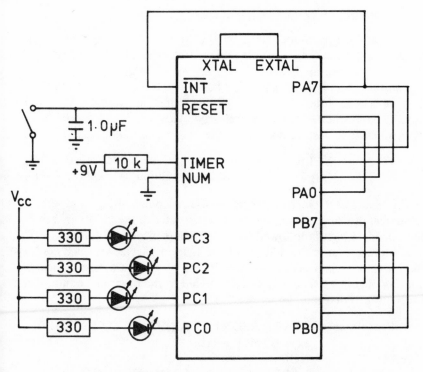

Fig. 2.14 Self-check circuitry for the MC6805P2.

Bit Set/Bit Clear
These instructions allow any bit in page zero, including bits in the I/O ports, but not always the data direction registers, to be set or cleared by one two-byte instructions.

Bit Test and Branch
These instructions allow any bit in page zero, including RAM, ROM and I/O to be tested and a branch to be carried out according to the result of the test. Also, the carry flag in the CCR contains the state of the tested bit after the test.

Although the DAA instruction was removed, two new branch instructions operating on the half carry flag have been added to facilitate decimal additions. The DAA instruction requires a lot of logic and hence silicon. It is much more cost effective to do this operation using software.

Branch if Interrupt High (BIH) or low (BIL) allow the interrupt pin to be used as an additional input line. Finally, Branch if Interrupt Mask Set (BMS) or Clear (BMC) have been added. This means that all bits of the Condition Code Register can be tested, and eliminates the need for instructions to transfer its contents to the accumulator.

2.6.3 M6805 Family Addressing Modes

All the addressing modes used by the M6801 family are used by the
M6805 family, but there are some minor differences in the ways in which
some of them are applied.

The bit set and clear instruction fall into the direct addressing mode.
Each of sixteen different opcodes specifies which of the eight bits is to be
modified and whether it be set or cleared. The opcode is followed by one
byte which specifies the address of the byte to be modified, e.g.:

| 11FA | BCLR | 0, $FA | Clear bit 0 of location FA_{16} |
| 1800 | BSET | 4, PORTA | Output a 1 on Port A bit 4. |

Bit test and Branch instructions use a combination of direct and
relative addressing. Again, the bit and the status of the bit are inherent in
the opcode which is followed by two bytes of address information. The
first address byte is the address of the byte in page zero which contains
the bit to be tested. The second address byte is the positive or negative
address offset ($+127$ to -128) to be added to the program counter if the
test is true. For example:

0A0001	BRSET 5,PORTA,LABEL1 GOTO LABEL1 if
	Port A, bit 0 is clear.
9D	NOP
09EAFD	LABEL1 BRCLR 4,$EA,LABEL1 GOTO
	LABEL1 if bit 4 of location EA_{16} is set.

In the MC6801 the 16-bit index register can be loaded with an address
to which can be added an 8-bit value to produce an effective address
anywhere in the 64 K memory map. Although the M6805 family index
register is only eight bits long, the instruction set allows the addition of a
zero, one or two-byte offset to produce an effective address anywhere
within the device's memory map. For example:

LDA	,X	Load A from address in X.
LDA	$FA,X	Load A from address in X plus FA_{16}.
LDA	$10FA,X	Load A from address in X plus $10FA_{16}$.

2.6.4 M6805 Family Hardware Features

Low-voltage Inhibit Circuitry (LVI)
Many of the HMOS family members have on-board circuitry which
monitors the voltage on the power supply pin and forces the device to
reset itself if this voltage falls below a specified minimum level, nominally
4 volts. This feature is not available on the CMOS versions due to the
greater tolerance of CMOS devices to fluctuations in supply voltage. LVI

is only one of many Masked Options which are available throughout the
M6805 family range. The customer may request that the LVI function be
enabled or disabled, and this feature is then built in or left out during the
manufacturing process along with the programming of the on-board
ROM.

I/O ports

All CMOS and HMOS family devices provide some input/output
capability. This may be in the form of bidirectional ports where each pin
may be configured as an input or output by setting or clearing the
appropriate bit in the Data Direction Register. In certain cases, such as in
the M6805R2, special I/O circuitry demands that some ports be
unidirectional, even if the special feature is not being used. Some ports
are TTL compatible, some are TTL and CMOS compatible, and others
are capable of providing the high sink and source output currents
required to drive LEDs or power devices directly. In many cases, the
customer may specify which configuration is required for the ports as a
Masked Option.

The M6805 family timer

The main elements of the M6805 timer are shown in Fig. 2.15. The 8-bit
timer data register may be loaded under software control and is
decremented by each clock input. A mask option allows the customer to
choose between two different sources of this clock: an external clock
signal may be applied directly to the timer input pin, or alternatively the
CPU's own internal $\phi2$ clock may be selected. In the latter mode, the
Timer Input Pin can be used to gate the $\phi2$ clock through to the timer, by
applying a logic high level, or to stop the clock by applying a logic low
level. This clock signal may be connected directly to the timer data
register or it may be connected to the timer via a 7-bit prescaler. The
prescaler tapping is again offered as a mask option and provides a
maximum division ratio of 128.

On all CMOS and EPROM versions, and on a number of HMOS parts
the Timer Clock Source and the prescaler value are software programmable rather than mask options. A mask option register (MOR) is
provided on these devices to allow the user to select the options required.
On reset, the CPU reads this register and configures the timer
accordingly.

When the timer decrements to zero, the Timer Interrupt Request bit in
the Timer Control Register is set. The state of the Timer Interrupt Mask
bit in the same register determines whether or not the interrupt is
processed. If the interrupt is to be serviced, the CPU stores the machine
state on the stack in RAM and fetches the start address of the timer
interrupt routine from the vector table in ROM. One other bit in the

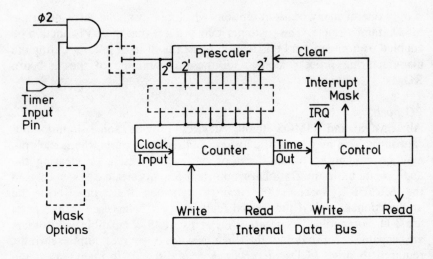

Fig. 2.15 The M6805 family timer.

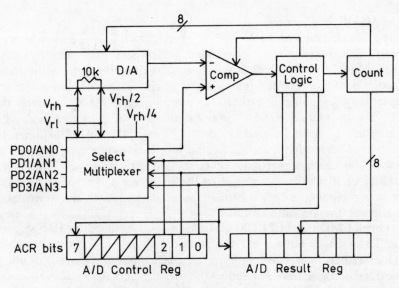

Fig. 2.16 The MC6805R2 analogue to digital converter.

Control Register can be used to clear the prescaler to zero at any time during processing.

Analogue-to-Digital Converter (A/D)
In many applications, analogue signals from external devices such as transducers and sensors have to be processed. Three family members, the MC6805R2, MC6805R3, and MC68705R3 EPROM have an 8-bit A to D converter implemented on the chip to allow such signals to be input with a minimum of preconditioning (see Fig. 2.16). Up to four external and four internal analogue signals may be selected via a multiplexer and applied to the conversion circuitry. The internal analogue signals are provided for calibration purposes. The multiplexer section is controlled by the A/D Conversion Register (ACR), three bits being used to select one of the eight analogue inputs and one bit (the Conversion Complete flag) being used to indicate when the conversion process is complete. The converter samples the analogue input and uses a successive approximation technique to convert this to digital form. Each conversion uses 30 machine cycles and, when complete, the resulting digital value is placed in the A/D Result Register, the Conversion Complete flag is set and the next conversion cycle is started. Whenever the ACR is written, the conversion in progress is aborted and a new one started.

The A/D is ratiometric. Two reference voltages (Vrh and Vr1) must be supplied via two pins on the device. An input voltage equal to Vrh converts to FF_{16}, and an input voltage equal to Vr1 converts to 00_{16}. An input voltage greater than Vrh converts to FF_{16}, and no overflow indication is provided.

Phase Lock Loop
The M6805T2 Phase Lock Loop provides a means of producing very stable local oscillator frequencies and of varying the frequency in discrete steps using software techniques under the control of the CPU. In the phase lock loop system shown in Fig. 2.17, the output frequency (f_{VCO}) of a Voltage Controlled Oscillator (VCO) is compared, using a phase comparator in the MC6805T2, with a very stable reference frequency (f_{Ref}). The phase comparator output causes the Varicap circuit to produce a voltage level which controls the VCO and modifies the output frequency to lock it into phase with fref.

A number of dividers or prescalers are provided in the PLL circuitry on the chip and the VCO frequency is usually divided down using an external prescaler, P. The reference frequency, f_{Ref}, is obtained from the basic crystal frequency using a reference divider, R, which has ten different division ratios selected by a mask option. This provides a wide range of reference frequencies and makes the device suitable for all television and VHF radio transmission frequency bands. The value of the

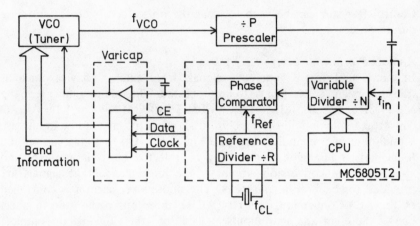

Fig. 2.17 A phase-lock loop system using the MC6805T2.

variable divider, N, can be controlled by software. It is loaded from a 14-bit latch which is loaded in turn from two read/write registers, PLLHI and PLLLO. PLLHI is a six-bit register and can be varied to provide coarse tuning. Fine tuning can be carried out by altering the 8-bit value in PLLLO.

2.6.5 M6805 CMOS Microcomputers

In many application areas, the unique properties of CMOS micro-computers are becoming increasingly attractive. With the advent of silicon-gate CMOS, this technology can now compete with the other technologies in terms of speed and, in terms of low power consumption it cannot be beaten. Motorola's CMOS M6805 microcomputers are ideal for portable battery-operated equipment, which demands very low current drain in order to preserve battery life, and applications where battery back-up is required for long periods of time when the equipment is not being used. Due to the excellent noise immunity and the tolerance to fluctuations in power supply exhibited by CMOS circuits, these micro-computers will function in electrically hostile environments, such as car engine compartments. Also, their fully static design allows them to operate at frequencies down to DC, thus benefiting from the fact that CMOS power consumption is almost directly proportional to the frequency of operation.

In the normal mode of operation, CMOS microcomputers may typically consume a few tens of milliwatts. The instruction set of Motorola's CMOS microcomputers has two additional instructions, WAIT and STOP, which place the devices in low power modes. In the

WAIT mode, the internal clock is disabled from all internal circuitry, except the timer which continues to count normally. All processing is suspended and all registers, memory and I/O lines remain in their last state. The STOP instruction eliminates all dynamic power consumption by stopping the oscillator and all on-board functions. The timer control register is altered to remove any pending timer interrupt requests, and the timer prescaler is cleared. All other static functions remain unchanged as in the WAIT mode. A $\overline{\text{RESET}}$ or external $\overline{\text{INT}}$ signal is required to bring the microcomputer back to the normal operating mode. A timer interrupt will also bring the microcomputer out of the WAIT state, provided the timer interrupt was enabled prior to issuing the WAIT instruction. The power consumed by the MCU in the WAIT and STOP mode is typically 5 mW and 25 μW respectively.

The user can choose between the 28-pin MC146805F2 (1,080 bytes or ROM, 64 bytes of RAM, 16 I/O lines and 4 input-only lines) and the 40-pin MC146805G2 (2,106 bytes of ROM, 112 bytes of RAM and 32 I/O lines). Both devices contain an 8-bit timer, with a 7-bit software programmable prescaler, which may be programmed to operate in four different modes by configuring two control bits in the timer control register. In mode 1, the input to the timer is from an internal clock via the prescaler and the timer input pin is disabled. In mode 2, the internal clock is gated to the timer by an external signal applied to the timer input pin. This mode can be used to measure external pulse widths. In mode 3, all inputs to the timer are disabled, effectively stopping the clock. In mode 4, the internal clock input to the timer is disabled and the timer is clocked by the signal applied to the timer input pin.

A number of mask options can be specified by the user when he orders these devices from the manufacturer. The on-board oscillator can be configured to accept either a crystal or an RC network connected to the oscillator input pins. Also, the customer may choose divide-by-two or divide-by-four circuitry to derive the bus frequency from the on-board oscillator. An external clock signal may be used with either the crystal or RC option. The last mask option configures the external interrupt pin ($\overline{\text{INT}}$) to be either edge- and level-sensitive or level-sensitive only. The first option is useful in applications where the $\overline{\text{INT}}$ input is pulsed because it does not require this input to be held low until the CPU recognises the interrupt request. Where a number of devices are wire-OR'd to the $\overline{\text{INT}}$ pin and each holds this input low until its interrupt request is acknowledged and serviced, the level-sensitive configuration is more appropriate.

Although the MC146805E2 has hardware and software features very similar to those on the other CMOS devices, it has no on-board ROM and cannot really be called a single chip microcomputer. It can address 8K bytes of external memory via a 13-bit expansion bus, the data bits being time-multiplexed with the eight low-order address lines. Multi-plexing of the bus is controlled by three control lines, and bus driver circuitry on the device eliminates the need for external bus driver hardware. The MC146805E2 uses divided-by-five circuitry on the oscillator to obtain the extra resolution required to generate the expansion bus interface and control signals.

Apart from the STOP and WAIT instruction, the CMOS micro-computers use the same instruction set as the HMOS devices and all are software compatible.

2.7   CASE STUDY – MC6805P2 CONTROLLED SPEEDOMETER/ TACHOMETER/ODOMETER

The following case study describes the design and development of a typical automotive application intended to demonstrate the capabilities of a single-chip microcomputer. The finished product was intended to replace existing electromechanical functions of a car dashboard, namely the speedometer, tachometer, odometer and the trip distance meter. The operation of each meter can be considered as three separate functions, Measurement, Conversion and Display.

Measurement
The speedometer and odometer both measure distance and consequently can both be driven by the same signal. In an electromechanical system, a flexible drive shaft connected to the final drive of the gearbox is magnetically coupled to the speedometer needle and mechanically coupled to the odometer. The tachometer measures the speed of rotation of the engine by monitoring an electrical waveform generated by the opening and closing of the contact breaker points in the distributor.

Conversion
Although the odometer and speedometer use the same input signal, they process this signal in different ways. The odometer uses a series of mechanical gears to count the number of rotations of the drive shaft and convert this value to miles or kilometres. Magnets attached to the drive shaft in the speedometer cause the speedometer needle to be deflected through an angle which is proportional to the road speed. Similarly, but using an electrical system, the tachometer needle is deflected through an angle proportional to the engine speed.

Display
The odometer displays distance in miles or kilometres on a mechanical meter with several digits. The trip meter does the same but has the

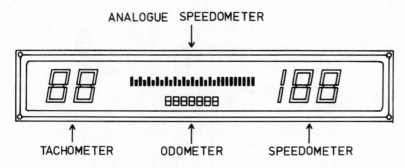

Fig. 2.18 The dashboard display layout.

facility to return the display to zero. The speedometer and tachometer normally display their information in an analogue fashion on circular, suitably calibrated dials.

The electronic system
The system uses an MC6805P2 microcomputer to receive signals from a distance sensor and convert these measurements to actual values of speed, r.p.m. and distance which can then be displayed on a suitable medium. Because of the wide range of M6805 and M6801 family microcomputers, the decision to use the MC6805P2 was made after the display medium was selected and the other requirements of the system were identified.

The main display chosen was a vacuum fluorescent dashboard display manufactured by Futaba (see Fig. 2.18.). This consists of a large 2-digit display, a similar 3-digit display, and a bar-graph. Road speed is displayed in digital form on the 3-digit display and in analogue form on the bar-graph. Each segment is constructed from a matrix of green and red dots. This provides the capability to display information in green or red or, by driving both sets of dots at once, in orange. This feature is used in the system to indicate low (green), medium (orange) and high (red) speeds. A small format, 7-digit, 7-segment display, mounted behind a window in the Futaba display, is used to display distance information.

Odometer and trip meter information must be retained indefinitely when the engine ignition is switched off and the microcomputer and display are powered down. To keep the system powered up permanently would cause an excessive current drain from the car battery. Fortunately, non-volatile memories are now available. Such devices will retain any information stored in them even when they are powered down, and can be read from, written to, and electrically erased when powered up. A push button is provided to allow switching between the odometer and the trip meter functions. Another push button allows the trip meter reading to be reset to zero.

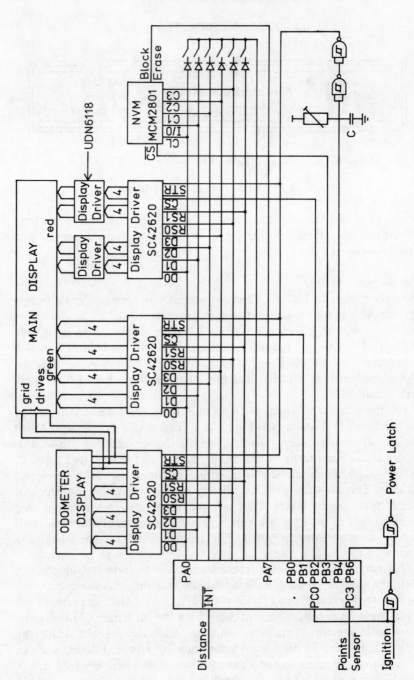

Fig. 2.19 The MC6805P2 controlled speedometer/tachometer/odometer.

2.7.1 Hardware Design

Figure 2.19 shows a simplified block diagram of the hardware.

An optical sensor connected to the drive shaft provides a distance signal which is connected to the interrupt input of the microcomputer. The engine speed signal from the contact breaker points is connected to bit 4 of Port C. A second signal indicates to the microcomputer whether the ignition is on or off. A 4 MHz crystal provides the basic system clock.

The Futaba display requires many more input signals to drive all the discrete segments of the display than are available on the I/O ports of the microcomputer. Also, the green elements of the display require a driving potential of the order of 25 V, while the red elements need around 50 V. Three Motorola SC42620 fluorescent display driver chips provide sufficient output signals to drive all the segments of the display. The output drive levels are about −21 V, and two of these devices are used to drive the green elements of the display directly. The outputs of the third SC42620 drive the inputs of two UDN6118 display drivers. These devices produce output potentials of 44 V by virtue of them being supplied from the −21 V and +23 V power supply lines. These outputs are used to drive the red elements of the display.

It is useful to examine the SC42620 to understand how so many segments can be controlled by the microcomputer. This device contains four pairs of 4-bit latches providing sixteen outputs (Fig. 2.20). Two inputs signals, RS0 and RS1, allow the microcomputer to select one pair of latches. Data applied to the four data inputs is loaded into a buffer and clocked into the first level latch of the selected pair. When the strobe line is taken high, the display driver outputs are switched off and the data in the latch is shifted into the output register. When the strobe line is taken low, the output drives are enabled. Therefore, only when the outputs are off can the output data be changed. This allows the strobe pin to pulse width modulate (or dim) all the outputs without introducing flicker when the data is changed. This feature is used in the design to automatically control the brilliance of the display. The strobe drive output from the microcomputer is connected to the display driver via two Schmidt trigger invertors. The display is switched on by the microcomputer switching this output low. This also discharges capacitor, C, which is then charged via a simple light-sensitive resistive circuit. As the ambient light level increases, the effective resistance of this circuit increases. Consequently, the time taken to charge up to the Schmidt trigger switching voltage increases and the strobe input signal is held low for a longer period of time. This means that the display segments are switched on for longer periods of time as the ambient light level increases, and ensures that the display is not washed out by brilliant sunlight and does not become dazzling at night.

Display data is output by the MC6805P2 on bits 0 to 3 of Port A and

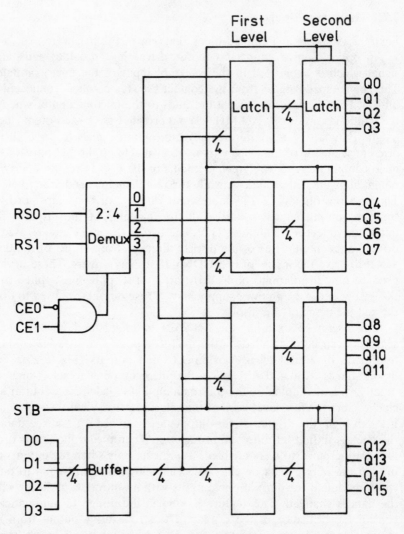

Fig. 2.20 The SC42620 fluorescent display driver.

bits 4 and 5 are used to select the display driver latch set via RS0 and RS1. Port B, bit 0, is used as a chip select line to select the SC42620 which drives the odometer display, and bits 1 and 2 select the SC42620 driving the green and red elements respectively. Port A also interfaces to the non-volatile memory and to the pushbuttons.

The non-volatile memory chosen is the Motorola MCM2801 which provides a memory array of sixteen 16-bit words. It also contains a 4-bit address register, which can be loaded with the address of any one of the sixteen internal memory locations, and a 16-bit data register. Data and address information is transferred serially on the I/O line using the CL line to clock each bit in, or out of, the memory. The microcomputer controls the memory by applying a 3-bit instruction code to its control pins, C1, C2 and C3. The memory's address register is loaded by outputting the address serially on Port A, bit 1, clocking each bit in turn by pulsing the clock line, while the SERIAL ADDRESS IN instruction code is applied to the control pins. To store data in the memory array, the microcomputer first writes the data into the memory's 16-bit data register, using the same procedure as above but with the SERIAL DATA IN instruction code on the control pins. It then moves the data from the data register to the location specified by the address register, by applying the WRITE instruction code and sending one clock pulse on the clock line. Data is retrieved in a similar manner using the READ instruction followed by a SERIAL DATA OUT instruction.

Port A, bit 7, controls the block erase feature of the non-volatile memory, allowing the whole or selected areas of the memory to be erased quickly and efficiently by the microcomputer. As the memory and fluorescent display driver interfaces are common, the memory is enabled using Port B, bit 3 as a chip select only when data transfers are being carried out. Similarly, diodes in the pushbutton circuits ensure that data being transmitted to the display or memory is not corrupted by the operation of these buttons. Although only two pushbuttons are used in the present system, four extra buttons are available for future software enhancement.

When the car ignition is switched off, the latest odometer and trip meter information must be securely stored in the non-volatile memory before the microcomputer is powered down. To ensure that this happens, the microcomputer holds Port B, bit 6 (POWER) low during the time when the ignition is switched on. This logic zero signal ensures that a logic high signal, from the output of a Schmidt trigger-input NAND gate, is applied to the power latch thus keeping the power on. When the ignition is switched off and the non-volatile memory is securely updated, the microcomputer switches the power signal high, making both inputs to the NAND gate low. The power latch signal, therefore, goes low and powers down the complete system. The 5 V supply needed to drive the microcomputer and other logic, and the -21 V and $+23$ V supplies to drive the fluorescent displays and to program the non-volatile memory, were generated from the car's 12 V battery using standard D.C. invertor circuits.

2.7.2 Software Considerations

Prior to writing the software, cross-reference tables were constructed to relate the binary coded decimal (BCD) digits, resulting from speed and distance calculations, to the individual segments of the display. These tables are located in the page zero ROM space to take advantage of the short direct mode of addressing, and are used by the microcomputer to output data on the four low-order bits of Port A in the correct format. Figure 2.21 shows the BCD to 7-segment display conversion table. (The table for the bar graph segments is similar.) This figure shows how each segment and decimal point is represented by one bit of an 8-bit byte. For example, to display a zero, all segments except G (bit 1) and DP (bit 0) must be driven. In this application a segment is off when a logic zero is applied, so the microcomputer must send FC_{16} (1111 1100) to the 7-segment display. FCB (Fix Constant Byte) is an instruction to the Assembler to allocate one byte of ROM to the following fixed data byte. A diagram showing the structure of the software is given in Fig. 2.22. It has three main sections, the Start-up procedure, the Main loop and the Shut-down procedure.

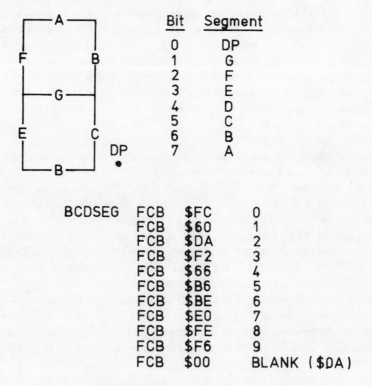

Fig. 2.21 BCD to 7-segment display conversion.

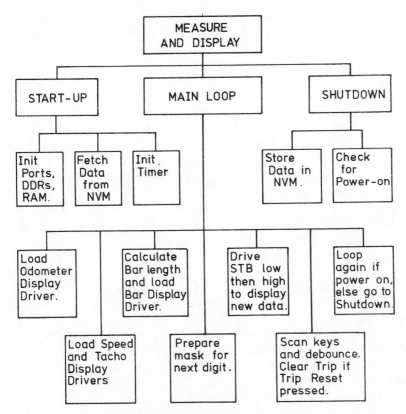

Fig. 2.22 Software structure diagram.

Start-up

Each Port is initialised by first of all loading an appropriate value into the accumulator and storing this in the data register, and then loading the accumulator with a byte representing the input (0) and output (1) lines and storing this in the data direction register. The RAM locations used by the microcomputer as temporary registers and flags are initialised by writing starting values into them. The contents of the non-volatile memory are retrieved and stored in temporary registers in RAM. All non-volatile memory data transfers are handled by a subroutine which may be entered from anywhere in the program, provided certain parameters are set up correctly prior to executing the jump-to-subroutine instruction. A flag bit in one of the temporary registers must be set up to indicate either a read or write operation on the non-volatile memory, the accumulator must be loaded with the number of bytes of data to be read or written, and the index register must contain the address of the first temporary register in RAM.

Because of the serial nature of the interface to the non-volatile memory, the microcomputer benefits from the power of the M6805 bit manipulation instructions. The following subroutines are used to write data from the accumulator to the non-volatile memory, clocking each bit in turn by setting then clearing the clock line:

SEROP	BCLR 1,	PORTA	Clear output.
	RORA		LSB of Acc into Carry.
	BCC	SEROP1	If Carry clear, O/P remains low.
	BSET 1,	PORTA	If Carry set, O/P goes high.
SEROP1	BSR	CLOCK	Clock out bit.
	DEC	TEMP2	Decrement bit counter (starts at 8).
	BNE	SEROP	If not zero get next bit.
	RTS		Return.
CLOCK	BSET 0,	PORTA	Clock line high.
	BCLR 0,	PORTA	Clock line low.
	RTS		Return.

When all the data in the non-volatile memory has been stored in RAM, the program enters a subroutine which erases the non-volatile memory.

Apart from the odometer and trip meter readings, the non-volatile memory also contains calibration factors for road speed, engine speed and distance. These values can be altered to make the system compatible with any vehicle. The distance calibration factor defines the number of interrupt pulses sent by the distance sensor per unit distance. The interrupt routine counts the pulses and increments the odometer and tripmeter values each time this value is reached. The interrupt routine also increments a temporary register called the Speed Counter. The speed and distance factors are used to generate a fixed time interval such that the contents of the speed counter at the end of each period are equal to the speed in m.p.h. or k.p.h. This time interval is made up from a number of 30-millisecond periods generated by the on-board timer. The timer is initialised by loading a value into its data register and then clearing its control register allowing the timer to be clocked by the microcomputer's internal 1 MHz clock. The interrupt mask is then cleared enabling a timer interrupt to occur when the data register counts down to zero. When the correct number of timer periods has expired, the speed counter is read then stored in the speed register ready for updating the speedometer displays. This is somewhat of an oversimplification because several speed measurements are averaged by the software to ensure that the display is 'debounced' and made visually acceptable to the driver. The engine speed is measured by a subroutine called during the main loop.

The main loop
This section of the program is entered immediately after the Start-up procedure is complete, and is only exitted when the ignition detect signal goes low. Its main purpose is to display the information obtained from the speed and distance measurements. Although the display appears to be continuous to the driver, it is actually time-multiplexed by the main loop software. This is necessary because many of the segment and grid drive inputs to the fluorescent displays are common.

The odometer/trip meter display driver is loaded by first fetching, from RAM, the BCD value of the next digit to be displayed and its position in the 7-digit display. The following routine is then used to look up the BCD to 7-segment display conversion table in page zero ROM.

```
LDX BCDVAL        Load BCD value into index register.
LDA BCDSEG,X      Get Segment drive data.
```

BCDSEG is the start address of the table shown in Fig. 2.21. As each latch in the display driver accepts four bits of data, the lower and upper nibbles of the resulting data byte are shifted into the four least significant bits of two temporary registers, TEMP1 and TEMP2. Bits 4 and 5 of TEMP1 are set to zero to select latch 0 in the display driver. The contents of TEMP1 are then output on Port A, and Port B, bit 0 is driven low to select the odometer display driver, and load the data into latch 0. Similarly, bits 4 and 5 of TEMP2 are set up to select latch 1 and the process is repeated. The position of the digit to be displayed is represented by a digit mask byte which is loaded into latches 3 and 4 in exactly the same way.

Before outputting speed information to the tachometer and speed-ometer display drivers, the engine speed signal is monitored by reading Port C, bit 4. If this signal has changed state since it was previously tested, the contents of a temporary tachometer register are incremented. This data is used in conjunction with the speedometer measurement period to determine the engine speed in revolutions per minute.

The digital speed and bar-graph information is loaded into the display drivers in exactly the same way as the odometer information by selecting the appropriate device. Each segment of the bar-graph represents 5 m.p.h. (or 5 k.p.h.) and a software routine effectively divides the speed by 5, to determine how many segments should be driven, before the display driver is loaded.

At this point in the program, all the display driver first level latches are loaded with new information, although this has not yet been displayed. Before displaying this information a number of digit position registers are updated in preparation for loading the display drivers on the next iteration of the main loop.

To transfer the latched data to the display, the microcomputer drives the strobe line high and then low again. As described earlier, driving this line high disables the driver outputs, thus switching off the display (this may have occurred already due to the brightness control circuitry), and latches the new data into the display output registers. This new data is displayed when the strobe line is driven low.

During the loading of the display drivers, all Port A pins are configured as outputs and bit 6 is held high to disable the keyboard. To scan the keyboard, pins 0 to 5 are reconfigured as inputs and pin 6 is driven low using the Bit Clear (BCLR) instruction. If any key is closed at this time, the logic zero output from pin 6 will be applied to the corresponding input pin. A logic one will be present on all other input pins. The microcomputer reads Port A into the accumulator, masks out the bits which do not correspond to keys, and compares the resulting byte with the byte obtained during the previous iteration of the Main Loop. If the bytes are the same it is assumed that a key has been pressed. If they differ, the latest reading is stored for comparison on the next keyboard scan. This effectively debounces the keyboard in software and obviates the need for expensive mechanically debounced keys. On completion, the keyboard is disabled by returning pin 6 to a logic one (BSET 6, PORTA). The key data is stored in RAM for use by other subroutines. If TRIP RESET has been pressed, the RAM locations storing the trip meter value are cleared to zero immediately. If TRIP has been pressed, a flag is set which causes the trip distance information to be loaded during the odometer display driver loading routine.

The final routine in the main loop simply tests Port C, bit 0, to determine whether the ignition is on or off. If it is still on, processing continues again from the start of the main loop. If the ignition is off, the program jumps out of the main loop to the Shut-down procedure.

Shut-down procedure

This routine is responsible for safely storing the latest odometer and trip meter values, and also the calibration factors, back in the non-volatile memory. As in the Start-up routine, when these values were fetched from the non-volatile memory, the index register and accumulator are loaded with the address of the first byte and the number of bytes to be saved. However, before jumping to the subroutine, the non-volatile memory flag is set to 'write' instead of 'read'. When this is complete, bit 6 of Port B is set to a logic one to release the power latch and switch off the power. Because a glitch on the ignition detect line may have caused a false power-down situation, this input is tested continuously until the power supply falls sufficiently to cause the microcomputer to stop processing. If, in this time, the ignition detect signal goes high again, the program jumps back to the Start-up routine and immediately latches the power supply on again. This power-down sequence is carried out by the following routine which includes debouncing to ensure that positive glitches on the ignition detect line do not cause a false restart:

PWROFF	BSET	6,PORTB	Switch off power.
END	BRCLR	0,PORTC,END	Test for ignition on.
	BRCLR	0,PORTC,END	Test for ignition on.
	BRCLR	0,PORTC,END	Test for ignition on.
	JMP	START	Ignition on, restart.

2.8 FUTURE TRENDS

The immediate future is not difficult to predict, because Motorola has a number of new single-chip microcomputers which are already well past the initial design stage. The M6805 family will continue to grow with the addition of new HMOS and CMOS parts. Already announced is the MC68HC05C4, a CMOS version featuring 4 K bytes of ROM, 176 bytes of RAM, a 16-bit timer similar to that used on the MC6801, a Standard NRZ format Serial Communications Interface and a four-wire Serial Peripheral Interface for multiprocessor applications. This part has been available since the end of 1983 and should find many uses in low-end and mid-range consumer and telecommunications applications.

In 1982, Motorola announced a new family of single-chip micro-computers – the M6804 family. Aimed at providing very low cost microcomputing power for low-end control applications, this family takes advantage of the very considerable savings in silicon that can be achieved by adopting a serial, rather than a parallel, architecture. Although, to the programmer, M6804 devices appear similar to the M6805 devices, internally, the hardware is very different. Whereas, in the MC6805P2, for example, the Arithmetic Logic Unit and the data bus are 8-bits wide, and the Program Counter incrementing logic and the address bus are 11-bits wide, in M6804 devices all these features are only 1-bit wide. Further savings in silicon have been achieved by using self-refreshing dynamic RAM instead of static RAM, and by implementing some of the special purpose registers in RAM locations rather than in dedicated registers which require a considerable amount of supporting logic circuitry. Whereas in the M6805 one cycle of the internal clock is equivalent to one machine cycle, the M6804, due to its serial architecture, requires twelve internal clock cycles for each machine cycle. This fact would have resulted in a very low performance microcomputer in terms of operating speed were it not for recent advances in HMOS technology and the advent of high-speed CMOS technology.

The M6804 devices are designed to operate at external frequencies up to 11 MHz, giving a minimum machine cycle of 4.36 μs. This, combined with the increased efficiency of the instruction set, means that the processing speed of the M6804 is not significantly less than that of the M6805. This family will provide ROM, RAM, Timer and I/O capabilities similar to the M6805 family and is currently available in HMOS and will be available in CMOS later in 1984. An EPROM version will also become available towards the end of 1984.

In the medium term future, we can expect to see the integration of many more hardware features onto silicon. More microcomputers will provide some form of serial interface to facilitate the design of distributed-intelligence multiprocessor control systems. High drive capability on output ports and the merging of different technologies will allow microcomputers to interface directly to many forms of display device without requiring expensive external display driver devices. The capability to merge different technologies will bring microcomputers with on-board electrically erasable-programmable ROM, and should make possible the integration of a processor and an uncommitted gate array on the same silicon chip, an extremely effective means of reducing the external logic circuitry normally required in any design.

The long-term future is more speculative but will obviously be influenced by a combination of what the microprocessor manufacturer can achieve on silicon and the demands of the market place. Motorola's investment in new manufacturing and testing plants in East Kilbride, Scotland, and in the U.S.A. will ensure that the most advanced CMOS and HMOS technologies can be supplied to future single-chip microcomputers.

The M6805 and M6804 families will continue to grow, reaching more new markets as they become more versatile and as they become cheaper and more cost effective in very low cost applications. The M6801 family will grow upwards, more powerful HMOS and CMOS devices being added as customers become more familiar with the microcomputer's potential and their application ideas become more complex and demanding.

As the 1-bit microcomputer was followed by the 4-bit microcomputer which was in turn followed by the 8-bit device, so the 16-bit single-chip microcomputer will follow the 8-bit device. However, it is unlikely that the 8-bit microcomputer will ever disappear entirely. Very few control applications, which are really the microcomputer's forte, merit the computing power of a 16-bit processor. The most likely application areas will be in the automotive industry for total engine management and vehicle condition monitoring systems and in systems requiring fast data manipulation and transfer, such as intelligent banking machines and point-of-sale terminals. Motorola will, no doubt, enter this field with a device based very much on the architecture of the MC68000 16-bit processor.

SUMMARY

In this chapter the Motorola M6801 and M6805 families are presented. Many of the concepts discussed, both of hardware and software, are highly relevant to all microcomputer families making this a detailed introduction to many general aspects of microcomputers. The case study of a car speedometer/tachometer/odometer highlights many aspects of application design in general, particularly display driving and the management of a peripheral circuit, in this case a non-volatile memory device. Some of the future trends hinted at in Chapter 1 are further discussed.

CHAPTER 3

Texas Instruments Microcomputers

By Chris Moller

3.1 THE TMS1000 – A LOW COST 4-BIT MICROCOMPUTER FAMILY

3.1.1 History and Product Range

Towards the end of the 1960s, the level of integration achievable had increased to the point where it became possible to integrate all the functions of a traditional computer onto one chip. The elements required were (and still are) a program memory store, a variable store, instruction interpretation logic, and an input/output structure. The significance of this was that for the first time, an alternative existed to designing special hardware for a given function. Designing hardware is a very labour-intensive and expensive process, and only a limited amount of previous experience can be used in designing a chip for a new application. The advent of the single-chip microcomputer meant that for the first time it was possible to define the desired function in software, and use standard hardware, only changing the contents of the program ROM for each new part. In time, of course, the prices of these new programmable parts came down and, as they did so, it became reasonable to review simpler and simpler functions, with a view to implementation using a micro-computer rather than custom hardware. Currently it is reasonable to consider a single-chip microcomputer to replace as few as a dozen standard TTL packages, if the quantity is sufficient.

Product milestones

1971	Single-Chip Microcomputer invented.
1972	First commercial application, in a hand-held calculator, using a PMOS part with buffered LED display.
1974	TMS1000 released for use by OEMs.
1975	Vacuum-fluorescent direct-drive parts released (TMS1070/1270).
1976	TMS1100/1300 2 K byte ROM parts released.
1978	CMOS parts introduced – allowing reduced power-consumption, auto power-off.
1980	TMS1400/1600/1700 4 K byte, 0.5 K byte parts introduced.

1981	2 K byte CMOS parts (TMS1100C/1300C).
	CMOS+ADC parts introduced (TMS2100/2300).
	First $1 priced parts shipped.
1982	1024 bit RAM part (TMS1304).
1983	LCD direct-drive parts (TMS2220/2240).

Despite its relatively modest performance, demand for the TMS1000 has not gone down as the demand for more exotic parts has gone up. On the contrary, continued erosion of the price has meant an ever-expanding market in areas where previously a microcomputer would never have been considered. In fact, it looks likely that the TMS1000 will be the first programmable integrated circuit to ship more than 100 million units. To support this market, new members of the family will be produced to permit even greater integration within one chip. Electronic products containing only one active component, a single-chip microcomputer, are already becoming commonplace, and this trend will continue.

3.1.2 Architecture and Design Philosophy

The TMS1000 family all have 4-bit wide data paths, and an 8-bit wide program ROM. This provides the most effective use of silicon, provided that 4 bits of data give adequate throughput capability for the application. Generally speaking, where design tradeoffs have involved a choice between lowering the silicon area needed (and hence cost), or providing greater programming convenience, the former choice has been taken. The rationale for this is that the design cost occurs only once, whereas the unit cost is repeated for each part produced. For the high-volume market for which the part is intended, the project development cost will be insignificant, when divided into the number produced. One of the repercussions of this is that the program counter is not sequential, as a pseudo-random binary sequence generator requires less space to implement than a full-blown counter. Fortunately, the assembler takes account of this, and allows the programmer to program in a conventional sequential manner. Other limitations on the hardware have a more immediate bearing on the application. The I/O structure has been designed with display and keyboard multiplexing in mind (see p. 88), without bringing out the internal busses, so interfacing to bus-orientated peripherals can be a little difficult. Also, the processing speeds of the parts are not spectacular; usually single-chip microcomputers are not required to process large amounts of data in a short time, and slower parts are, of course, cheaper to produce. A typical TMS1000 family PMOS part, shown in Fig. 3.1, runs with a 330 kHz oscillator frequency, and executes an instruction in 18 microseconds, regardless of the instruction.

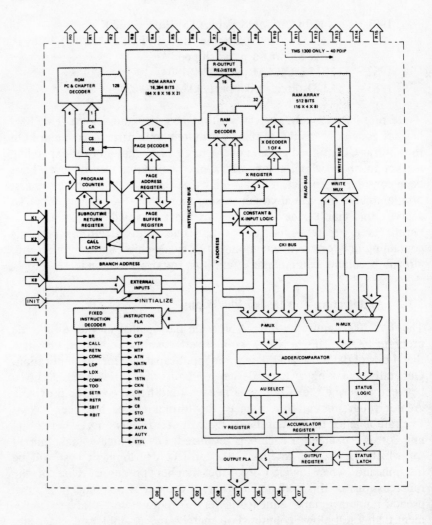

Fig. 3.1 Typical TMS1000 family member block diagram.

There are also some limitations on the software, again imposed to simplify the internal chip design. The instruction sets (there are actually two distinct TMS1XXX instruction sets, TMS1000/1200 and TMS1000/1300) do not attempt to compete with the instruction set of a mainframe. The instructions which are necessary are there, but there are few concessions to structured programming. For example, only limited subroutine nesting is permitted. No high-level target program is supported. (There's seldom enough room in the ROM for an interpreter package anyway.) Also, the development system does not support programming in a high-level language, for subsequent conversion to native code in the target system. This is because when using a limited instruction set, every feature of an instruction must be exploited, to make the most of the available ROM space, and native-code generators tend to be too conservative in this respect.

Another respect in which the TMS1XXX family differ from conventional microprocessors in their architecture is the absence of a memory map as such for the RAM. Instead, referencing a particular 4-bit word in the RAM is achieved by setting two internal registers, called X and Y, to the co-ordinate of the desired word in a memory array. Some of the commands permit auto-incrementing of one of the registers, allowing easy access to successive locations. A similar scheme exists for the program ROM. This is divided into 'pages', each of sixty-four bytes. Execution of the software within a page is determined by the program in the conventional way, but branching to another page requires a pre-load of a page-register before branching (the load doesn't occur until the branch is executed).

The power-up aspect of single-chip microcomputer applications is frequently neglected during program development and system emulation. All microcomputers begin execution on power-up at a location in program memory defined in the hardware. (During system emulation, it's defined in software.) For the TMS1000 family, this location is always Page F, Location 00. The power-up condition is detected by an internal capacitor time-delay, but this is only functional if the power-supply rise-time is short. If this is not the case, an external capacitor on the INIT pin will be required. Note particularly that initialisation only happens correctly if the K-inputs and R10 are all at logic zero during the reset cycle; failure to observe this rule is a common cause of design problems!

3.1.3 Instruction Sets

The two TMS1000 family instruction sets are listed in Tables 3.1 and 3.2. There are a number of features of the instructions that differ appreciably from more conventional microprocessor instructions. Conditional jumps, in particular, are achieved in an unusual manner. A single status bit is provided. It is normally set to one, but may be set to zero by some instructions. In any event, it will be set to one at the end of the next instruction. All BRanch and CALL instructions are conditional on this status bit being one. Arithmetic instructions set the status bit to the value of the Carry bit from the ALU. Memory-compare instructions set the bit if the results differ, and clear it if they are equal. Further details can be found in Ref. 3.1 (see end of this chapter).

The program memory (ROM) is divided into 64-byte pages. The CALL and BRanch instructions use only the two most significant bits of

Table 3.1 TMS1000/1200/1700 instruction summary.

Function	Mnemonic	Status* Effect C8	NE	Description
Register to	TAY			Transfer accumulator to Y register.
Register	TYA			Transfer Y register to accumulator.
	CLA			Clear accumulator.
Transfer	TAM			Transfer accumulator to memory.
Register to	TAMIY			Transfer accumulator to memory and increment Y register.
Memory	TAMZA			Transfer accumulator to memory and zero accumulator.
Memory to	TMY			Transfer memory to Y register.
Register	TMA			Transfer memory to accumulator.
	XMA			Exchange memory and accumulator.
Arithmetic	AMAAC	Y		Add memory to accumulator, results to accumulator. If carry, one to status.
	SAMAN	Y		Subtract accumulator from memory, results to accumulator. If no borrow, one to status.
	IMAC**	Y		Increment memory and load into accumulator. If carry, one to status.
	DMAN**	Y		Decrement memory and load into accumulator. If no borrow, one to status.
	IA			Increment accumulator, no status effect.
	IYC	Y		Increment Y register. If carry, one to status.
	DAN	Y		Decrement accumulator. If no borrow, one to status.
	DYN	Y		Decrement Y register. If no borrow, one to status.
	A8AAC	Y		Add 8 to accumulator, results to accumulator. If carry, one to status.
	A10AAC	Y		Add 10 to accumulator, results to accumulator. If carry, one to status.
	A6AAC	Y		Add 6 to accumulator, results to accumulator. If carry, one to status.
	CPAIZ	Y		Complement accumulator and increment. If then zero, one to status.
Arithmetic	ALEM	Y		If accumulator less than or equal to memory, one to status.
Compare	ALEC	Y		If accumulator less than or equal to a constant, one to status.
Logical	MNEZ		Y	If memory not equal to zero, one to status.
Compare	YNEA		Y	If Y register not equal to accumulator, one to status and status latch.
	YNEC		Y	If Y register not equal to a constant, one to status.
Bits in	SBIT			Set memory bit.
Memory	RBIT			Reset memory bit.
	TBIT1		Y	Test memory bit. If equal to one, one to status.

Table 3.1 continued

Funtion	Mnemonic	Status* Effect C8	Status* Effect NE	Description
Constants	TCY			Transfer constant to Y register.
	TCMIY			Transfer constant to memory and increment Y.
Input	KNEZ		Y	If K inputs are not equal to zero, one to status.
	TKA			Transfer K inputs to accumulator.
Output	SETR			Set R output addressed by Y.
	RSTR			Reset R output addressed by Y.
	TDO			Transfer data from accumulator and status latch to O-outputs.
	CLO			Clear O-output register.
RAM X	LDX			Load X with a constant.
Addressing	COMX			Complement X.
ROM	BR			Branch on status = one.
Addressing	CALL			Call subroutine on status = one.
	RETN			Return from subroutine.
	LDP			Load page buffer with constant.

***NOTE A:**

C8 (microinstruction C8 is used) – Y (Yes) means that if there is a carry out of the MSB, status output goes to the ONE state. If no carry is generated, status output goes to the ZERO state.

NE (microinstruction NE is used) – Y (Yes) means that if the bits compared are not equal, status output goes to the ONE state. If the bits are equal, status output goes to the ZERO state.

A ZERO in status remains through the next instruction cycle only. If the next instruction is a branch or call and status is a ZERO, then the branch or call is not executed.

****NOTE B:**

Execution of the DMAN or IMAC instruction does not change (increment or decrement) the content of the addressed memory cell.

Table 3.2 TMS1100/1300/1400/1600 instruction summary.

Function	Mnemonic	Status Effect C8	Status Effect NE	Description
Register to	TAY			Transfer accumulator to Y register.
Register	TYA			Transfer Y register to accumulator.
Transfer	CLA			Clear accumulator.

Table 3.2 continued

Function	Mnemonic	Status Effect C8	NE	Description
Register to Memory	TAM			Transfer accumulator to memory.
	TAMIYC	Y		Transfer accumulator to memory and increment Y register. If carry, one to status.
	TAMDYN	Y		Transfer accumulator to memory and decrement Y register. If no borrow, one to status.
	TAMZA			Transfer accumulator to memory and zero accumulator.
Memory to Register	TMY			Transfer memory to Y register.
	TMA			Transfer memory to accumulator.
	XMA			Exchange memory and accumulator.
Arithmetic	AMAAC	Y		Add memory to accumulator, results to accumulator. If carry, one to status.
	SAMAN	Y		Subtract accumulator from memory, results to accumulator. If no borrow, one to status.
	IMAC	Y		Increment memory and load into accumulator. If carry, one to status.
	DMAN	Y		Decrement memory and load into accumulator. If no borrow, one to status.
	IAC	Y		Increment accumulator. If carry, one to status.
	DAN	Y		Decrement accumulator. If no borrow, one to status.
	A2AAC	Y		Add 2 to accumulator. Results to accumulator. If carry one to status.
	A3AAC	Y		Add 3 to accumulator. Results to accumulator. If carry one to status.
	A4AAC	Y		Add 4 to accumulator. Results to accumulator. If carry one to status.
	A5AAC	Y		Add 5 to accumulator. Results to accumulator. If carry one to status.
	A6AAC	Y		Add 6 to accumulator. Results to accumulator. If carry one to status.
	A7AAC	Y		Add 7 to accumulator. Results to accumulator. If carry one to status.
	A8AAC	Y		Add 8 to accumulator. Results to accumulator. If carry one to status.
	A9AAC	Y		Add 9 to accumulator. Results to accumulator. If carry one to status.
	A10AAC	Y		Add 10 to accumulator. Results to accumulator. If carry one to status.
	A11AAC	Y		Add 11 to accumulator. Results to accumulator. If carry one to status.
	A12AAC	Y		Add 12 to accumulator. Results to accumulator. If carry one to status.

Table 3.2 continued

Funtion	Mnemonic	Status* Effect C8	NE	Description
	A13AAC	Y		Add 13 to accumulator. Results to accumulator. If carry one to status.
	A14AAC	Y		Add 14 to accumulator. Results to accumulator. If carry one to status.
	IYC	Y		Increment Y register. if carry, one to status.
	DYN	Y		Decrement Y register. If no borrow, one to status.
	CPAIZ	Y		Complement accumulator and increment. If then zero, one to status.
Arithmetic Compare	ALEM	Y		If accumulator less than or equal to memory, one to status.
Logical Compare	MNEA		Y	If memory is not equal to accumulator, one to status.
	MNEZ		Y	If memory not equal to zero, one to status.
	YNEA		Y	If Y register not equal to accumulator, one to status and status latch.
	YNEC		Y	If Y register not equal to a constant, one to status.
Bits in Memory	SBIT			Set memory bit.
	RBIT			Reset memory bit.
	TBIT1		Y	Test memory bit. If equal to one, one to status.
Constants	TCY			Transfer constant to Y register.
	TCMIY			Transfer constant to memory and increment Y.
Input	KNEZ		Y	If K inputs are not equal to zero, one to status.
	TKA			Transfer K inputs to accumulator.
Output	SETR			Set R output addressed by Y.
	RSTR			Reset R output addressed by Y.
	TDO			Transfer data from accumulator and status latch to O outputs.
RAM X Addressing	LDX			Load X with file address.
	COMX			Complement the MSB of X.
ROM Addressing	BR			Branch on status = one.
	CALL			Call subroutine on status = one.
	RETN			Return from subroutine.
	LDP			Load page buffer with constant.
	COMC			Complement chapter buffer.

the instruction byte to specify the opcode, leaving six bits to specify an absolute destination within the page. BRanching and CALLing outside a page are achieved with the LDP (Load Page) instruction. This causes the page to switch simultaneously with the execution of the next BRanch or CALL instruction that occurs. Note that in the case of a CALL to a subroutine, the corresponding RETN restores the page buffer to its former value. (If a RETN is executed, without a previous CALL, execution continues in-line, but the page buffer is still restored.) In TMS1000 Assembler source-code, the mnemonics BL, CALL L (Branch Long, CALL Long) are used to generate the appropriate LDP, BR, or LDP, CALL instructions. This makes the paging relatively transparent to the programmer, although it is still necessary to ensure that the program does not attempt to execute past the end of a page.

3.1.4 Input/Output Structures

As mentioned above, the Input and Output ports do not form part of either the RAM or ROM memory maps. They are specifically designed with multiplexed displays and keyboards in mind, and for this reason are statically latched by specific commands.

The outputs are of two kinds, arbitrarily named 'O-' and 'R-lines'. In each case, they are numbered starting with zero, but that is where the similarity ends. R-lines are controlled with two commands:

SETR .... Set R-line, addressed by current Y-reg, contents to ONE.

RSTR .... Clear R-line, addressed by current Y-reg, contents to ZERO.
(Note that on Power-Up, all R-lines are at ZERO.)

The O-lines are a little more complicated. Two instructions are provided which control the contents of the 5-bit-wide O-latch. They are:

TDO .... Transfer contents of A (LSN) and SL (MSB) to O-register.

CLO .... Clear O-register to ZERO (power-up state) −TMS1000/1200 only.

The five bits of the O-register are not brought out directly, however. Eight O-outputs are provided. An OPLA (O-output Programmable Logic Array) is mask-programmed to generate up to twenty possible 8-bit output patterns. The most obvious application of this is to drive a set of 7-segment displays, where ten 7-bit output patterns are required. In this case, the contents of the O-register represent BCD numbers directly, and

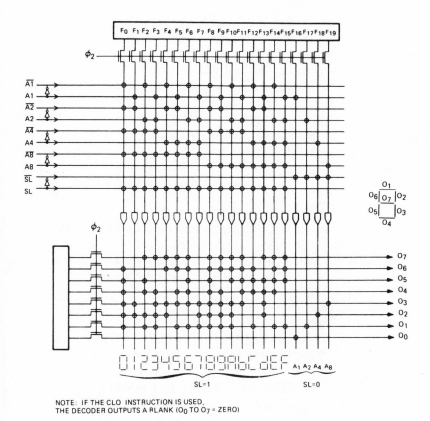

Fig. 3.2 Typical coding example of O-Output PLA.

the O-outputs are the segment drives to the display. An example, with this principle extended to displaying all the hexadecimal digits, is given in Fig. 3.2. It should be noted that the O-outputs have frequently been used for other purposes, and by suitable use of the 'don't care' option, some or all of the O-lines may be used to directly echo bits of the O-register.

The principal input structure for the TMS1000 family is the 'K-line'. Four are provided, labelled K1,2,4,8. They can be transferred to the Accumulator directly by the TKA instruction, or tested to see if any of them are at logic-ONE by the KNEZ instruction. (Some members of the family allow a mask option frequency-divider on the K8 input, for measuring high-frequency inputs.) In addition to these, some members have four 'L-inputs', which may be selected instead of the K-inputs, using yet another input pin. They may also be latched, to catch transient events.

In order to minimise the necessary interface hardware, some flexibility has been built into the electrical structure of the I/O pins. All I/O pins adhere to the convention that more-positive voltages represent a logic-ONE, and more negative voltages a logic-ZERO, regardless of the technology used, and the polarity of the supplies. Programming will probably be simplified if logic-ZERO is adopted as the inactive state, both for input and output. The K-inputs are provided with pull-down resistors to guarantee that they are inactive when left open-circuit (subject only to noise considerations). The O- and R-outputs are 'open-drain' types on PMOS parts, (but complementary on CMOS). Optional pull-down resistors can be provided, but inevitably the ability to sink current is much more limited than the ability to source it.

3.1.5 Product Types

There are many parameters which can be changed to suit a given application, and this means that the total number of family members which could be built is very large. The parameters which determine the part number of the part required for a particular design are:

Process:

TMS1XXXC	5 volt CMOS
TMS1XXXNLL	9 volt PMOS
TMS1XXXNLP	15 volt PMOS

Output structure:

TMS1X00	Vol (min) = Vdd
TMS1X70	Vol (min) = −35 volts

Program ROM size:

TMS17XX	512 bytes
TMS10XX/12XX	1024 bytes
TMS11XX/13XX	2048 bytes
TMS14XX/16XX	4096 bytes
TMS21XX/23XX	2048 bytes, extended I/O

(For a given ROM size, the second part number has a larger package, and more I/O pins.) Other variables which need to be specified are:

Required operating temperature range.
Ceramic or Plastic Package.
Dual-In-Line or Chip-Carrier Package.
70 or 100-mil Pin Spacing (If Plastic DIL Package).
(or reduced-pinout 20-pin version).

As can be seen with so many variables, it is not just the ROM code which guarantees that a part is unique! Table 3.3 shows the various parts of the TMS1000 series.

Table 3.3 TMS1000 family product chart.

		Quick-reference Selection Guide						
PART NUMBER		10XX	11XX	12XX	13XX	14XX	16XX	17XX
ROM	512 × 8 Bits							P,L
	1024 × 8 bits	P,L,C		P,L,C				
	2048 × 8 bits		P,L,C		P,L,C			
	4046 × 8 bits					P,L	P,L	
RAM	32 × 4 bits							P,L
	64 × 4 bits	P,L,C		P,L,C				
	128 × 4 bits		P,L,C		P,L,C	P,L	P,L	P,L
OUTPUTS	R lines — 9 lines							P,L
	10 lines	C	C			1470P		
	11 lines	P,L	P,L			1400P/ 1400L		
	13 lines			P,L				
	16 lines			C	P,L,C		P,L	

92

Table 3.3 continued

Quick-reference Selection Guide

PART NUMBER			10XX	11XX	12XX	13XX	14XX	16XX	17XX
	O lines	8 lines	P,L,C	P,L,C	P,L,C	P,L,C	P,L	P,L	P,L
		10 lines			1270P				
INPUTS	K lines	non-latching	P,L,C	P,L,C	P,L,C	P,L,C	P,L	P,L	P,L
	L lines	latching			C	C		P,L	
SUBROUTINES		1 level, same page	P,L	P,L	P,L	P,L			P,L
		3 levels, any page	C	C	C	C	P,L,	P,L	

P: 15 VOLT PMOS   L: 9 VOLT PMOS   C: CMOS

All devices have:
   8-bit Analogue-to-Digital Converter.
   Zero-crossing Detector.
   Interval Timer.
   Input Frequency Divider.
   PMOS Technology, −9 V supply.
   2048 × 8 bits Program ROM.
   128 × 4 bits Data RAM.
   TMS1100-compatible instruction set (with additions).
   4 levels of subroutines.

They differ as follows:

Table 3.4 TMS2100/2300 family product chart.

	TMS2100	TMS2300	TMS2170	TMS2370
Number of Pins	28	40	28	40
Output R-lines	7	15	6	14
O-lines	8	8	8	8
Input K,J,R-lines	8	12	8	12
Analogue	1	2	1	2
Most negative O/P	−15v	−35v	−15v	−35v
Event Counter	No	Yes	No	Yes

The TMS2100/2300 family shown in Table 3.4 are TMS1100 derivatives with additional I/O features. In particular, an integral 8-bit Analogue-to-Digital converter (ADC) has been included, and an interrupt, specially configured to be driven by a 50 Hz or 60 Hz synchronising input.

3.1.6 A Typical Application

Fig 3.3 shows a circuit diagram for use with the TMS2372 climate controller, a pre-programmed TMS2370. It includes all the basic interfacing techniques.

(1) *Outputs*

Both vacuum-fluorescent and LED displays are driven, in a multiplexed mode, using O-lines via the OPLA to drive segments and R-lines to drive digits. The vacuum-fluorescent display can be driven directly, using the chip's high-voltage output capability. The LEDs, which also look to the 2372 like additional digits, need transistor buffers to provide adequate current. (The SN75491 is a quad transistor driver package.) The heating, air-conditioning and fan control lines are R-lines from the microcomputer. Of course, all of these will need buffering, probably via a triac, or solid-state relay.

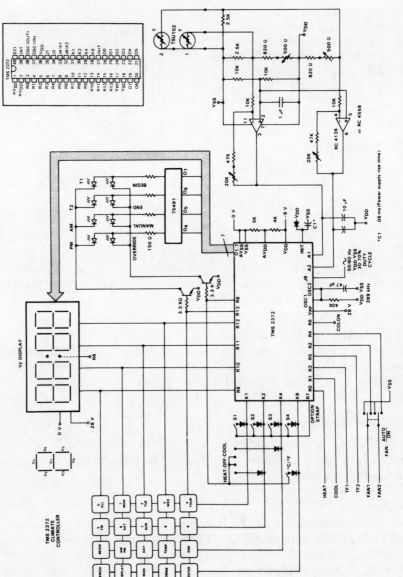

Fig. 3.3 A typical TMS2300 application.

(2) *Inputs*

Both control and user inputs are needed in this application. The control inputs are analogue voltages, using the TMS2300's internal ADC. The two channels are used to monitor two temperatures. A small amount of analogue buffering is needed, to increase the voltage range for a given temperature variation, and also to filter out any noise which might creep into the signal. The user inputs are a multiplexed array of twenty momentary keys, and a selection of switches. Each switch needs a diode associated with it, whereas the keys, which are also simple contact closures, do not. The reason for this is that the switches may remain closed while valid inputs at the keyboard are attempted. Were, for example, switches S1 and S4 closed, without diodes, they would effectively short together input lines K1 and K8, making keypresses in the left-hand column indistinguishable from those in the right-hand column.

In contrast, there should only ever be one key pressed at a time, obviating the need for diodes associated with them. The key- and switch-multiplexing is driven from the display digit-drive R-lines – a very common way of multiplexing both input and output with the same hardware and software. Care must be taken when using this technique to ensure that the voltage swings on the R-lines are still sufficient to produce good logic-level inputs on the K-lines via the diodes, even when driving the maximum current into the display. One further special input needs mentioning. The TMS2300 family has a special 'J8' input which is used to synchronise the program with an externally applied 50/60 Hz waveform, thereby providing accurate program timing without a crystal-controlled oscillator for the microcomputer.

3.2 THE TMS7000 8-BIT MICROCOMPUTER FAMILY

3.2.1 History and Product Range

The TMS7000 family is a recently-introduced 8-bit single-chip micro-computer family. It draws on many of the features of older 8-bit families, and also adds a few of its own. It is intended primarily as a single-chip solution, with RAM and ROM on-board, but may also be used as a regular microprocessor with up to 64 K bytes of external memory space. It does not aspire to being as inexpensive as the TMS1000 family described above, but aims rather to provide a huge leap in performance for only a slight increase in price.

Product milestones

| 1980 | TMS7000, 7020 NMOS 5 MHz parts. |
| 1981 | TMS7040 4 K byte ROM NMOS. |

	TMS7020-8 8 MHz TMS7020.
1982	TMS70C20 CMOS TMS7020.
	TMS7041 −TMS7040 + UART.
1983	TMS70E40 −TMS7040 + EPROM.
	TMS70120 −12 K byte ROM.
	TMS70PX41 −prototyping part.

3.2.2 Architecture and Design Philosophy

The TMS7000 family grew out of the realisation that a large part of the area on a typical microprocessor chip was wasted in interconnects between the various elements. By reducing this interconnect area to a minimum, the size of the chip, and hence its cost, could be reduced. The result was 'SCAT' (Strip Chip Architecture Topology), which bears more resemblance to a memory device than a traditional microprocessor. The parts contain two ROM arrays, one for the user's program, and a second 'microcode' store, which defines the instruction set, and how it should be interpreted.

The standard instruction set is a logical extension of traditional 8-bit instruction sets, and quite powerful, so most users will not want to redefine the instructions, but for those applications where speed or code-size are paramount, or the user is anxious that his proprietary software should not be bootlegged, this flexibility exists. In theory, all the instructions could be redefined, but in practice only a few will be changed, especially as a totally custom instruction set would probably be quite untestable!

Most of the cost-cutting compromises made for the TMS1000 family have been avoided. The instruction set is easy to use for anyone who has been brought up on more traditional 8-bit parts. The program counter is sequential, and there is only one address space, partitioned as shown in Fig. 3.4.

Another very significant extension in capability arises from the availability of a conventional multiplexed address/data bus (which is not available on the TMS1000). Of course, this feature uses up a large number of pins, which is most undesirable, if the bus is not needed. To counter this, an internal flag can be set which specifies whether any or all of the bus signals should be brought out. The modes are:

(a) *Microcomputer mode*
  Microcomputer mode is used when the chip needs to appear as a self-contained random-logic component, driving output lines according to what is received on input lines. As many pins as possible are devoted to statically-latched I/O ports, and the expansion bus and memory space are not accessible to the user. The I/O supported is:

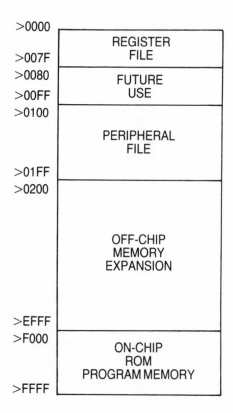

Fig. 3.4 Typical TMS7XXX memory map.

1	8-bit input port.
1	8-bit output port.
1	8-bit bitwise-bidirectional ports.
2	Interrupts.

(b) *Peripheral expansion mode*

Peripheral Expansion mode is used when more I/O is needed than can be provided by the ports alone. The additional I/O may be provided by memory-mapped latches, or by special purpose peripheral chips, or it may consist of a small amount of additional RAM, or an external FIFO buffer. To achieve this, one port is sacrificed, to provide an 8-bit multiplexed address/data bus, giving an external address space of 256 bytes. The I/O then supported is:

1	8-bit input port.
1	4-bit output port.
1	8-bit bitwise-bidirectional port.

244   bytes of external address space.
2   interrupts.

(c) *Full expansion mode*

This mode is used for prototyping, where all the program memory resides off-chip, and also in applications where more than 256 bytes of address space are needed. In this mode, two ports are given up to provide a full 64 K address space, as with a regular microprocessor. However, the internal RAM and ROM may still be enabled. The I/O supported is:

1   8-bit input port.
1   4-bit output port.
61   Kbytes of external address space.
2   interrupts.

3.2.3   TMS7000 Standard Instruction Set

The standard TMS7000 instruction set contains many powerful features. The instructions are listed in tabular form in Table 3.5.

This does not attempt to be a comprehensive description of the instructions; this is adequately described elsewhere (Ref. 3.2 – see end of this chapter). However, a few unusual features should be highlighted.

MPY – Multiply Instruction

This powerful instruction takes two unsigned 8-bit values and generates a 16-bit result. At 5 MHz, it requires 18 microseconds to do this.

DECD – Decrement-Double

Decrement a pair of registers, treating them as a 16-bit value (lsb at LABEL, msb at LABEL−1) – this is very useful for indexing through the 64 K address space.

MOVD – Move-Double

Move a 16-bit value to a contiguous register-pair. The 16-bit value may be a 2-byte immediate operand.

BTJO, BTJOP, BTJZ, BTJZP – Bit Test and Jump

Test specified bits of a register or peripheral file address, and if result is a zero/non-zero, perform a short-jump – allows very fast response to a single bit change on a peripheral port, or a compare-and-jump on a register value.

XORP – Exclusive-Or Peripheral File

Toggle a bit or bits of a specified peripheral-file location.

Table 3.5 TMS7000 instruction set.

	SINGLE OPERAND			DUAL OPERAND											PERIPHERAL				EXTENDED				OTHER		STATUS WORD
	A	B	Rn	A,B	B,A	Rn,A	%n,A	Rn,B	%n,B	Rn,Rn	%n,Rn	A,Rn	B,Rn	A,Pn	Pn,A	B,Pn	Pn,B	%n,Pn	DIRECT	INDIRECT	INDEXED	OTHER	COND. BITS	INT. EN.	
additional bytes needed	0	0	1	0	0	1	1	1	2	2	1	1	1	1	1	1	2	2	1		2	0			
ADC				69	19	29	39	59	49	79													x		0
ADD				68	18	28	38	58	48	78													x		0
AND				63	13	23	33	53	43	73													x		0
ANDP														83		93		A3					x		0
BTJO				66	16	26	36	56	46	76													x		1
BTJOP														86		96		A6					x		2
BTJZ				67	17	27	37	57	47	77													x		1
BTJZP														87		97		A7					x		2
BR																			8C	9C	AC				0
CALL																			8E	9E	AE				0
CLR	B5	C5	D5																				x		0
CLRC																						B0	x		0
CMP				6D	1D	2D	3D	5D	4D	7D													x		0
CMPA																			8D	9D	AD		x		0
DAC				6E	1E	2E	3E	5E	4E	7E													x		0
DEC	B2	C2	D2																				x		0
DECD	BB	CB	DB																				x		0
DINT																						06	x	x	0
DJNZ	8A	CA	DA																						1
DSB				6F	1F	2F	3F	5F	4F	7F													x		0
EINT																						05	x	x	0
IDLE																						01			0
INC	B3	C3	D3																				x		0
INV	B4	C4	D4																				x		0
JMP																						E0			1
JC/JHS																						E3			1
JN																						E1			1
JNC/JL																						E7			1
JNZ/JNE																						E6			1
JP																						E4			1
JPZ																						E5			1
JZ/JEQ																						E2			1
LDA																			8A	9A	AA		x		0
LDSP																						0D			0
MOV			CD	62	12	22	32	52	42	72	D0	D1											x		0
MOVD									98	88											A8		x		1
MOVP														82	80	92	91	A2					x		0
MPY				6C	1C	2C	3C	5C	4C	7C													x		0
NOP																						00			0
OR				64	14	24	34	54	44	74													x		0
ORP														84		94		A4					x		0
POP	B9	C9	D9																			08	x		0
PUSH	B8	C8	D8																			0E	x		0
RETI																						0B			0
RETS																						0A			0
RL	BE	CE	DE																				x		0
RLC	BF	CF	DF																				x		0
RR	BC	CC	DC																				x		0
RRC	BD	CD	DD																				x		0
SBB				6B	1B	2B	3B	5B	4B	7B													x		0
SETC																						07	x		0
STA																			8B	9B	AB		x		0
STSP																						09			0
SUB				6A	1A	2A	3A	5A	4A	7A													x		0
SWAP	B7	C7	D7																				x		0
TSTA																						B0	x		0
TSTB																						C1	x		0
TRAP																						E8FF			0
XCHB	B6		D6																				x		0
XOR				65	15	25	35	55	45	75													x		0
XORP														85		95		A5					x		0

* additional bytes needed

DAC/DSB – Decimal Add-Subtract with Carry/Borrow

Treat register contents as two BCD digits, and produce a BCD result.

TRAP n – Short-form call to common subroutines

Common subroutines can be called using a single byte instruction, where five bits of the opcode define which of twenty-four subroutines is to be called, and the subroutine start address is contained in a 16-bit vector held in high-memory. For well-structured code, the space saving can be very significant.

3.3   CASE STUDY – TMS7000 TO SPEECH SYNTHESISER INTERFACE

A frequent requirement in single-chip microcomputer applications is an interface to a 'slow peripheral' device, i.e. one that responds more slowly than the bus cycle time. This may be achieved with the minimum of components with the TMS7000, by using the various expansion modes to advantage. This section describes a simple method for interfacing a TMS5220 Speech Synthesiser to any TMS7000 family member, but the technique could be adapted to other 8-bit microcomputers. It only requires eight resistors in addition to the components already present. The speech data can reside either in serial ROM (e.g. TMS6100) or in general system memory, or a mixture of the two. There is no requirement for mask-programmed parts, although their use will further lower the total system cost.

3.3.1   General Principles

The TMS5220 cannot reside on the microprocessor bus as a regular 8-bit peripheral chip, as it requires the data on its I/O lines to remain stable for at least 30 microseconds when writing, and has an access time of 23 microseconds when reading, both of which imply that there must be some way of freezing the data. Conventional design techniques employ a bidirectional octal latch (e.g. SN74LS2646) or a PIA (e.g. MC6821) to latch the data, but these methods are expensive, and use up board area.

All members of the TMS7000 family have RAM on board, and can operate in single-chip mode, where all the I/O pins function as statically latched ports. In this mode, interfacing to the TMS5220 is very easy; provided that the 5220 is powered from ±5 V, the I/O pins of the synthesiser can be connected directly to the appropriate port on the microcomputer. The only things to watch for are that D0 of the 5220 is the most significant bit (unlike the TMS7000!), and V in (high) for the 5220 is 4.4 V, which is higher than V out (high) of the TMS7000. This is readily fixed by the addition of pull-up resistors on the bus lines and $\overline{RS}$ (read strobe) and $\overline{WS}$ (write strobe). A value of 6.8 Kohms should suffice. Also, operating margins are improved by the addition of 4.7 Kohms pull-ups on the output lines from the synthesiser, $\overline{READY}$ and $\overline{INT}$.

However, it may not be possible to put the program into ROM in a specific application, and hence to use the single-chip mode in normal operation. Fortunately, the TMS7000, whilst retaining the conventional 8-bit microprocessor architecture internally, can dynamically reconfigure its external bus as statically latched ports, even when normally executing program resident in EPROM. It achieves this by loading a program template from the external EPROM into its internal RAM, and then executing it from there. The first few opcodes of this template tell the TMS7000 to go into its statically latched mode, and then the byte is read or written to the TMS5220 as necessary. Finally, the program restores the full-expansion mode of the processor, and returns to the calling program which is resident in EPROM. The template uses twenty-eight of the available 128 locations in the internal RAM, leaving 100 free for program variables, stack, etc.

3.3.2 Hardware Implementation

The sample routines shown below assume that the hardware is connected as shown in Fig. 3.5.

Note that the TMS5220 is connected directly to the expansion bus, meaning that in normal program execution, things will be happening on the bus at a far greater rate than it can respond to. However, provided that the TMS5220's chip select pin is false throughout this time, this is of no consequence.

3.3.3 Software Techniques

Sample subroutines to perform common functions are listed in Fig. 3.6. In normal program execution, the bus lines will be fetching program and data from the EPROM, via the external bus, in full-expansion mode. When reading or writing a byte to the TMS5220, the program first checks to see if the appropriate RAM template program is resident. If it is not, it copies it in from the EPROM. Then it branches to the program in RAM, the first instruction of which tells it to go out of expansion mode, and appear to be a single-chip microcomputer. The program is then able to statically latch the pins that had just been used for talking to the EPROM, and hold data on them for as long as the slow peripheral chip needs it. Finally, it switches back into full-expansion mode, and execution continues as normal.

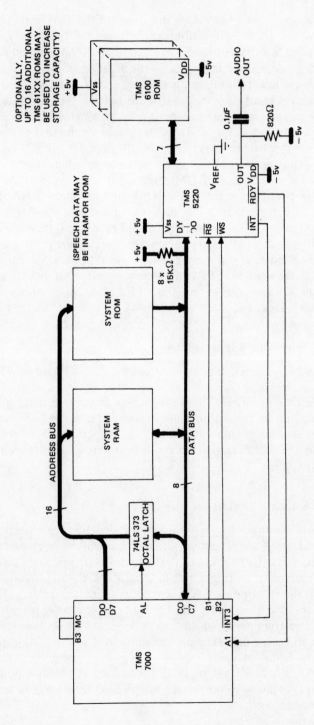

Fig. 3.5 TMS7000-TMS5200 interface circuit

```
0001              ************************************************************
0002              *                                                          *
0003              *            SPEECH I/O WITH THE TMS7000                    *
0004              *                                                          *
0005              ************************************************************
0006              *        INITIAL DEFINITIONS
0007              ************************************************************
0008              *
0009 0040                   DORG   >40                SUITABLE PLACE IN RAM FILE
0010              *
0011 0040    00   WRFLAG BYTE   0                     SYN WRITE FLAG REGISTER.
0012              *
0013 0041        RAMST  BSS    28                     RAM PROGRAM SPACE START
0014              *
0015              ************************************************************
0016              * I/O PORT DEFINITIONS
0017              ************************************************************
0018      0000   IOCNTL EQU    P0                     I/O CONTROL REGISTER
0019      0080   FULLEX EQU    >80                    I/O CTRL REG FULL EXPANSION
0020      0000   SINGCH EQU    >00                    I/O CTRL REG SINGLE-CHIP
0021              *
0022      0004   PORTA  EQU    P4
0023      0002   READY  EQU    >02                    READY LINE IS A1 INPUT
0024              *
0025      0006   PORTB  EQU    P6                     BPORT BIT DEFINITIONS
0026      00FD   RS     EQU    >FD                    SET -RS (B1)
0027      00FB   WS     EQU    >FB                    SET -WS (B2)
0028      0006   NORSWS EQU    >06                    DENY -RS, -WS
0029      0008   EXPOFF EQU    >08                    TURN MC EXP EN OFF (MC=B3)
0030      00F7   EXPON  EQU    >F7                    TURN MC EXPANSION ENABLE ON
0031              *
0032      0008   SYN    EQU    P8                     SYN BUS CONNECTED TO C-PORT
0033      0009   DDRC   EQU    P9                     C-PORT DATA DIRECTION REG.
0034              *
0035              *
0036 F000              AORG >F000
0037 F000    D5   START  CLR    WRFLAG               CLEAR WRITE SYN TEMPLATE
     F001    40
0038 F002    8E          CALL @RSTSYN
     F003 F064
0039              *
0040              *       :
0041              *       :
0042              *       :                            (MAIN PROGRAM)
0043              *       :

0045              ************************************************************
0046              *                    RDSYN
0047              *        READ A BYTE FROM THE SYN INTO A
0048              * THIS BLOCK READS A BYTE FROM SYN. IT COPIES A TEMPLATE TO
0049              * THE REGISTER FILE, AND THEN EXECUTES IT. THIS IS DONE
0050              * TO ALLOW D PORT TO BE STATICALLY LATCHED UNTIL READY
0051              * GOES TRUE. (TEMPLATE IS COPIED EVERY TIME, TO ALLOW A
0052              * MODEST DELAY BETWEEN READS)
0053              ************************************************************
0054 F005    52   RDSYN  MOV    %RDSPC,B             WRITE ROUTINE NO LONGER...
     F006    1C
0055 F007    D5          CLR    WRFLAG               ..RESIDENT IN RAM.
     F008    40
0056 F009    AA   RDLP   LDA    @RDROM-1(B)          TRANSFER...
     F00A F013
0057 F00C    AB          STA    @RAMST-1(B)          ..ROM INTO RAM...
     F00D 0040
0058 F00F    CA          DJNZ   B,RDLP               ...AND LOOP TILL DONE.
     F010    F8
0059 F011    8C          BR     @RAMST
     F012 0041
0060              *****                READ TEMPLATE
0061              * THIS IS ALWAYS COPIED TO RAM BEFORE EXECUTION
```

Fig. 3.6 Example speech synthesiser I/O routines.

```
0062 F014   A3    RDROM  ANDP   %EXPON,PORTB      SET MC=1.
     F015   F7
     F016   06
0063 F017   A2           MOVP   %SINGCH,IOCNTL    SET TO S/ALONE MODE
     F018   00
     F019   00
0064 F01A   A2           MOVP   %>00,DDRC         SET DDC=INPUT
     F01B   00
     F01C   09
0065 F01D   A3           ANDP   %RS,PORTB         ASSERT -RS (=B1)
     F01E   FD
     F01F   06
0066 F020   A6           BTJOP  %READY,PORTA,$    SPIN UNTIL -READY (A1) =0
     F021   02
     F022   04
     F023   FC
0067 F024   80           MOVP   SYN,A             READ INPUT
     F025   08
0068 F026   A4           ORP    %NORSWS,PORTB     MAKE BOTH -RS AND -WS HIGH
     F027   06
     F028   06
0069 F029   A2           MOVP   %>6A,IOCNTL       FULL-EXPN MODE CLR INTRPTS!
     F02A   6A
     F02B   00
0070 F02C   A4           ORP    %EXPOFF,PORTB     SET MC=0
     F02D   08
     F02E   06
0071 F02F   0A           RETS
0072        F030  RDEND  EQU    $
0073        001C  RDSPC  EQU    RDEND-RDROM       SIZE OF RD PROG IN RAM
0074              *



0076              ****************************************************************
0077              *               WRSYN
0078              *        WRITE A BYTE TO THE SYN
0079              * THIS BLOCK SENDS A TO SYN. IT COPIES A TEMPLATE INTO THE
0080              * REGISTER FILE IF NECESSARY, AND THEN EXECUTES IT.
0081              ****************************************************************
0082 F030   77    WRSYN  BTJZ   %>01,WRFLAG,WRCON  IS WRITE ROUTINE IN RAM?
     F031   01
     F032   40
     F033   03
0083 F034   8C           BR     @RAMST             YES, IT IS...
     F035   0041
0084 F037   B8    WRCON  PUSH   A                  SAVE CHAR, LOAD WRITE S/R
0085 F038   52           MOV    %WRSPC,B
     F039   1C
0086 F03A   AA    WRLP   LDA    @WROM-1(B)         ...COPY ROM INTO RAM...
     F03B   F047
0087 F03D   AB           STA    @RAMST-1(B)
     F03E   0040
0088 F040   CA           DJNZ   B,WRLP             ...LOOP TILL DONE.
     F041   F8
0089 F042   B9           POP    A                  GET CHARACTER BACK AND...
0090 F043   D3           INC    WRFLAG             SHOW WRITE ROUTINE PRESENT
     F044   40
0091 F045   8C           BR     @RAMST             JUMP TO TEMPLATE
     F046   0041
0092              *** WRITE TEMPLATE -LOAD INTO RAM AT RAMST BEFORE EXECUTION
0093 F048   A3    WROM   ANDP   %EXPON,PORTB       ENABLE MODE CONTROL BITS
     F049   F7
     F04A   06
0094 F04B   A2           MOVP   %SINGCH,IOCNTL     S/ALONE MODE, DISABLE INTS
     F04C   00
     F04D   00
0095 F04E   A2           MOVP   %>FF,DDRC          SET PORT-C TO OUTPUT MODE.
     F04F   FF
     F050   09
0096 F051   82           MOVP   A,SYN              LATCH OUT DATA.
     F052   08
0097 F053   A3           ANDP   %WS,PORTB          ASSERT -WS. (=PORT B2)
     F054   FB
```

Fig. 3.6 continued

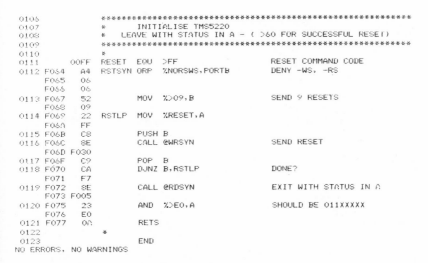

```
           F055  06
0098 F056  A6              BTJOP  %READY,PORTA,$      LOOP UNTIL -READY (A1) =0
     F057  02
     F058  04
     F059  FC
0099 F05A  A4              ORP    %NORSWS,PORTB       MAKE -WS AND -RS HIGH
     F05B  06
     F05C  06
0100 F05D  A2              MOVP   %FULLEX,IOCNTL      SELECT FULL EXPANSION MODE
     F05E  80
     F05F  00
0101 F060  A4              ORP    %EXPOFF,PORTB       SET MC=0
     F061  08
     F062  06
0102 F063  0A              RETS
0103       F064  WREND     EQU    $
0104       001C  WRSPC     EQU    WREND-WROM          CALC SIZE OF PROG


0105              **************************************************************
0107              *        INITIALISE TMS5220
0108              *    LEAVE WITH STATUS IN A - ( >60 FOR SUCCESSFUL RESET)
0109              **************************************************************
0110              *
0111       00FF  RESET     EQU    >FF                 RESET COMMAND CODE
0112 F064  A4    RSTSYN    ORP    %NORSWS,PORTB       DENY -WS, -RS
     F065  06
     F066  06
0113 F067  52              MOV    %>09,B              SEND 9 RESETS
     F068  09
0114 F069  22    RSTLP     MOV    %RESET,A
     F06A  FF
0115 F06B  C8              PUSH   B
0116 F06C  8E              CALL   @WRSYN              SEND RESET
     F06D  F030
0117 F06F  C9              POP    B
0118 F070  CA              DJNZ   B,RSTLP             DONE?
     F071  F7
0119 F072  8E              CALL   @RDSYN              EXIT WITH STATUS IN A
     F073  F005
0120 F075  23              AND    %>E0,A              SHOULD BE 011XXXXX
     F076  E0
0121 F077  0A              RETS
0122              *
0123              END
NO ERRORS, NO WARNINGS
```

Fig. 3.6 continued

Summary

The TMS1000 series of devices is one of the most widely used microcomputers for high-volume applications. They have characteristics, in terms of process technology, I/O, and processor features, that make them suitable for many applications where processing requirements are not too demanding. A significant increase in performance is offered by the TMS7000 family of 8-bit devices. These devices have a comprehensive instruction set that can be customised. The example presented, illustrates interfacing to the TMS7000 family both in terms of the hardware arrangement and the software routines.

REFERENCES
3.1. TMS1000 Family Design Manual.
3.2. TMS7000 Assembly Programmer's Guide, Texas Instruments.

CHAPTER 4

Zilog – The Z8 Family

By Dr Brian Jasper

4.1 INTRODUCTION

The Z8 single-chip microprocessor, which is the second 8-bit micro offered by Zilog, was introduced in 1978, two years after the introduction of Zilog's first microprocessor, the Z80. The identification Z8 stands for a family of products which can be used either as single-chip computers or as processors in a small system. Features of the device include up to 4 K bytes of internal program memory, two counter timers, a UART, four I/O ports and the provision to configure I/O ports to function as Z-Bus, the standard bus used by the majority of Zilog processors and peripherals. The instruction set of the Z8, although incorporating some useful Z80 features, is optimised for bit and byte processing.

When the Z80 was designed, the rationale for defining the architecture was maintenance of software compatibility with the earlier 8080 family. This allowed users to transport their application packages, often quite large portions of software, over to the superset architecture of the Z80 with little or no modification of firmware or system support software. (A good example of this is the transportation of the CP/M operating system from 8080 to Z80 systems.)

In the case of the Z8 design, the options open to the designers included making a single-chip version of the Z80, copying another existing architecture (8048, etc.) or defining a completely new architecture embodying useful features from other microprocessor designs and some new ideas which, from consideration of performance studies of software on other machines, would appear to offer some overall benefit. The approach that Zilog chose was to go for a new architecture and thus gain some advantages from a number of architectural innovations, particularly in the implementation of the instruction set and in the way internal registers are organised.

When considering the issues involved in selecting a suitable architecture for a microprocessor, historically designers have concentrated on CPU capabilities while neglecting I/O or memory requirements. In many multi-chip microcomputer designs, this philosophy may have some merit, since the ROM, RAM and I/O mix can be tailored to the application through selective choice of memory and, providing the devices are available, appropriate peripheral circuits. For the single-chip computer, the selection process is constrained by the available on-chip memory and I/O resources so that as a result, the use and efficiency of these resources, in particular the interface between I/O and CPU, becomes as important as the CPU architecture itself. However, the single-chip microcomputer architect needs to bear in mind that generally designs fall into two categories; I/O intensive or computational/communications intensive. Designs that fall into the first category may be achieved with a single-chip device, but often multi-chip solutions are needed if a large amount of I/O is required. If the design falls into the second category, data manipulation and arithmetic functions become more important. In this situation the software requirements often exceed the capabilities of a single-chip device, so that again a multi-chip solution is required to provide for extra memory or communications functions.

In the Z8 design, it was decided to provide a device capable of working either as a self-contained processor, with an efficiently organised memory and I/O structure on chip, or as the main processing element in a multi-chip design. The latter ability not only allows external memory to be accessed, but also allows the architecture to take advantage of a companion family of special peripheral devices.

To make the on-chip I/O resources as flexible and efficient as those of the CPU and at the same time improve the I/O to CPU interface, emphasis has been placed on minimising the time involved during data transfers between I/O registers and CPU registers (accumulators). Moreover I/O registers have been given the same access privileges as CPU data registers, allowing them to be directly operated on by the CPU's arithmetic functions. This mechanism helps to improve data throughput by reducing intermediate data storage, when it is required to manipulate data in I/O registers.

These I/O improvements have been implemented by mapping all the control data registers of the I/O functions into the same register file as the CPU data registers. This method of combining CPU resources and I/O resources into one memory block is probably best described as accumulator mapping. In a multi-chip scheme, an analogous memory organisation would be memory mapped I/O. However, for small dedicated control type applications, the accumulator mapping method is considerably more efficient since the number of time-consuming data accesses to external memory can be minimised to just program memory accesses or the occasional data access.

4.2 Z8 ARCHITECTURE

The main features of the Z8 architecture include a 144-byte register file of which 124 are general purpose accumulators, 2 K or 4 K bytes of internal memory (ROM), external memory expansion capability up to 126 K bytes, four 8-bit I/O ports, one UART, two counter-timers and six maskable, selectable priority vectored interrupts.

At the time of introduction the maximum clock speed that could be used was 8 MHz (4 MHz internal). However, devices are now available which will operate as 12 MHz (6 MHz internal) and which will allow most instructions to execute in 1 or 1.7 microseconds (6 to 10 machine cycles), with the longest instruction taking 3.3 microseconds (20 cycles). The remainder of this section covers the details of the Z8 architecture, the block diagram of which is shown in Fig. 4.1.

4.2.1 Memory Organisation

For a minimum chip application, memory in the Z8 is split into two separate memory spaces, the internal register file and the program memory ROM. However, if external memory is enabled, then it is possible to separate memory into three spaces. This is shown in Fig. 4.2.

In order to use the external memory, it is necessary for the I/O ports to be reconfigured so that they function as address and data lines. To achieve this, the appropriate bits must be programmed in a special control register known as the Port 01 Mode register. If the full 64 K of address range is required, then two of the I/O ports need to be configured. However, intermediate memory sizes may be accommodated by only partially configuring the I/O address outputs. Thus I/O port wastage can be minimised when only a small amount of extra memory is required.

Port 1 can be reprogrammed to provide eight multiplexed address and data lines (A/D0 to A/D7) and so allow a block of 256 bytes of external memory to be accessed. Port O, which is used to supply the upper address bits (A8 to A15), can be enabled in two halves, upper and lower 4-bits, to allow access either to an extra 4 K bytes of memory if the lower 4-bits is enabled, or if all 8-bits are enabled the full address range of 64 K. Usually this range of addresses is adequate for most applications. If a design required more memory, or if it is necessary to distinguish between external data space and external program space, a further single bit output signal is available for Port 3. This output, known as DM (Data memory), becomes true when a special group of load instructions are executed (LDE and LDEI) or when stack operations occur (CALL PUSH POP RET and IRET).

To provide for address references ranging up to 64 K, a 16-bit program counter is available. For memory accesses via the load group instructions (LDE, LDEI, LDC and LCDI), indirection through a pair of 8-bit registers is used.

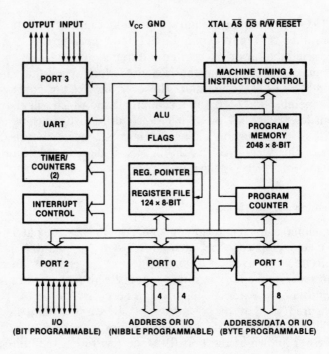

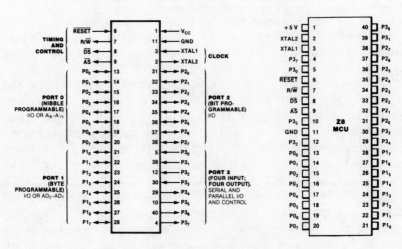

Fig. 4.1 Z8 architecture and pin functions.

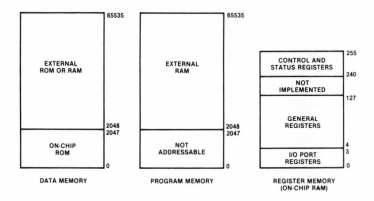

Fig. 4.2 Z8 memory spaces.

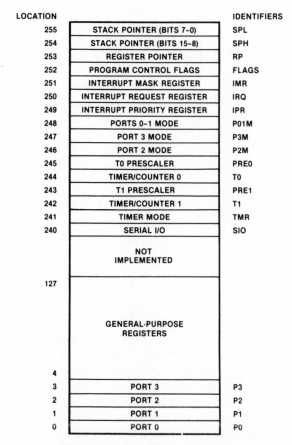

Fig. 4.3 Register file organisation.

4.2.2 Register File

Fig. 4.3 shows the layout of the 144-byte register file. Mapped into this file are four I/O ports, two counter/timers, the input buffers of a UART, thirteen control registers and 124 general purpose registers (accumulators). Since the register file is the main mechanism for manipulating data, of the forty-three instructions in the Z8, thirty operate exclusively on this file, while the remainder are concerned with program control or transferring data to external memory.

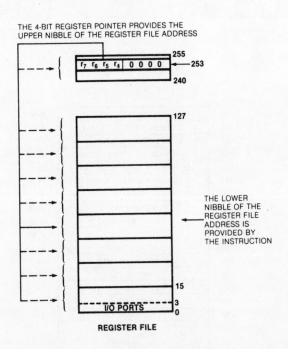

Fig. 4.4 Register pointer mechanism.

Z8 instructions can access registers directly or indirectly using an 8-bit address field. Consequently, an instruction like LD 56,72 which transfers the contents of register 72 to register 56, will require three bytes of program code memory. Shorter codes can be written since the Z8 can also address registers using a 4-bit register pointer mechanism. In the 4-bit addressing mode, the register file is divided into nine working register groups, each occupying sixteen contiguous locations (Fig. 4.4). A register pointer (one of the control registers) addresses the starting location of the active working-register group. Any instruction that can alter the contents of the register file can be used to alter the register pointer. The Z8 instruction set also provides a special Set Register Pointer instruction to initialise or alter the register pointer contents. Consequently, a register within the active working register group is specified by a 4-bit register designator in the instruction.

4.2.3 Stack

Either the internal register file or the external data memory can be used for stacks. The selection is made by programming a bit in mode register R248. A 16-bit stack pointer (R254 and R255) is used for the external stack which can reside anywhere in data memory between locations 2048 (4096) and 65535. When the stack is located in the register file, an 8-bit stack pointer (R255) is used for the general purpose registers (R4 to R127).

The program counter during a CALL instruction, or the program counter and the flag registers during an interrupt cycle are automatically saved on the stack. PUSH and POP instructions can save and restore any register of the register file, with the exception of write-only registers. When returning from a subroutine the RET and IRET instructions pop the saved value of the program counter and of the flag register and program counter respectively.

4.2.4 General I/O Structure

The Z8 has thirty-two lines which can be configured as to inputs or outputs. These lines are grouped into four ports (0, 1, 2 and 3) of eight lines each and are configurable as input, output or address/data. Under software control, the ports can be programmed to provide address outputs, timing, status signals, and serial parallel I/O features with or without handshake. All ports have active pull-ups and pull-downs compatible with TTL loads.

Port 1 can be programmed as a byte I/O port with or without handshake, or an address data port for interfacing external memory. The configuration is set using the mode register for Ports 0 and 1 (P01M) R248. In the byte output mode, the port is accessed as general register R1. The port is written by specifying R1 in the register file as the destination register of an instruction. The port is read by specifying R1 as a source register of an instruction. When used as an I/O port, Port 1 may be placed under handshake control by programming the Port 3 Mode register (P3M) R247. In this configuration, Port 3 pins P33 and P34 are used as the handshake control lines DAV1 and RDT1 for input handshake, or RDY1 and DAV1 for output handshake.

For external memory references, Port 1 must be programmed for the multiplexed address data modes (AD0-AD7). In this configuration, the lower eight bits of address (A0-A7) are multiplexed with the data (D0-D7). Associated with Port 1 are the timing and control signals address Strobe (AS), Data Strobe (DS) and Read/Write (R/W). The timing relationships of these signals during memory read and write operations is discussed later. It should be noted that when Port 0 and 1 are configured as address/data ports, the parts which are used for the addresses cannot be accessed as registers.

In addition to the I/O and address/data modes, Port 1 can be placed in the high-impedance state (along with control lines AS, DS and R/W), allowing the Z8 to share common resources for multiprocessor and DMA applications. This mode is totally under software control and is programmed using the P01M register (R248).

Port 0 can be programmed as a nibble I/O port or as an address output port for addressing external memory. The selection is made by programming the mode register for Ports 0 and 1 (P01M) R248. When a Port 0 nibble is used in the I/O mode, it is accessed as the corresponding nibble of register RO. Like Port 1, Port 0 is read or written to by specifying RO as the source or destination register of an instruction. In this mode, Port 0 may be placed under handshake control by programming the Port 3 Mode register (P3M) R247. In this configuration, Port 3 pins P32 and P35 are used as the handshake control lines DAVO and RDYO for input handshake, or RDYO and DAVO for output handshake. The handshake signal assignment for lines P32 and P35 is dictated by the direction (input or output) assigned to the upper nibble of Port 0. For external memory references, when Port 0 nibbles are defined as address bits, they can be set to the high-impedance state alone with Port 1 and the control signals AS, DS and R/W by programming P01M Register.

Port 2 can be configured so that individual bits can be either inputs or outputs by programming the Port 2 Mode register (P2M) R246. This port is accessed as general register R2. Handshake control can be enabled by programming the Port 3 Mode register (P3M) R247. In this configuration Port 3 pins P31 and P36 are used as the handshake control lines DAV2 and RDY2 for input handshake, or RDY2 and DAV2 for output handshake. The handshake signal assignment for lines P31 and P36 is dictated by the direction of data flow. Port 2 can also be configured to provide open-drain outputs.

Because external memory addresses only originate from Ports 0 and 1, Port 2 is always available for I/O operations in both the memory-intensive and I/O-intensive configurations. The organisation for ports 0, 1 and 2 is shown in Fig. 4.5.

Port 3 lines can be configured as I/O or control lines by programming the associated Mode register (P3M) R247. In either case the direction of the eight lines is fixed as four input (P30-P33) and four output (P34-P37) as shown in Fig. 4.6.

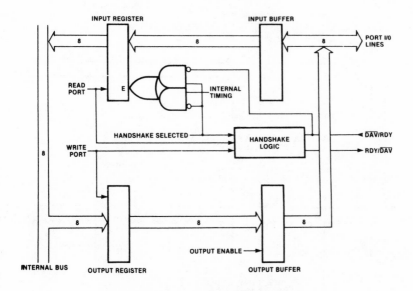

Fig. 4.5 Ports 0, 1 and 2 block diagram.

Table 4.1 Port 3 control functions.

Function	Line	Signal
Handshake	P31	$\overline{\text{DAV2}}$/RDY2
	P32	$\overline{\text{DAV0}}$/RDY0
	P33	$\overline{\text{DAV1}}$/RDY1
	P34	RDY1/$\overline{\text{DAV1}}$
	P35	RDY0/$\overline{\text{DAV0}}$
	P36	RDY2/$\overline{\text{DAV2}}$
Interrupt Request	P30	IRQ3
	P31	IRQ2
	P32	IRQ0
	P33	IRQ1
Counter/ Timer	P31	Tin
	P36	Tout
Status Out	P34	$\overline{\text{DM}}$

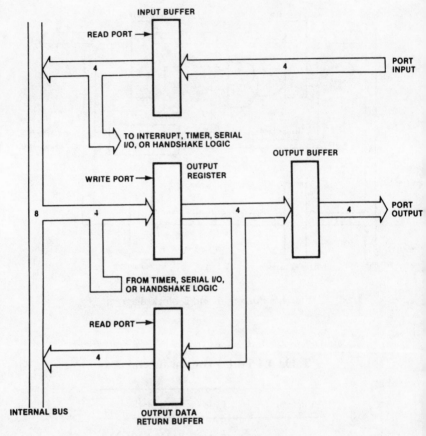

Fig. 4.6 Port 3 block diagram.

When data accesses are made, the port is accessed as general register R3. Consequently the data which is transferred during a read is the data present on the four input pins (P30-P33) along with the data stored in the output register (P34-P37). The four bits of the output register can be written only if they are used as data outputs. For serial I/O, lines P30 and P37 are programmed as serial in and serial out respectively.

Port 3 control functions (see Table 4.1) are defined by programming the P3M register. These control functions can provide the following signals:

1. Handshake for Ports 1 and 2 (DAV and RDY);
2. Four external interrupt request signals (1RQ0-1RQ3);
3. Timer input and output signals (Tin and Tout);
4. Signal DM to identify external data memory.

Ports 0, 1 and 2 can be used to transfer data using the interlocked handshake signals Ready (RDY) and Data Available (DAV). A pair of Port 3 lines (one handshake output and one handshake input) is required for each of the other ports used in the handshake. The handshake signals function as Ready (output) and Data Available (input) when the port is in the input mode, or as Data Available (output) and Ready (input) when the port is in the output mode.

4.2.5 Counter/Timers

The Z8 contains two 8-bit programmable counter-timers (T0 and T1), each driven by its own 6-bit programmable prescaler (Fig. 4.7). The T1 prescaler can be driven by internal or external clock sources; the T0 prescaler is driven by the internal clock only. Both counter/timers can

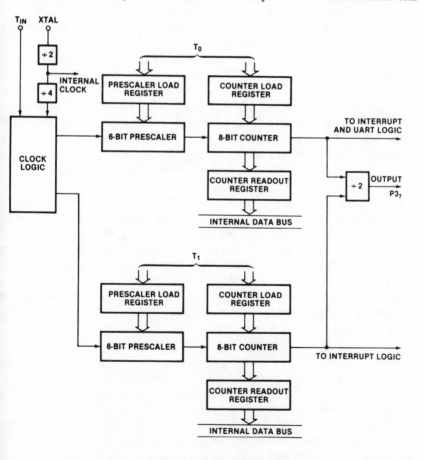

Fig. 4.7 Counter/timer block diagram.

operate independently from the processor instruction sequence, thereby unburdening the program from time-critical operations such as event counting or elapsed-time calculations.

Registers R243 and R245 program the 6-bit prescalers to divide the input frequency of the clock source by any number from 1 to 64. Each prescaler drives its counter (R244 for T0; R242 for T1), which decrements the value (1 to 256) that has been loaded into the counter. When the counter reaches the end of count, a timer interrupt request, IRQ4 (T0) or IRQ5 (T1) is generated.

The counters can be started, stopped, restarted to continue, or restarted from the initial value by programming the Timer Mode register (TMR) R241. The counters can also be programmed to stop upon reaching zero (single-pass mode), or to automatically reload the initial value and continue counting (modulo-n continuous mode) by programming Prescaler 0 (PRE0) and Prescaler 1 (PRE1) control registers. The counter, but not the prescaler, can be read any time without disturbing their value or count mode.

The clock source for T1 is user-definable and can be the internal microprocessor clock (4 or 6 MHz maximum) divided by four, or an external signal input via Port 3. The Timer Mode register configures the external time input as an external clock 1 or 1.5 MHz maximum), a trigger input that can be retriggerable or non-triggerable, or as a gate input for the internal clock. The counter/timers can be cascaded by connecting the T0 output to the input of T1.

Port 3 line P36 also serves as a timer output (Tout) through which T0, T1, or the internal clock can be output. The timer output toggles at the end of count. If the timer is programmed in a continuous count mode, P36 generates a 50% duty cycle output. Tout resets whenever new initial values are loaded in T0 or T1 from the count load registers either by a software load command or by an external trigger input (T1 only).

In the modulo-n count mode, new values for both counters can be written into the count load register without affecting the on-going countdown operation. When end-of-count is reached, the new initial values are loaded for subsequent counting operations.

4.2.6 Serial Input/Output

Port 3 lines P30 and P37 can be programmed as serial I/O lines for full-duplex serial asynchronous receiver/transmitter operation. The bit rate is controlled by counter/timer 0 (T0), and has a maximum data rate of 62.5 kilobits per second (fXTAL/128 with an 8 MHz clock). The data to be transmitted is loaded into register R240 and shifted out via P37 (Fig. 4.8) The serial data is received through P30, assembled into an 8-bit character, and transferred to the receive buffer. Register R240 is actually two

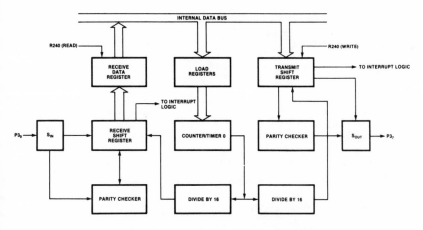

Fig. 4.8 Serial I/O block diagram.

registers; when written into, it is the transmitter; when read, it is the receiver buffer.

The T0 counter/timer runs at 16 times the bit rate to synchronise the incoming data stream. For easy derivation of commonly used asynchronous data communications bit rates, a 7.3728 MHz crystal can be used for the Z8 clock input. Table 4.2 lists the different bit rates and their required T0 initial values.

Table 4.2 Derivation of common bit rates.

Bit Rates	T0 Preset Value
19200	1
9600	2
4800	4
2400	8
1200	16
600	32
300	64
150	128
110	175 (error 0.3%)

Notes: 7.3728 MHz crystal; T0 prescaler=3

In the transmit mode, the Z8 automatically adds a start bit and two stop bits to the transmitted data. The Z8 also provides odd parity if control register R247 (P3M) is programmed accordingly. Eight data bits are always transmitted, regardless of parity selection. If parity is enabled,

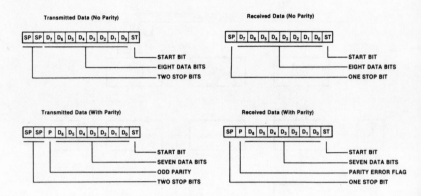

Fig. 4.9 Serial data formats.

the eighth bit is the odd parity bit. Between characters, the P37 output is held High to maintain the mark condition.

In the receive mode, the data format must have a start bit, eight data bits, and at least one stop bit (Fig. 4.9). If parity is on, bit 7 of the data received (parity bit) is replaced by a parity error flag. An error sets the flag to a logic 1.

An interrupt request (IRQ3) is generated whenever a character is transferred into the receive buffer. A transmitted character also generates an interrupt request (IRQ4) and, like the receive buffer, the transmit buffer can also be overwritten.

4.2.7 Interrupts

To support interrupt driven programs, the Z8 allows six different interrupts from eight sources: the four Port 3 lines P30-P33, serial in, serial out, and the two counter/timers. These interrupts can be masked and prioritied using the Interrupt Mask Register (IMR) R251 and the Interrupt Priority Register (IPR) R249. All six interrupts can be globally disabled by resetting the master interrupt enable bit in the Interrupt Mask Register (IMR) R251.

All Z8 interrupts are vectored through an Index table at the bottom of memory (Fig. 4.10). When an interrupt occurs, control passes to the service routine pointed to by the specific location in program memory reserved for that interrupt. This location and the next byte contain the 16-bit address of the service routine for that particular interrupt request.

Table 4.3 lists the available interrupts, their sources, types and vector locations. Since T0 supplies the clock for serial I/O operation, the interrupts from the T0 counter and Serial Out are mutually exclusive and both use the same interrupt request line IRQ4. Similarly, the Serial in

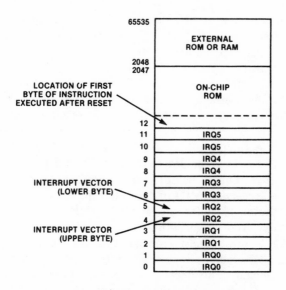

Fig. 4.10 Program memory map.

Table 4.3 Interrupts types, sources and vector locations.

Name	Source	Vector Location	Comments
IRQ0	$\overline{\text{DAV0}}$, IRQ0	0,1	External (P3$_2$), ↓ Edge Triggered
IRQ1	$\overline{\text{DAV1}}$, IRQ1	2,3	External (P3$_3$), ↓ Edge Triggered
IRQ2	$\overline{\text{DAV2}}$, IRQ2, T$_{\text{IN}}$	4,5	External (P3$_1$), ↓ Edge Triggered
IRQ3	IRQ3	6,7	External (3$_0$), ↓ Edge Triggered
	Serial In	6,7	Internal
IRQ4	T$_0$	8,9	Internal
	Serial Out	8,9	Internal
IRQ5	T$_1$	10,11	Internal

interrupt is combined with IRQ3 since serial data is input through P30 (IRQ3). The four inputs of Port 3 (P30-P33) are the interrupt request inputs IRQ0-IRQ3. A High-to-Low transition on their inputs generates an interrupt request.

Six-bits in the Interrupt Mask Register R251 can be used to individually enable or disable the six interrupt requests IRQ0-IRQ5. Bit 7 globally disables all interrupts. When more than one interrupt is pending, priorities are resolved by a programmable priority encoder that is controlled by the Interrupt Priority Register R249. The output of the priority encoder points to the program memory vector location associated with the interrupt request being serviced. Before the contents of the Interrupt Mask Register (IMR) or the Interrupt Priority Register (IPR) are changed, the enable interrupt bit of the IMR must be reset by the Disable Interrupt (DI) instruction.

When an interrupt request is granted, the Z8 enters an interrupt machine cycle that globally disables all subsequent interrupts, saves the program counter and status flags, and branches to the address contained within the vector location for the interrupt. Only at this point does control pass to the interrupt service routine. Fig. 4.11 illustrates the interrupt cycle process when an interrupt request occurs.

Interrupts can be re-enabled by the interrupt handling routine (EI instruction) to allow interrupt nesting. Interrupts can also be re-enabled automatically by issuing an Interrupt Return (IRET) instruction as the last instruction of the interrupt handling routine. IRET also restores the program counter and status flags.

The Z8 supports both polled and interrupt/driver systems. To accommodate a polled structure, any or all of the IRQ inputs can be masked and the Interrupt Request Register polled to determine which of the normal interrupt requests needs service.

4.2.8 Status Flags

Flags register, R2542, contains eight flags:

C Carry	S sign	D Decimal Adjust	F1 User Flag 1
Z Zero	V Overflow	H Half Carry	F2 User Flag 2

User flags F1 and F2 are available to the programmer for general use. The Half carry and decimal adjust flags are specialised flags that are used only by specific instructions. The remaining flags can be used by the programmer with Jump and Jump Relative instructions to provide a repertoire of nineteen conditional tests.

The flags can be set or reset by instructions. However, only those instructions that do not affect the flags as an outcome of the execution

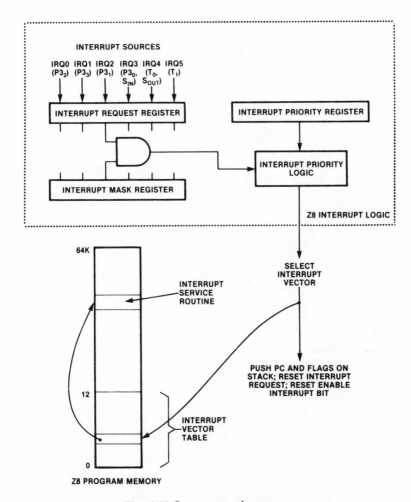

Fig. 4.11 Interrupt cycle process.

should be used (e.g. Load Immediate). In addition, the carry flag can be set to 1 by the Set Carry Flag (SCF) instruction, cleared to 0 by the Reset Carry Flag (RCF) instruction, or complemented by the Complement Carry Flag (FFC) instruction.

4.2.9 Instruction Timing

The basic time periods used by the Z8 are machine cycles (Mn), timing states (Tn) and clock periods. All Z8 timing references are made with respect to the output signals AS and DS. The clock is shown in the following illustrations for clarity only, and does not have a specific timing

Table 4.4 Z8 opcode map.

Lower Nibble (Hex)

Upper Nibble (Hex)	0	1	2	3	4	5	6	7	8	9	A	B	C	D	E	F
0	6,5 DEC R_1	6,5 DEC IR_1	6,5 ADD r_1,r_2	6,5 ADD r_1,Ir_2	10,5 ADD R_2,R_1	10,5 ADD IR_2,R_1	10,5 ADD R_1,IM	10,5 ADD IR_1,IM	6,5 LD r_1,R_2	6,5 LD r_2,R_1	12/10,5 DJNZ r_1,RA	12/10,0 JR cc,RA	6,5 LD r_1,IM	12/10,0 JP cc,DA	6,5 INC $r1$	
1	6,5 RLC R_1	6,5 RLC IR_1	6,5 ADC r_1,r_2	6,5 ADC r_1,Ir_2	10,5 ADC R_2,R_1	10,5 ADC IR_2,R_1	10,5 ADC R_1,IM	10,5 ADC IR_1,IM								
2	6,5 INC R_1	6,5 INC IR_1	6,5 SUB r_1,r_2	6,5 SUB r_1,Ir_2	10,5 SUB R_2,R_1	10,5 SUB IR_2,R_1	10,5 SUB R_1,IM	10,5 SUB IR_1,IM								
3	8,0 JP IRR_1	6,1 SRP IM	6,5 SBC r_1,r_2	6,5 SBC r_1,Ir_2	10,5 SBC R_2,R_1	10,5 SBC IR_2,R_1	10,5 SBC R_1,IM	10,5 SBC IR_1,IM								
4	8,5 DA R_1	8,5 DA IR_1	6,5 OR r_1,r_2	6,5 OR r_1,Ir_2	10,5 OR R_2,R_1	10,5 OR IR_2,R_1	10,5 OR R_1,IM	10,5 OR IR_1,IM								
5	10,5 POP R_1	10,5 POP IR_1	6,5 AND r_1,r_2	6,5 AND r_1,Ir_2	10,5 AND R_2,R_1	10,5 AND IR_2,R_1	10,5 AND R_1,IM	10,5 AND IR_1,IM								
6	6,5 COM R_1	6,5 COM IR_1	6,5 TCM r_1,r_2	6,5 TCM r_1,Ir_2	10,5 TCM R_2,R_1	10,5 TCM IR_2,R_1	10,5 TCM R_1,IM	10,5 TCM IR_1,IM								
7	10/12,1 PUSH R_2	12/14,1 PUSH IR_2	6,5 TM r_1,r_2	6,5 TM r_1,Ir_2	10,5 TM R_2,R_1	10,5 TM IR_2,R_1	10,5 TM R_1,IM	10,5 TM IR_1,IM								
8	10,5 DECW RR_1	10,5 DECW IR_1	12,0 LDE r_1,Irr_2	18,0 LDEI Ir_1,Irr_2												6,1 DI
9	6,5 RL R_1	6,5 RL IR_1	12,0 LDE r_2,Irr_1	18,0 LDEI Ir_2,Irr_1												6,1 EI
A	10,5 INCW RR_1	10,5 INCW IR_1	6,5 CP r_1,r_2	6,5 CP r_1,Ir_2	10,5 CP R_2,R_1	10,5 CP IR_2,R_1	10,5 CP R_1,IM	10,5 CP IR_1,IM								14,0 RET
B	6,5 CLR R_1	6,5 CLR IR_1	6,5 XOR r_1,r_2	6,5 XOR r_1,Ir_2	10,5 XOR R_2,R_1	10,5 XOR IR_2,R_1	10,5 XOR R_1,IM	10,5 XOR IR_1,IM								16,0 IRET
C	6,5 RRC R_1	6,5 RRC IR_1	12,0 LDC r_1,Irr_2	18,0 LDCI Ir_1,Irr_2				10,5 LD r_1,x,R_2								6,5 RCF
D	6,5 SRA R_1	6,5 SRA IR_1	12,0 LDC r_2,Irr_1	18,0 LDCI Ir_2,Irr_1	20,0 CALL* IRR_1		20,0 CALL DA	10,5 LD r_2,x,R_1								6,5 SCF
E	6,5 RR R_1	6,5 RR IR_1		6,5 LD r_1,Ir_2	10,5 LD R_2,R_1	10,5 LD IR_2,R_1	10,5 LD R_1,IM	10,5 LD IR_1,IM								6,5 CCF
F	8,5 SWAP R_1	8,5 SWAP IR_1		6,5 LD Ir_1,r_2		10,5 LD R_2,R_1										6,0 NOP

Bytes per instruction: 2   3   2   3   1

Lower Opcode Nibble

Execution Cycles   Pipeline Cycles

Upper Opcode Nibble → A   10,5
CP
R_2,R_1 ← Mnemonic

First Operand   Second Operand

Legend:
R = 8-Bit Address
r = 4-Bit Address
R_1 or r_1 = Dst Address
R_2 or r_2 = Src Address

Sequence:
Opcode, First Operand, Second Operand

Note: The blank areas are not defined.

*2-byte instruction; fetch cycle appears as a 3-byte instruction

relationship with other Z8 timing signals.

The important Z8 timing relationships relate to the instruction pipeline accesses, instruction cycles, external memory (or I/O accesses, interrupt cycles and the reset cycle.

The high rate of Z8 throughput is due, in part, to the use of instruction pipelining, where the instruction fetch and execution cycles are overlapped. During the execution cycle of an instruction, the opcodes for the next instruction are fetched. The overlap of instruction fetch and execution makes the Effective Execution Time of an instruction shorter than the Instruction Completion Time by the amount of overlap. The amount of overlap is called Hidden Delay Until Completion. This delay is the amount of time incurred by an instruction until its results are valid.

When a program is running, the instruction overlap time is completely hidden in the total program execution time. Consequently, this amount of time can be subtracted from the instruction completion time to calculate the effective execution time of instructions in a program. However, when testing the results of a single instruction, the hidden delay must be taken into account.

The Z8 Opcode map in Table 4.4 has two columns pertinent to instruction time calculations; Execution Cycles (effective execution time) and Pipeline Cycles (hidden delay until completion). Because of the effects of pipelining described above, only the execution time column is used in program throughput calculations. Because the hidden delay does not affect any instruction except the last executed instruction, it should not be used in throughput calculations.

Figs. 4.12 and 4.13 show instruction cycle timing for instructions fetched from external memory. The addresses, Address Strobe (AS) and Read Write (R/W) are output at the beginning of each machine cycle (Mn). The addresses output via Port 0 (if used) remain stable throughout the machine cycle, whereas addresses output via Port 1 remain valid only

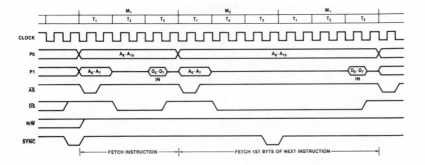

Fig. 4.12 Instruction cycle timing (one-byte instructions).

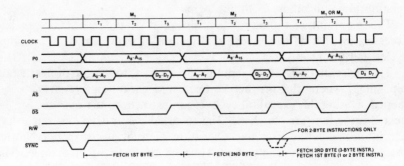

Fig. 4.13 Instruction cycle timing (two and three-byte instructions).

during MnT1. The addresses are guaranteed valid at the rising edge of AS, which should be used to latch the Port 1 output. Port 1 is then placed in an input mode at the end of MnT1. The Data Strobe is output during MnT2, allowing data to be placed on the Port 1 bus. The Z8 accepts the data during MnT3 and DS is terminated.

An instruction synchronisation pulse SYNC is output one clock pulse period prior to the beginning of an opcode fetch machine cycle (M1). This output is directly available on the 64-pin version of the Z8; whereas, on the 40-pin version, the Data Strobe pin outputs SYNC only if external memory is not used.

Note that all instruction fetch cycles have the same machine timing regardless of whether the memory is internal or not. If configured for external memory and internal memory is referenced, the addresses are still output via Ports 0 and 1; however DS and R/W are inactive. If configured for internal memory only, Ports 0 and 1 are used for I/O, DS outputs SYNC and R/W is inactive.

4.2.10   External Memory or I/O Timing

When external memory is addressed, Ports 0 and 1 are configured to output the required number of address bits. Port 1 is used as a multiplexed address/data bus for AD0-AD7 and Port 0 outputs address bits A8-A15. The timing relationships for addressing external memory and I/O are illustrated in Fig 4.14. An added timing cycle that extends external memory timing to allow for slower memory can be interposed between T1 and T2. Address bits A0-A15 are valid on Ports 0 and 1 at the trailing edge of AS for both the read and write memory cycles. Because Port 0 is not multiplexed, address bits A8-A15, if used, are present all through the read/write memory cycle.

During the read cycle, the input data must be valid on Port 1 at the

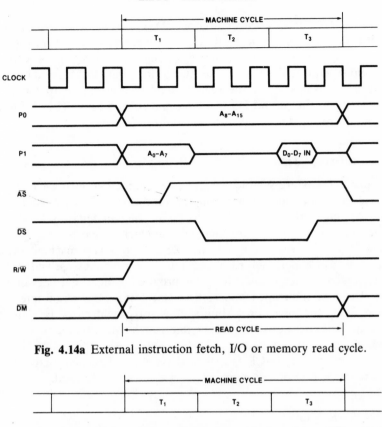

Fig. 4.14a External instruction fetch, I/O or memory read cycle.

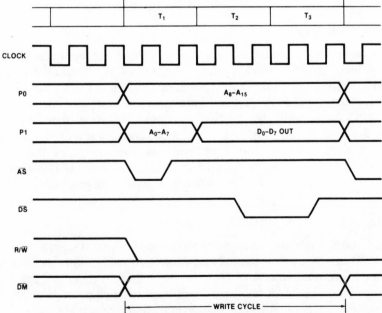

Fig. 4.14b External I/O or memory write cycle.

trailing edge of the Data Strobe output (DS). The Data Memory Select output (DM) is used to select external data memory or external program memory. If selected, DM is active during the execution of certain instructions. During the write cycle, the address outputs follow the same timing relationships as for the read cycle. However, the output data is valid for the entire period DS is active, and R/W is active (Low) during the entire write cycle.

4.2.11 Interrupt Timing

Interrupt requests are sampled before each instruction fetch cycle. First, external interrupt requests are sampled four clock periods prior to the active AS pulse that corresponds to an instruction fetch cycle. Then, internal interrupt requests are sampled one clock period preceding AS.

If an interrupt request is set, the Z8 spends seven machine cycles (forty-four clock periods) resolving interrupt priorities, selecting the proper interrupt vector, and saving the program counter and flags on the stack. The total interrupt response time (including the external interrupt sample time) for an external interrupt is forty-eight clock periods, at which time the first instruction of the interrupt service routine is fetched.

When an interrupt request is detected in the Z8602 or Z8612 development device, IACK is activated (High) and remains active until the first instruction of the interrupt service routine is fetched.

4.2.12 Reset Timing

The internal logic is initialised during reset if the Reset input is held Low for at least eighteen clock periods (see Fig. 4.15). During the time RESET is Low, AS is output at the internal clock rate, DS is forced Low, R/W is inactive and Ports 0, 1 and 2 are placed in an input mode. AS and DS both Low is normally a mutually exclusive condition; therefore, the coincidence of AS Low and DS Low can be used as a reset condition for other devices. Zilog Z Bus peripherals take advantage of this reset condition. Following a reset signal program, execution is restarted at location 12 which is the first address available to user programs.

4.2.13 Alternative Control Signal Uses

In addition to their uses in memory transfers, the control signals AS, DS and R/W can be used in the following interface applications. AS can be modified to provide the RAS (Row Address Strobe) signal for dynamic memory interface. RAS can be derived from the trailing edge of DS to the trailing edge of AS. DS has several alternative uses: as a CAS (Column Address Strobe) for dynamic memory interface, as a Chip

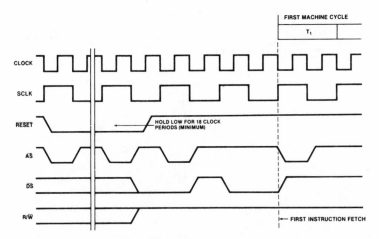

Fig. 4.15 Reset cycle timing.

Enable for memory and other interface devices, and as an Enable input for 3-state bus drivers/receivers for memory and interface devices. R/W can be used as Write input to memory interfaces, and as an Early Status output to switch the direction of 3-state bus drivers/receivers.

4.3 ADDRESSING MODES

With the exception of immediate data and condition codes, all operands are expressed as register file addresses, program memory addresses or data memory addresses. The various addressing modes provided by the Z8 are:

Register	Direct
Indirect Register	Relative
Indexed	Immediate

The Summary of Instructions shown in Table 4.5 specifies the applicable addressing modes for each Z8 instruction.

4.3.1 Register Address

In the register addressing mode, the operand value is the contents of the specified register. The register can be addressed in one of two ways: by an 8-bit address in the range of 0-127, 240-255, see Fig. 4.16, or by a 4-bit working-register address in the range of 0-15.

Table 4.5 Instruction summary.

Instruction and Operation	Addr Mode dst	Addr Mode src	Opcode Byte (Hex)	C	Z	S	V	D	H
ADC dst,src / dst ← dst + src + C	(Note 1)		1□	•	•	•	•	0	•
ADD dst,src / dst ← dst + src	(Note 1)		0□	•	•	•	•	0	•
AND dst,src / dst ← dst AND src	(Note 1)		5□	-	•	•	0	-	-
CALL dst / SP ← SP - 2 @SP ← PC; PC ← dst	DA IRR		D6 D4	-	-	-	-	-	-
CCF / C ← NOT C			EF	•	-	-	-	-	-
CLR dst / dst ← 0	R IR		B0 B1	-	-	-	-	-	-
COM dst / dst ← NOT dst	R IR		60 61	-	•	•	0	-	-
CP dst,src / dst - src	(Note 1)		A□	•	•	•	•	-	-
DA dst / dst ← DA dst	R IR		40 41	•	•	•	X	-	-
DEC dst / dst ← dst - 1	R IR		00 01	-	•	•	•	-	-
DECW dst / dst ← dst - 1	RR IR		80 81	-	•	•	•	-	-
DI / IMR (7) ← 0			8F	-	-	-	-	-	-
DJNZ r,dst / r ← r - 1 if r ≠ 0 PC ← PC + dst Range: +127, -128	RA		rA r=0-F	-	-	-	-	-	-
EI / IMR (7) ← 1			9F	-	-	-	-	-	-
INC dst / dst ← dst + 1	r R IR		rE r=0-F 20 21	-	•	•	•	-	-
INCW dst / dst ← dst + 1	RR IR		A0 A1	-	•	•	•	-	-
IRET / FLAGS ← @SP; SP ← SP + 1 PC ← @SP; SP ← SP + 2; IMR(7) ← 1			BF	•	•	•	•	•	•
JP cc,dst / if cc is true PC ← dst	DA IRR		cD c=0-F 30	-	-	-	-	-	-
JR cc,dst / if cc is true, PC ← PC + dst Range: +127, -128	RA		cB c=0-F	-	-	-	-	-	-
LD dst,src / dst ← src	r r R r X r Ir R R R IR IR	Im R r X r Ir r R IR Im Im R	rC r8 r9 r=0-F C7 D7 E3 F3 E4 E5 E6 E7 F5	-	-	-	-	-	-
LDC dst,src / dst ← src	r Irr	Irr r	C2 D2	-	-	-	-	-	-
LDCI dst,src / dst ← src r ← r + 1; rr ← rr + 1	Ir Irr	Irr Ir	C3 D3	-	-	-	-	-	-

Instruction and Operation	Addr Mode dst	Addr Mode src	Opcode Byte (Hex)	C	Z	S	V	D	H
LDE dst,src / dst ← src	r Irr	Irr r	82 92	-	-	-	-	-	-
LDEI dst,src / dst ← src r ← r + 1; rr ← rr + 1	Ir Irr	Irr Ir	83 93	-	-	-	-	-	-
NOP			FF	-	-	-	-	-	-
OR dst,src / dst ← dst OR src	(Note 1)		4□	-	•	•	0	-	-
POP dst / dst ← @SP SP ← SP + 1	R IR		50 51	-	-	-	-	-	-
PUSH src / SP ← SP - 1; @SP ← src	R IR		70 71	-	-	-	-	-	-
RCF / C ← 0			CF	0	-	-	-	-	-
RET / PC ← @SP; SP ← SP + 2			AF	-	-	-	-	-	-
RL dst	R IR		90 91	•	•	•	•	-	-
RLC dst	R IR		10 11	•	•	•	•	-	-
RR dst	R IR		E0 E1	•	•	•	•	-	-
RRC dst	R IR		C0 C1	•	•	•	•	-	-
SBC dst,src / dst ← dst - src - C	(Note 1)		3□	•	•	•	•	1	•
SCF / C ← 1			DF	1	-	-	-	-	-
SRA dst	R IR		D0 D1	•	•	•	0	-	-
SRP src / RP ← src		Im	31	-	-	-	-	-	-
SUB dst,src / dst ← dst - src	(Note 1)		2□	•	•	•	•	1	•
SWAP dst	R IR		F0 F1	X	•	•	X	-	-
TCM dst,src / (NOT dst) AND src	(Note 1)		6□	-	•	•	0	-	-
TM dst, src / dst AND src	(Note 1)		7□	-	•	•	0	-	-
XOR dst,src / dst ← dst XOR src	(Note 1)		B□	-	•	•	0	-	-

Note 1

These instructions have an identical set of addressing modes, which are encoded for brevity. The first opcode nibble is found in the instruction set table above. The second nibble is expressed symbolically by a □ in this table, and its value is found in the following table to the left of the applicable addressing mode pair.

For example, to determine the opcode of an ADC instruction using the addressing modes r (destination) and Ir (source) is 13.

Addr Mode dst	Addr Mode src	Lower Opcode Nibble
r	r	2
r	Ir	3
R	R	4
R	IR	5
R	IM	6
IR	IM	7

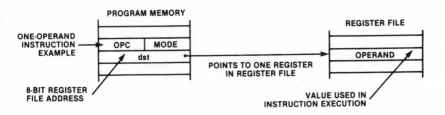

Fig. 4.16 Register addressing.

4.3.2 Working Register Address

Designating a register by a 4-bit working-register address, rather than an 8-bit register-file address, reduces the length of an instruction and results in a shorter execution time. In this case, the full register-file address is formed by concatenating the 4-bit field (address range 0-15) with the upper four bits of the register pointer (Fig. 4.17). Thus, the working-register set can be varied dynamically by changing the value of the register pointer (R253).

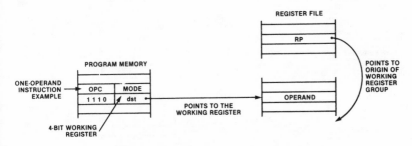

Fig. 4.17 Working-register addressing.

4.3.3 Register Pair Address

Registers can be used in pairs to designate 16-bit values or memory addresses. A register pair must be specified as an even number in the range 0, 2, 4 . . . 126 or 240, 242, 244 . . . 254.

Working-register pairs can also be used to designate 16-bit values or memory addresses. The allowable register pairs begin with an even number and are in the range 0, 2, 4 . . . 14.

4.3.4 Indirect-Register Address

In indirect addressing, the value of the operand is not the contents of a register. Instead, the register (register pair, working-register or working-register pair) contains the address of the location whose contents are to be used as the operand value (Fig. 4.18).

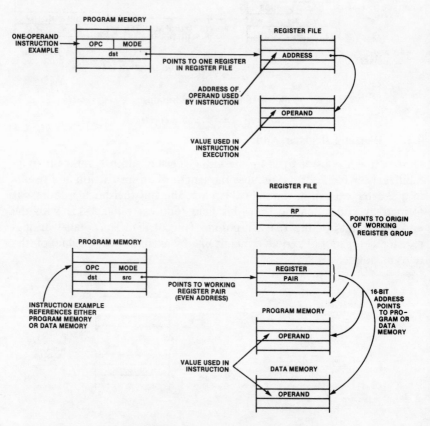

Fig. 4.18 Indirect register addressing.

Depending on the instruction selected, the address may point to a register, program memory, or external data memory location.

Register pairs or working-register pairs are used to hold the 16-bit addresses when accessing program or external data memory. Pairs are indicated by an even number (see the lower part of Fig. 4.18).

4.3.5 Indexed Address

An indexed address consists of a register address offset by the contents of a designated working register (the index). This offset is added to the register address and the resulting address points to the location whose value is used by the instruction (Fig. 4.19). This address mode is used only by the Load (LD) instruction to address the register file.

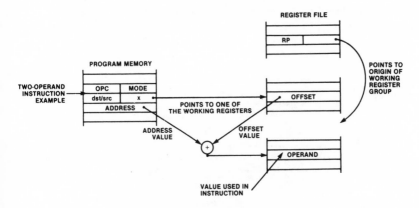

Fig. 4.19 Indexed addressing.

4.3.6 Direct Address

Direct addressing is used only by Conditional Jump (JP) and Call (CALL) instructions to specify the destination where program control is to be transferred (Fig. 4.20).

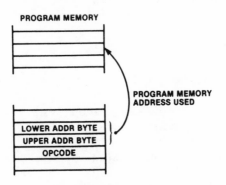

Fig. 4.20 Direct addressing.

4.3.7 Relative Address

The relative address mode is implied by its instruction. It is used only by the Jump Relative (JR) and the Decrement and Jump (DJNZ) instructions, and is the only mode available to these instructions. In this case, the operand contains a two's complement offset that is added to the contents of program counter to form the destination address (the program address where control is to be transferred). The content of the program counter is the address of the instruction following the JR or DJNZ instruction. The offset value is an 8-bit signed value in the range of −128 to +127 (Fig. 4.21).

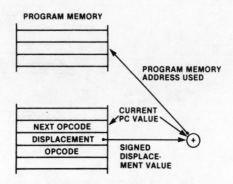

Fig. 4.21 Relative addressing.

4.3.8. Immediate Data

Immediate data is considered an 'address mode' for the purposes of this discussion. The operand value used by the instruction in this case is the value supplied in the operand field itself.

4.4 INSTRUCTION SET

Z8 instructions are functionally divided into eight groups:

Load	Bit Manipulation (Test)
Arithmetic	Block Transfer
Logical	Rotate and Shift
Program Control (Branch)	CPU Control

The summary in Table 4.6 shows the instructions belonging to each group and the number of operands required for each, where 'src' is the source operand, 'dst' is the destination operand and 'cc' is a condition code.

4.5 THE Z8 FAMILY

In its basic form the Z8 family consists of the Z8601 and the Z8611 which are, respectively, the 2 K byte and 4 K byte custom masked ROM devices. These are used when a design is fully debugged and large

Table 4.6 Z8 instruction set: functional groups.

Instruction	Operand (s)	Name of Instruction
Load Instructions		
CLR	dst	Clear
LD	dst, src	Load
LDC	dst, src	Load Constant
LDE	dst, src	Load External Data
POP	dst	Pop
PUSH	src	Push

Instruction	Operand (s)	Name of Instruction
Arithmetic Instructions		
ADC	dst, src	Add with Carry
ADD	dst, src	Add
CP	dst, src	Compare
DA	dst	Decimal Adjust
DEC	dst	Decrement
DECW	dst	Decrement Word
INC	dst	Increment
INCW	dst	Increment Word
SBC	dst, src	Subtract with Carry
SUB	dst, src	Subtract

Instruction	Operand (s)	Name of Instruction
Logical Instructions		
AND	dst, src	Logical And
COM	dst	Complement
OR	dst, src	Logical Or
XOR	dst, src	Logical Exclusive Or

Instruction	Operand (s)	Name of Instruction
Program-Control Instructions		
CALL	dst	Call
DJNZ	r, dst	Decrement and Jump if Nonzero
IRET		Interrupt Return
JP	cc, dst	Jump
JR	cc, dst	Jump Relative
RET		Return

Table 4.6 continued

Bit-Manipulation Instructions		
Instruction	Operands	Name of Instruction
TCM	dst, src	Test Complement Under Mask
TM	dst, src	Test Under Mask
AND	dst, src	Logical And
OR	dst, src	Logical Or
XOR	dst, src	Logical Exclusive Or

Block-Transfer Instructions		
Instruction	Operands	Name of Instruction
LDCI	dst, src	Load Constant Autoincrement
LDEI	dst, src	Load External Data Autoincrement

Rotate and Shift Instructions		
Instruction	Operand	Name of Instruction
RL	dst	Rotate Left
RLC	dst	Rotate Left Through Carry
RR	dst	Rotate Right
RRC	dst	Rotate Right Through Carry
SRA	dst	Shift Right Arithmetic
SWAP	dst	Swap Nibbles

CPU Control Instructions		
Instruction	Operand	Name of Instruction
CCF		Complement Carry Flag
DI		Disable Interrupts
EI		Enable Interrupts
NOP		No Operation
RCF		Reset Carry Flag
SCF		Set Carry Flag
SRP	src	Set Register Pointer

production quantities are required. For the development phase of a design, the Z8602, 3, 12 and 13 ROMless devices are available and allow the user to develop software for the internal memory space (2 K or 4 K bytes), external to the device. This is achieved in two ways. In the Z8602 and Z8612, access to internal memory space is provided by packaging the micro into a 64-pin package and routing the address and control signals through the extra pins. In the earlier versions, a 64-pin Quip package was used. However, this has now been superseded by a dual-in-line package with 70 mil pin spacing, which in many instances can be used in the final production design.

The Z6803 and Z8613 are similar to the Z8602 and Z8612 except that they are housed in a 40-pin package which has a 24-pin socket situated on the top to provide for direct interface to 2716 and 2732 EPROMS. The advantages that this type of package (known as a Protopak) has over the 64-pin version is that when the final program is established, the user can then switch directly to the 40-pin mask programmed Z8601 or Z8611 devices.

Other variants of the basic Z8 architecture include the Z8681 and Z8682 devices, also ROMless, like the Z8602 to Z8613 devices, but designed to operate in a multichip configuration where external memory is provided. In the Z8681, Port 1 is always configured as an address/data bus and Port 0 is nibble programmable. Consequently, after a reset or power-on has occurred, the device expects 256 bytes of memory to be resident on the bus. The Z8682 is similar except that Port 0 is also configured for external address so that the device expects memory decode logic to decode sixteen address bits.

The remaining members of the family, which are discussed in the following sections, include the Z8671 BASIC/DEBUG device, which is suitable for use in applications which are user interactive such as industrial control, and the Z809X and Z859X Universal peripheral controllers, which are slave peripheral processors. These two latter groups of devices consist of a slightly modified Z8 architecture, altered to function as close support slaves to Z80 and Z8000 microprocessors. Table 4.7 summarises the various devices which are available.

4.6 THE Z8671

The Z8671 member of the Z8 family is a Z8601 which has a Basic interpreter, known as BASIC/DEBUG, programmed into the 2 K ROM. This Basic interpreter is a descendant of Dartmouth Basic and so has a similar syntax and is therefore easy to learn and use. However, because BASIC/DEBUG is designed specifically for industrial control applications, some of the Dartmouth Basic features which are inappropriate to

Table 4.7 Z8 family variants.

Part Number	Package	Description
Z8601	40-pin	2 K bytes of internal mask-programmable ROM
Z8602	64-pin	No internal ROM; interface to 2 K bytes of external ROM/PROM
Z8603	40-pin Protopak	No internal ROM; 24-pin socket for 2 K bytes of external EPROM
Z8611	40-pin	4 K bytes of internal mask-programmable ROM
Z8612	64-pin	No internal ROM; 42-pin socket for 2 K bytes of external ROM/PROM
Z8613	40-pin Protopak	No internal ROM; 24-pin socket for 4 K bytes of external EPROM
Z8681	40-pin	No internal ROM; port 1 pins an interface to external memory
Z8671	40-pin	Z8601 with a BASIC debugger/interpreter

N.B. An A designation indicates that the device will run at clock speeds up to a maximum of 12 MHz. Parts without A designation operate to a maximum of 8 MHz (e.g. Z8601A).

Z8671 applications have been omitted. (Remember the Z8 is optimised for bit and byte manipulation.) Among these are trigonometric and other transcendental functions, array and character string handling, and fractional numbers. Moreover to conserve memory space, all redundant commands and statement types which can be duplicated by combining other commands, have also been eliminated. On the credit side, BASIC/DEBUG allows first hardware tests, examination and modification of any memory locations of I/O port at the bit or byte level and the capability to process decimal or hexadecimal input/output values.

A BASIC/DEBUG program may access machine language code as either a subroutine or as a user-defined function. Another useful feature, and unlike Dartmouth Basic, is that BASIC/DEBUG accepts expressions following the Keyword GOTO or GOSUB, thus allowing a variable to be used to select a line number, as opposed to line numbers being fixed at edit time. Hence:

GOTO A+B   GOTO 3*4,   GOSUB A*Z,   etc.

The following listing represents all the expressions, operators, functions and statements that can be used with BASIC/DEBUG.

Expressions:
Variable Names A-Z.
Signed decimal numbers in the range −32768 to +32767.
Hexadecimal numbers (preceded by "%") in the range 0 to 65535.

Operators:		*Arithmetic Operators*:	
=	equal.	+	addition.
<=	less than or equal.	−	subtraction.
<	less than.	*	multiplication.
<>	not equal.	/	division.
>	greater than.	\	unsigned division.
>=	greater than or equal.		

Memory Operators:

@   Any byte may be referenced by placing the byte signal character
    "@" in front of the address. For example, LET X = @ 1000
    assigns the value at address 1000 to X; LET @ (C*100) = A
    assigns the value of A to the byte at address (C*100).

    Sixteen-bit words may be referenced with an address preceded
    by the word signal character " ↑ ". For example, PRINT ↑ 8 will
    print the sixteen-bit value pointed to by the contents of the word at
    location 8.

Functions:

AND (a,b)   Performs a logical AND of the expressions a,b.
USR (a,b,c) Calls an assembly language routine at address a. The
            expressions b,c may be used to pass arguments to the
            routine. The assembly language routine must return a
            value.

Statements:

GO@   Branches to an assembly language routine. This statement
        is similar to USR except no value is returned by the
        assembly language routine.
GOSUB   Calls a subroutine at line number.
GOTO   Branches to a line number.
IF/THEN Used for conditional operations and branches.
INPUT   Inputs expressions separated by commas.
IN   Same as INPUT except values remaining in the input
        buffer are used first, then new data is requested.
LET   Assigns the value of an expression to a variable or memory
        location.
LIST   Lists the current program.
NEW   Establishes a new start-of-program address.
PRINT   Lists its arguments, which may be text messages or
        numerical values, on the output terminal.

REM   Used to insert comments.
RETURN   Returns control to line following GOSUB statement.
RUN   Initiates sequential execution of all instructions in current program.
STOP   Gracefully ends program execution.

BASIC/DEBUG operates in one of the two modes; 'immediate' or 'run'. In the immediate mode, a line editor is operating and allows the Basic line numbers and program instructions to be entered:

$$100 \quad A=B*C \qquad 110 \quad PRINT \ A.$$

Commands may also be executed in immediate mode, some exclusively such as RUN and NEW. Most others, however, can be used in both modes.

In the 'run' mode, which is entered from the immediate mode by typing RUN, commands previously entered via the line editor are executed in order of ascending line number. Program control then returns to the immediate mode when the interpreter completes the execution of a program or when an error condition occurs.

The Z8671 is configured at power-on/reset by the BASIC/DEBUG interpreter to work with external memory and to estimate its nature (RAM or ROM) and size (up to 64 K bytes). If no external memory exists, the device will place all the interpreter parameters into the register file, along with an internal stack, the input line buffer and the user variables. With this configuration a limited number of commands can be executed in the immediate mode.

Once the application program has been developed and tested, the Z8671 system may be converted from a development/debug mode to an automatic mode. To do this, the developed program is stored in a ROM and located at a special location in memory. The BASIC/DEBUG interpreter will then execute the Basic program in the ROM every time the system is powered-up or reset.

4.7 COMPANION PERIPHERAL DEVICES AND Z BUS

So far, the discussion of the Z8 has centred on the aspects of the device which are relevant to single-chip applications. When it becomes necessary to add extra memory or peripheral capabilities, the Z8's ports 0 and 1 must be reconfigured so that they function as a parallel address/data bus which conforms with the Zilog bus standard, Z Bus.

Z Bus, which came about with the introduction of the Z8000, is used by the majority of devices made by Zilog (Z8, Z800, Z8000, Z80K and their family members) and was designed to ease the problems involved when adding extra peripheral features or when mixing dissimilar CPUs. By using Z Bus, a Z8 design can take advantage of Z8000 family peripheral members. For instance, counter-time and I/O port capabilities can be increased by the addition of the Z8036 CIO. If on the other hand, extra serial I/O is required, then the Z8030 SCC (dual channel serial communications controller) can be added. Apart 'from the CIO and SCC, other peripherals exist, some of which will be described in the following sections.

Z Bus, which is a multiplexed address/data bus, was designed to support an addressing range up to thirty-two bits (4 Gigabytes) and data transfers of bytes, words and long words. However, current peripheral devices are designed for byte data transactions, with the Z8000 as the only CPU capable of supporting both byte and word transfers with address references up to 8 Mbytes. In a Z8 system only byte data formats can be used with addressing limited to 64 Kbytes (sixteen bits).

One of the major advantages of Z bus is that the devices which use this bus, CPUs and peripherals alike, can be encapsulated into smaller packages than would otherwise be possible if address and data information required separate pins. As a corollary of this, registers in the various peripheral devices can be directly addressed, up to 256 registers, since address information is available to the peripherals on the address/data bus. This does away with a pointer register mechanism or the use of multiple register reads or writes used by earlier designs (Z80, PIO, Intel 8257, etc.).

The signals address strobe AS, data strobe DS and read/write R/W are provided to facilitate transfers between the Z8 CPU and external memory or peripheral devices. When a transfer is required from an external device into the CPU, address information is put onto the bus and is indicated true by the presence of the signal AS going low. After AS goes high, the CPU puts DS low (true), which is the signal to the external device to place its data on the bus. During an input to the CPU, R/W remains high, while for an output R/W will go low before the start of AS and after the end of DS. These signals, and others which are not used by the Z8 but which are required by other Z Bus processors, are described in reference 4.1 (see end of this chapter). In Fig. 4.22 it can be seen how a Z8 might be connected to a Z Bus peripheral device.

A8 – 15		
A/D0-7	:	Address/data bus bits 0 – 7.
AS	:	Address strobe.
DS	:	Data strobe.
R/W	:	Read/Write signal.
INT	:	Interrupt – Connected to one of the Ports repeat lines.
INTACK	:	Interrupt Acknowledge – tied high (inactive).

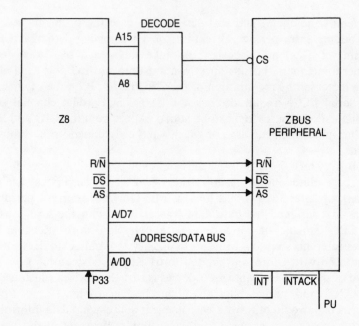

Fig. 4.22 Z8 connected to a Z bus peripheral.

In this configuration the Z8 can either poll the peripheral or the peripheral can interrupt the Z8 via one of Port 3 input lines. CS is provided by decoding address lines A8 to A15.

4.7.1 Z8036 (CIO)

The CIO (counter timer input/output device) consists of two bit ports, one 4-bit port and three 16-bit counters. Each 8-bit port, ports A and B, can be programmed to be doubled buffered, byte input/output, bidirectional or bit input/output. In the bit input/output mode, each bit can be inverted/non-inverted, input/output push-pull or open drain, or operate as a '1's catcher in the input mode. In addition, pattern recognition can be performed on each bit so that a pattern match will occur when either a '1' or '0' is present, or when a positive transition has occurred.

Port C, which is four bits, is bit programmable and is also used to supply handshake lines to ports A and B. The handshake modes supported include strobed, pulsed (uses one of the counter timers), two wire interlocked and three wire (IEEE 488) handshake. Two 4-bit deskew timers are also available for delaying the handshake readyline until data has been set-up for some prescribed period.

The three 16-bit counter timers each consist of a 16-bit down counter,

16-bit time constant register and a 16-bit current count register. Each time can be externally gated, triggered or clocked, and each can be operated in pulsed, one shot or square wave output modes. Counter timers 1 and 2 can be combined to form a 32-bit counter where counter 2 is either gated, triggered or clocked by counter 1. The device can be operated in interrupt, interrupt vectored or polled modes. By using the pattern recognition capability of the ports A or B and the interrupt logic the CIO can be used as a 16-input interrupt controller.

4.7.2   Z8030 (SCC)

The SCC (Serial Communications Controller) consists of two independent 0 to 1 Mbit/second, full duplex serial communications controllers. Each channel has its own Baud rate generator, crystal oscillator and digital phase-locked loop, which can be used to recover the clock from the incoming data stream. The protocols supported include Async, with provision for five to eight bits per character, Bisync and Monosync, SDLC and HDLC. Each Baud rate generator consists of a 16-bit counter whose output may be used either as the TX clock, the RX clock or both. It can also drive the Digital Phase-Locked Loop (DPLL). Inputs to the Baud rate generator can come from either the RX clock or the crystal oscillator.

The DPLL can be used to recover clock information from a data stream which is encoded in FM, FMO, NRZ and NRZI. In addition to these four methods, the SCC can be used to decode Manchester (biphase level) data by using DPLL in the FM mode and programming the receiver for NRZ data. Other features which are available include full DMA capability for full duplex on both channels, local loopback and auto echo.

The Z8031 ASCC (Asynchronous only Communications Controller) is functionally similar to the Z8030 SCC except for the synchronous modes of operation, which have been omitted.

4.7.3   Z8038 (FIO)

The FIO (First In/First Out I/O device), which will work at data rates greater than 1 Mbyte/second, consists of a 128 bytes bidirectional FIFO buffer placed between two programmable interface ports. Port 1 side is capable of functioning as a Z Bus interface or as a general purpose microcomputer interface. Port 2 can function in an identical manner, but in addition it will also function as a buffer with two-wire handshake or with a three-wire (IEEE 488) handshake. These features enable the designer to easily implement CPU to CPU or CPU to peripheral interfaces. For CPU to CPU interfaces, two mailbox registers are available, one for each direction, so that control parameters can be exchanged outside of the FIFO buffer. Either port can support an interrupt, vectored interrupt or polled environment. Seven sources of interrupt are available. These include pattern match, byte count, buffer empty, buffer full, underflow/overflow, data direction change and mailbox message available. Other features include DMA request signals, DMA requests initiated by byte count match and features for FIFO width and depth expansion.

4.7.4   Z8068 (DCP)

The DCP (Data Cipher Processor) contains the circuitry necessary to encrypt and decrypt data using the National Bureau of Standards encryption algorithms. It is designed to be used in a variety of environments, including dedicated controllers, communication concentrators and peripheral task processors in general purpose systems. Data rates greater than 1 Mbytes/second can be handled using Cipher Feedback, Electronic Code Book, or Cipher Block Chain operating modes.

Other devices which conform to the Z bus standard but which are not discussed here include the Z8016 DMA Controller, the Z6132 4 K Quasi-static RAM, the Z8070 Floating Point Processor and the Z8116 and Z8216 CPUs. Detailed technical descriptions of the aforementioned devices can be found in Reference 4.1 (see end of this chapter).

4.8   THE UNIVERSAL PERIPHERAL CONTROLLER

Often a particular computing application requires the use of more than one processor in order to increase data throughput or to cope with complex data formats. In some instances the appropriate method of increasing the processing power is by configuring the computing system as an array of similar processors so that any member of the array is able to process any given task.

Such arrangements are common in mainframe designs. However, other situations occur where it is more appropriate to use a special-purpose processor for one particular aspect of a computing task (and free the main processor so that it can handle the remaining tasks more efficiently). In a Z80, 68000 or Z8000, multitasking system subtasks which are concerned with serving disc memory units or network controllers, are best suited to some form of I/O processor where the I/O processor is optimised for bit, 4-bit and byte data manipulation.

The interface between the I/O processor and the system CPU for such schemes can be implemented in a number of ways. Assuming that a Z8 is used, the most straightforward method is for the host CPU to treat the Z8 as an I/O device interfaced via some sort of parallel I/O device (PIO) which can provide the handshake signals to a port in the Z8, and the appropriate interface to the host CPU. This PIO can be either a member of the host CPU's family (the host could be an 8086 or 68000) or a device such as the Zilog Z8036, Z8536 or Z8038. A second method would be to make the Z8 a bus master on the same bus as the host CPU with communications between the two via data exchanges in global memory.

For situations where data throughput is not of prime importance, the aforementioned configurations are usually satisfactory. However, when a high data throughput is required, these methods can introduce severe bottlenecks due to the single data path constraint in the PIO network, or problems with arbitration overhead for the shared memory scheme.

To provide a Z8 type architecture but with an efficient host CPU interface, Zilog introduced the Z809X and Z859X Universal Peripheral Controllers. The Z809X UPC is designed for systems which use a multiplexed bus such as Z bus or the bus used by the 8086. The other version of the UPC, the Z859X, is designed for systems which operate with a non-multiplexed bus such as the 68000 or the Z80.

Architecturally, the UPC is similar to the Z8, the instruction set is the same, but some of the later features have been deleted and new ones added to suit the UPC's role as a slave processor. The differences between the two architectures include the sacrifice of an I/O port to free pins for an 8-bit data bus, omission of the UART so that more space can be provided for an increased register file (256 registers over the 144 in the Z8) and the re-assignment of some of the control registers, some of which are now redundant, to other roles.

One other important modification of the architecture is the provision for the host processor to access the majority of registers in the UPC's register file as if the file was a dual-port memory. This mechanism allows the host processor to gain access to data in the UPC with minimal delay in the transfer process.

Figs. 4.23 and 4.24 show respectively the functional block diagram for the UPC and the register file. All communications between the master CPU and the UPC, except interrupts to the host CPU, are initiated by the host CPU. This means that the host CPU can issue read or write commands to the UPC, but the UPC cannot issue these commands back to the host CPU. If the UPC needs to gain the attention of the host CPU, it can do this by issuing an interrupt.

When the UPC allows it, the host CPU can gain access for reads or writes, to the UPC register file. If the UPC is in the midst of an instruction, the wait line of the host (assuming it has one) is activated, causing the host CPU to insert wait cycles into the read and write commands. Once the UPC has completed the instruction, the wait signal is deactivated and the host CPU is allowed to proceed with its read or

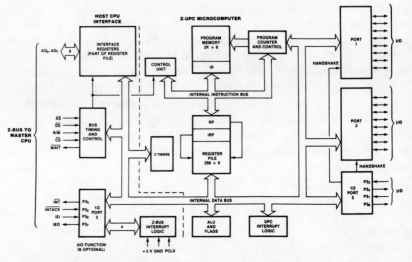

Fig. 4.23 Z8090 UPC functional block diagram (Z bus version).

LOCATION		IDENTIFIER (UPC Side)
FFH	STACK POINTER	SP
FEH	MASTER CPU INTERRUPT CONTROL	MIC
FDH	REGISTER POINTER	RP
FCH	PROGRAM CONTROL FLAGS	FLAGS
FBH	UPC INTERRUPT MASK REGISTER	IMR
FAH	UPC INTERRUPT REQUEST REGISTER	IRQ
F9H	UPC INTERRUPT PRIORITY REGISTER	IPR
F8H	PORT 1 MODE	P1M
F7H	PORT 3 MODE	P3M
F6H	PORT 2 MODE	P2M
F5H	T0 PRESCALER	PRE0
F4H	TIMER/COUNTER 0	T0
F3H	T1 PRESCALER	PRE1
F2H	TIMER/COUNTER 1	T1
F1H	TIMER MODE	TMR
F0H	MASTER CPU INTERRUPT VECTOR REG.	MIV
EFH		
	GENERAL-PURPOSE REGISTERS	
6H		
5H	DATA INDIRECTION REGISTER	DIND
4H	LIMIT COUNT REGISTER	LC
3H	PORT 3	P3
2H	PORT 2	P2
1H	PORT 1	P1
0H	DATA TRANSFER CONTROL REGISTER	DTC

Fig. 4.24 UPC register file.

write command. If the host CPU does not have a wait input, special provision must be made to avoid the access conflicts with the UPC when the UPC's wait line is active.

Three UPC registers, Data Transfer Conrol (DTC), Master Interrupt Vector (MIV) and Master Interrupt Control (MIC), are mapped directly into the host CPU address space. The host CPU is able to access these registers via the address shown in Table 4.8.

Table 4.8 Master CPU/Direct access register map.

Z-UPC/UPC Register File Address			Master CPU Addresses	
Decimal	Hex	Identifier	Address	Shifted Address (Z-UPC Only)
0	0	DIC	xxx11000	xx11000x
5	5	DIND	xxx10101	xx10101x
240	FO	MIV	xxx10000	xx10000x
254	FE	MIC	xxx11110	xx11110x
n+0*		DSC0	xxx00000	xx00000x
n+1		DSC1	xxx00001	xx00001x
n+2		DSC2	xxx00010	xx00010x
n+3		DSC3	xxx00011	xx00011x
n+4		DSC4	xxx00100	xx00100x
n+5		DSC5	xxx00101	xx00101x
n+6		DSC6	xxx00110	xx00110x
n+7		DSC7	xxx00111	xx00111x
n+8		DSC8	xxx01000	xx01000x
n+9		DSC9	xxx01001	xx01001x
n+10		DSCA	xxx01010	xx01010x
n+11		DSCB	xxx01011	xx01011x
n+12		DSCC	xxx01100	xx01100x
n+13		DSCD	xxx01101	xx01101x
n+14		DSCE	xxx01110	xx01110x
n+15		DSCF	xxx01111	xx01111x

*The DSC registers can be any contiguous 16 registers on a 16-byte boundary.

There are two ways in which the host CPU can access the UPC control registers; direct access and block access. As can be seen from the table, the host CPU has direct access to sixteen registers known as the data, status and command (DSC) registers as well as the three mentioned above and an address specified by the Data Indirection Register (DIND). The DSC registers, which are numbered 0 to F (DSC0-DSCF), can be any contiguous 16-register file registers beginning on a 16-bit boundary. The base address of the DSC group is the I/O register pointer (IPR), which is bits D4 to D7 of the Data Transfer Control register. Fig. 4.25

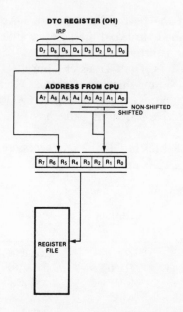

Fig. 4.25 DSC register addressing scheme.

shows how the register address is made up of the 4-bit IRP field combined
with the low-order four bits of the address from the host CPU.

If data transfers are to take place via block access mode, the host CPU
can transmit or receive blocks of data via address XXX10101 (XX10101X
if the decode is shifted for a Z8000) to a register address specified by the
Data Indirection register (DIND). Consequently, when the host CPU
accesses this address, the UPC register pointed to by DIND is accessed
and DIND is incremented. This scheme is well suited to the Z8000 CPU
and allows the Z8000 to read or write blocks of data efficiently.

If the UPC wants to control the number of bytes transferred in a block
transfer, the maximum number transferred may be programmed into a
register known as the Limit Count Register (LC). The contents of LC is
decremented by one for each byte transferred. If the host CPU attempts
to read or write to the UPC after LC reaches 0, a Limit Count Error bit
(LERR) (D2) of the Data Transfer Control register is set, indicating a
limit count error. The LERR error also causes an interrupt on IRQ0.

The registers MVI and MIC define the value of the interrupt vector, if
used, and the status and control information relating to the UPC
interrupts sent back to the host CPU. When the IP (Interrupt Pending)
bit in MIC is set by the UPC, an interrupt is sent to the host CPU. The
UPC can set this bit, but only the host CPU can reset it.

Memory space for the UPC is either 2048 or 4096 bytes of internal
program memory. Any address reference above 4K is currently

undefined even though the UPC can manipulate 16-bit addresses. Table 4.9 describes the possible combinations of the UPC in both 859X and 809X forms. The 859X devices differ from the 809X devices mainly in the definition of the bus. For the 859X devices, the signals A/D (address/data), RD (read) and WR (write) replace AS, DS and R/W.

Table 4.9 UPC variants.

80/8590	=	Masked programmed UPC. (40-pin package.)
80/8591	=	No internal ROM; interface to 4 K bytes of external ROM/PROM. (64-pin package.)
80/8592	=	36-byte internal ROM holds bootstrap program; interface to 4 K bytes of external RAM.
80/8593	=	No internal ROM; 24-pin socket for 4 K bytes of external EPROM. (40-pin package.)
80/8594	=	36-byte internal ROM holds bootstrap program; 24-pin socket for 4 K bytes of external RAM. (40-pin package.)

Detailed technical descriptions of these devices are given in References 4.1 and 4.3 (see end of this chapter).

4.9   CASE STUDY – DATA LOGGER

In this section, the design of a simple data logger using the Z8601 version of the Z8 is discussed.

4.9.1   Objective

The design specification calls for a data logger which will record switch closures on any one of ten channels, labelled A to J. For every occurrence of a closure, the channel and time of occurrence should be displayed on a VDU screen or back to a computer or a printer, both of which are coupled via an RS232 link to the logger.

4.9.2   Specification of Design Task

The connection to the switches should consist of two terminal connectors for each channel, with each switch being monitored, making a short circuit between the two connectors to indicate closure to the data logger. When the short occurs, the time is recorded at the moment of closure.

No record is made when the switch is open, after closure has occurred, or when the switch changes from closed to open. When the switch closes, it must remain closed for 50 milliseconds to ensure that any switch bounce has ceased. (Switch bounce is normally no longer than 10 milliseconds.)

For the terminal connection, an RS232 type is assumed with baud rates ranging from 150 baud to 19.6 k baud. Baud rate detection should be done automatically upon receipt of the first character from the terminal. This first character should be a carriage return. All characters typed to the terminal should be echoed back from the logger.

Fig. 4.26 shows the format that would be displayed for various switch closures on three channels.

	Hours		Minutes		Seconds
B:	14	:	01	:	21
A:	22	:	20	:	05
B:	09	:	04	:	17
G:	10	:	06	:	41

Fig. 4.26 Logger display format.

There are several commands that the data logger should expect to receive from the terminal. The listing below explains these commands. Only the letters shown in parentheses are actually entered into the terminal, and only the letters shown in square brackets are printed out by the terminal.

CMD : (READY ?)
RESPONSE : [READY]
This command verifies that the logger is operating and talking to the terminal.

CMD : (DUMP)
RESPONSE :[C 12:445:00]
               [D 01:30:01]
               [END DUMP]
This command prints the times of all switch closings and the channels on which they have occurred.

CMD : (All B 12:45:01   14:43:02)
RESPONSE [20]
The result of this command is a printout of the number of switch closures for channel B between the times 12:45:01 and 14:43:02.

CMD : (T 12:35:01)

RESPONSE : [TIME ENTERED]
With this command the time of day clock is initialised.

For the computer connection, a second RS232 link is used with the transmit data and receive data connections reversed and its modem signals RTS and CTS set active.

4.9.3 Design Overview

Given the preceding description of the data logger, it can be decided what hardware and software modules will be needed to create the logger. This can be done by breaking the design into a number of smaller modules and working on each one independently. Finally, all of these modules must be merged to make them function together. The first division made is between the hardware design and the software design.

A UART can be used to enable the data logger to receive the serial data from the terminal and the computer connection. The UART is interrupt-driven, so the microcomputer can apply full attention to scanning for switch closures. The UART requires a baud rate generator to clock the sending and receiving of serial data. A timer chip is required to provide the pulses to maintain a time-of-day clock. An interrupt controller chip co-ordinates interrupts between the UART and timer. A microprocessor performs logical operations and computation. Read-Only Memory (ROM) holds the program for the microprocessor. Random Access Memory (RAM) is provided for storage of temporary data. These parts constitute the bulk of the design and are all LSI.

There are some less complex parts that are also critical to the design. The oscillator is needed as a source for the baud rate clock and to provide a system clock for the LSI devics. A TTL/RS232 converter is used to convert TTL voltage levels to RS232 levels. An RS232/TTL converter is used to convert RS232 levels from the terminal and computer to RTL levels required by the data logger logic. The Optoisolators isolate the logger circuitry from high voltages that might enter from switches. They also provide for a convenient interface to the switches. Fig. 4.27 shows a block diagram summarising the hardware requirements.

The next step in the design is to determine how to implement the various modules required. The classic approach is to buy each component (UART, PROM, RAM, etc.) separately and then to connect all the parts together on a printed circuit board. However, the Z8601 interrupt control block satisfies the requirement of the interrupt controller in Fig. 4.27. Interrupts from the UART and timer are routed through the Z8601 just as required. The Register File in Fig. 4.3 contains 124 bytes. The bytes in this block that are not used as registers can be used as RAM with the remaining registers used as a stack area. The program memory of Fig.

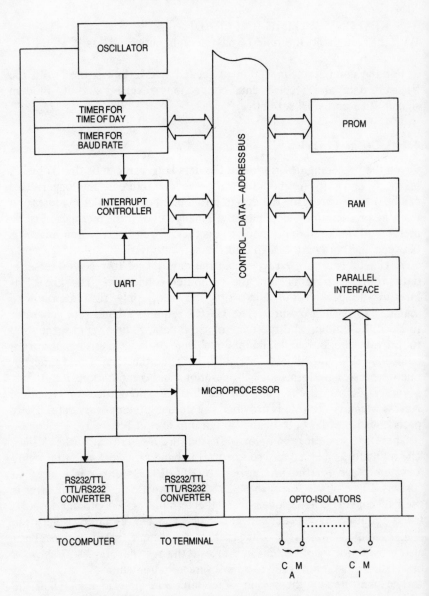

Fig. 4.27 Data logger hardware block diagram.

4.10 should hold the program easily. The diagram shows 2 K available bytes. If this is not enough, Zilog has a 4 K byte part called the Z8611. Ports 2 and 3 provide the parallel lines needed in Fig. 4.27. A oscillator on the Z8601 only needs a crystal to operate.

All of the major components needed for the application are contained

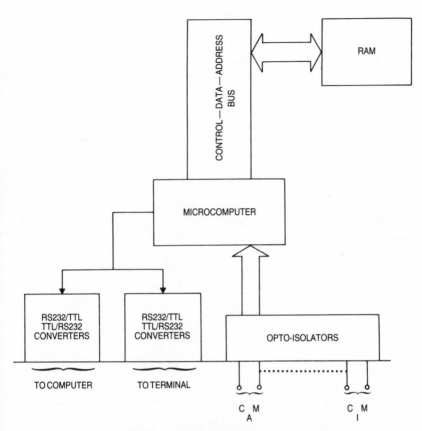

Fig. 4.28 Block diagram data logger using Z8601.

in the Z8601, which reduces the hardware design to a trivial task. Fig. 4.28 shows the block diagram that results from using the Z8601.

The software is the other major part of the design and, like the hardware, it, too, can be partitioned into modules. The first module is the initialisation routine which is used to set RAM and flags to their initial values.

The second software module is the baud rate routine, which analyses the first character received from the terminal or computer and determines the baud rate of each.

The third module is the real time clock routine and is driven by an interrupt sent from the T1 timer every 10 milliseconds. This routine maintains the time of day in hours, minutes and seconds after the initial value is loaded through the terminal via the T command.

The fourth software module, which is called the scanner and runs continuously except when interrupts occur, checks the ten switches for contact closure, it stores the channel letter and the time of closure in memory.

The fifth module is activated by an interrupt that is generated when the UART receives a character. The routine reads the character and stores it in an input buffer. If the received character is a carriage return, the program jumps to a command processor that will interpret the command in the receive buffer and perform the action requested.

The sixth and last routine is the transmit character routine. This routine is activated when the UART becomes empty and generates an interrupt. It is used to send characters to the UART. Once the routine is started it continues to move characters and generate interrupts until it reaches an end-of-message character (FE_{16}). This routine is started by a character being loaded into the UART by the command processor routine. Fig. 4.29 shows a summary of the modules in the software design.

INITIALISATION
ROUTINE

BAUD RATE
ROUTINE

REAL TIME CLOCK
ROUTINE

SCANNER
ROUTINE

RECEIVE CHARACTER
ROUTINE

TRANSMIT CHARACTER
ROUTINE

Fig. 4.29 Software modules.

4.9.4 The Hardware Design

Using the Z8601 greatly simplifies the hardware design, since most of the features required are available in the chip.

Some additional design is needed to connect the external RAM, since the 124 bytes of RAM on the chip are not enough for this application. This task is easy when using the Zilog 6132 RAM, which is 4 K bytes by eight bits. The 6132 RAM's interface is perfectly matched to the Z8601;

to make the connection between the two, only four lines are needed with no external logic.

The instruction LDE dst, src, allows access to the external RAM attached to the Z8601. LDE is the mnemonic for 'Load External Data'. Src is the source of the byte from one of the 62 K possible external RAM locations into a register, and can be any of sixteen registers in a selected group. The group is selected by another instruction loading the RP (Register Pointer) register at another time. Dst stands for a register pair holding a 16-bit value that specifies one of the 62 K bytes of RAM.

To move a byte from one of 124 registers to one of the 62 K RAM locations, the dst specifies a register pair that is holding a 16-bit value. The 16-bit value determines which of 62 K RAM locations is to be loaded. Src then specifies one of the sixteen registers in the group selected by the RP register.

The schematic diagram of Fig. 4.30 shows the arrangement of the Z6132s and the various interface devices. The ten input channels are interfaced to the outside world via optoisolators. RS232 connections are made via appropriate RS232 (V24) drivers.

4.9.5 Software

This section details each of the six software modules mentioned in the design overview. Listings for only two of the modules will be given. These will allow the designer to see some of the available instructions in action. The other modules will be described with flow charts.

4.9.5.1 INITIALISATION SOFTWARE

The first software module considered is intialisation. In initialisation, the peripherals (UART, timer, etc.) on the Z8601 must be set to the desired mode of operation. This is done via the sixteen control registers. The program listing is not given for this routine, but the function of each of these registers and how they are programmed is discussed below.

The control registers, which are closely tied to the hardware, comprise addresses $F0_{16}$ and FF_{16} (in decimal, registers 240 to 255). These are illustrated in Fig. 4.31.

Register 240 is the register associated with UART. A read from register 240 gives the byte received by the UART. Likewise, a write to 240 is the data sent out from the UART.

Register 241 is used to set the timer to its desired mode of operation. In this register, bits 7 and 6 select one of three waveforms to be output on pin P36. The three possible waveforms are the output from the TO counter, the output from the T1 counter, and the internal clock. When bits 7 and 6 are both zero, no waveforms are output to the pin and it functions as a normal I/O pin. In this application, pin P36 is used to drive

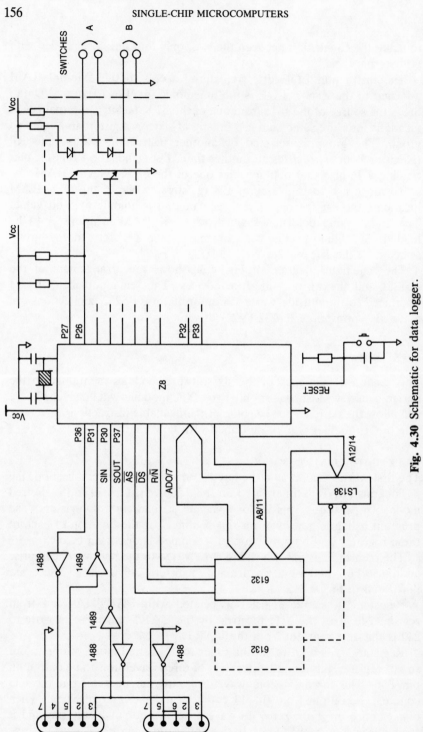

Fig. 4.30 Schematic for data logger.

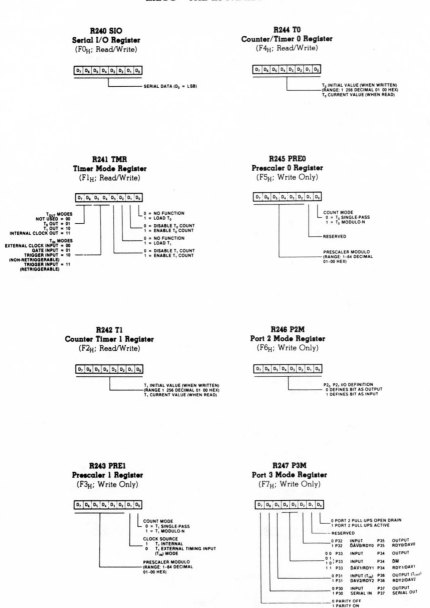

Fig. 4.31 Z8 control registers.

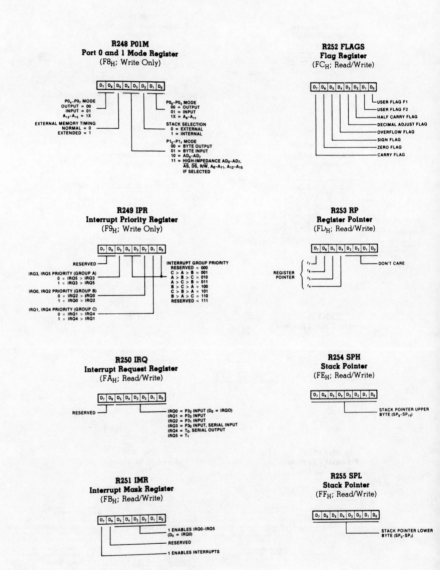

Fig. 4.31 continued

the RTS modem signal, so bits 7 and 6 must be set to 0.

Bits 5 and 4 of register 241 select one of four operating modes for the T1 timer. In one mode, P34 provides the clock to drive the T1 timer. In a second mode, the T1 timer is driven by an internal clock and pin P34 can be used to gate this clock on or off. In the third mode, the T1 timer is driven again by an internal clock and when pin P34 receives a high-to-low transition, the timer will be loaded and enabled regardless of whether it was running or not.

Bit 3 of register 241 enables the T1 counter, which will be set later in this application when our time-of-day clock routine is executed. Bit 2 is used to load the counter value, which sits in a temporary buffer. The temporary buffer is loaded through register 242. In this application, bit 2 will be set once when the time-of-day routine is started. Since T1 will run in a continuous mode, the time will be reloaded every time it reaches 0. Bits 1 and 0 perform the enable and load functions for the T0 counter. Since the T0 counter will be operating in continuous mode, bit 1 and bit 0 must be set to 1 to enable the counter, so that it will reload itself whenever it counts down to 0.

Register 242 is the count register for timer. A read from the register will give the count value of this timer. If a byte is loaded into register 242, it will not be loaded into the timer. Instead, it will be placed into a count load register. The timer is loaded by setting a bit in register 241, which will transfer the byte in the count load register into the timer. The 8-bit value loaded into the timer will be decremented by each rising edge of the clock coming from the prescaler.

Register 243 is used to load six bits directly into the T1 prescaler. There is no count load register as with the timer count value, so six bits are loaded directly into the prescaler. In this application, the frequency of the square wave going into the T1 prescaler is the microcomputer crystal frequency divided by eight. This mode of operation was specified by setting bit 1 of register 243 to 1. The prescaler can be thought of as a box with a square wave whose output frequency is equal to the input frequency divided by the prescale value.

The T1 prescaler output is fed into the T1 counter. In this application, the T1 prescaler is loaded with the value 36. Since the crystal frequency is 7.3728 MHz, 0.9216 MHz (crystal frequency divided by eight) goes into the prescaler and 25.6 KHz (0.9216/36) is available at the output of the prescaler and is fed into the T1 timer. Bit 0 is set to 1 so the T1 timer runs in modulo-n mode, otherwise known as continuous mode. This mode causes the counter to be reloaded automatically with its count value when decremented to 0. In this application, 256 is loaded every 10 milliseconds as the T1 count value. When the count reaches 0, a T1 timer interrupt is generated and the count value is reloaded automatically.

Register 244 is identical to register 242 except that it works with the T0 timer. The T0 timer is used as a baud rate generator and calculates the count value to be loaded.

Register 245 is equivalent to register 243 except that it is the prescaler for the T0 timer. For this application, it is loaded with the value 3. The input to this prescaler is always the microcomputer crystal value divided by eight.

Register 246 is set to FF_{16}, since all these pins are required to be input because they constitute eight of the inputs from the optoisolators. Register 247 controls the functions for the Port 3 pins and the UART.

Bit 7 is set to 0 since parity is not required during UART operation. Bit 6 is set to 1 to connect the UART output to pin P37 and to connect the UART input to P30. Bit 5 is set to 0 to make pin P31 act as an input pin. In this design, pin P31 is connected to the modem control CTS (Fig. 4.28).

Bits 4, 3 and 2 are set to 0,1 and 0 respectively, so that pin P33 and P32 act as inputs from the optoisolators.

Register 248 is used to select how Port 0 and Port 1 will operate. Since we need more than 2 K bytes of RAM for this application, ports 0 and 1 must be programmed to give sixteen bits of address. To do this, bit 7 is set to 1 and bit 6 to 0 in register 248 so that Port 1 acts as a multiplexed data and address bus (AD0-AD7). Bit 5 of register 248 is set to 1 to give us normal memory access timing. If this bit were set to 0, one extra cycle (composed of two clock periods) would be inserted in the middle of all external memory accesses. This extended memory fetch is used to access slower memories. The Z8601 does not need a WAIT pin, since the extended fetch can be selected to slow the memory access to match the speed of slower memories.

Register 249 is used to set priorities for the interrupt controller. Fig. 4.11 shows how the interrupt logic is arranged in the Z8601. In this application, only three interrupts are used. These are discussed next.

Since the T1 timer is generating an interrupt every 10 milliseconds and this interrupt is the basis for the time-of-day clock, its interrupts (IRQ5) are required to have highest priority so that the clock will not miss counts and lose time. The UART full interrupt (IRQ3) is assigned higher priority than the UART empty interrupt (IRQ4). These two interrupts never occur together, so their relationship to one another is not important. To see how the above-mentioned hierarchy is achieved, refer to Fig. 4.31, register 249. This shows that bit 5 must be 0 and bits 4, 3 and 0 must be 0, 1 and 1 respectively. The value of bit 2 does not matter, since neither of the interrupts associated with it is used. Bits 7 and 8 are not used by the Z8601 at this time.

Bits 7 and 6 of register 250 are not used by the Z8601. Bits 5 to 0 of register 250 show which interrupts are requesting service. These bits are used to operate the peripherals in a polled manner. If it is desired to operate the UART in a polled manner, the bit corresponding to this interrupt would have its mask bit set in register 251 (bit 3). The mask bit prevents the serial input interrupt from being acted on, but the interrupt request bit is still set in register 250. This bit can be polled until it becomes 1, at which time a character is available to be read in the UART. After the character is read, the bit remains set and must be reset by writing a 0 over it.

Register 251 contains the masks for the six interrupts. Bit 7 is used to disable or enable all interrupts. In this application, the bit is set at the start of the scanner routine to allow the UART and time-of-day timer to interrupt when they need service. The easiest way to set the bit is by executing an EI (Enable Interrupt) instruction.

The remainder of the bits enable or disable the interrupts on an individual basis. For this design, bits 2, 1 and 0 are set to 1 at the start of the scanner routine to allow the UART and time 1 interrupts to occur. Since there is no interest in the remaining interrupts, those mask bits are reset to 0 to assure that the processor is not able to give them service.

The interrupts in the Z8601 are vectored, which means the address of the processing routine associated with each interrupt is stored somewhere in the program. When an interrupt occurs, the address stored for that interrupt is fetched and execution begins at that address. Remember, for the Z8601, the vectors for its six interrupts are stored in the first twelve program locations in the PROM within the processor. Each interrupt has a 16-bit address associated with it. The arrangement of these addresses in memory and their relation to the interrupts is shown in Fig. 4.10.

Register 252 contains the flags that show the status of the Z8601, with bits 0 and 1 available to the user for whatever use is desired.

The Register Pointer, register 253, is used to select one of eight groups of registers (group 0 to group 7). Each register group contains sixteen registers. Fig. 4.4 shows how these registers are arranged. The programmer selects the group desired by loading the appropriate value into register 253. All the instructions that follow only need to select one of sixteen registers. Since sixteen registers can be selected with only four bits, this addressing method allows the addresses to be shortened in many instructions of the Z8601 to four bits.

Register 254 and 255 specify where the stack is to begin. Since the stack has been selected to reside in the internal RAM, the Stack Pointer need only be initialised with eight bits. In this application, the value in register 254 is irrelevant. Register 255 is loaded with $7F_{16}$, which is the location in internal RAM where the stack begins. As bytes are put on to the stack, the pointer is decremented. This internal RAM is register space. If the stack had been placed in external memory by setting bit 2 of register 248 to 0, it would be necessary to load both registers 254 and 255 with the initial stack value. When internal stack is selected, all stack accesses are made internally as if they were register transfers, which is why only eight bits are needed to specify the beginning of the stack. If an external stack was specified, all stack accesses would be to external memory.

4.9.5.2 BAUD RATE ROUTINE

The second software module is the baud rate routine. The listing for this routine (Fig. 4.32) shows some of the instructions available in the Z8601. After the data logger has been reset, the baud rate routine processes the first character received from the terminal or computer, determines what baud rate the character was sent at, and then sets the data logger baud rate generator to the same rate. This first character must be a carriage return.

The philosophy behind the baud rate routine is to set the UART initially at the maximum data rate for the Z8601, which is 19,200 baud. Typing a carriage return causes a 0 (start bit) to enter the Z8601's UART: a 1 bit follows immediately after the 0. This is the least significant bit of the ASCII value for the carriage return (OD_{16}). The routine will gauge how long this first received 0 is by counting the number of zero bits gathered at the 19,200 baud rate until the 1 bit is received (Fig. 4.33). Now that the number of zero bits at 19,200 baud that span the first zero bit is known, the value that must be loaded into the baud rate generator can be determined. There is a relation between the number of zeros received and the count value to be loaded into the baud rate generator. This relationship can be seen by examining Fig. 4.34, which shows the number of 0s received and the associated T0 count value. The number of zero bits collected were determined for each baud rate using the waveforms shown in Fig. 4.33. Note the diagonal of ones running through the T0 counter column of data. The same diagonal appears in the number of zero bits collected as data bits. This relation is the basis of the routine used to calculate the T0 count value from the number of zero bits that have been counted.

4.9.5.3 TIME-OF-DAY CLOCK ROUTINE

The third software module is the time-of-day clock routine used to maintain the time of day in hours, minutes and seconds. The hours are stored in register 12, the minutes in register 13, and the seconds in register 14. A listing of this routine (Fig. 4.35) gives a quick overview of some of the available instructions in the Z8601. The section of code labelled TOD_INIT actually resides in the initialisation module, since this code is configuring the operation of the timer. The description of the initialisation routine will be helpful if following through the TOD_INT section of code.

LOC   OBJ   CODE   STMT SOURCE STATEMENT

LOC	OBJ	CODE		STMT	SOURCE STATEMENT			
				1	bit-rate		MODULE	
				2	EXTERNAL			
				3	DELAY	PROCEDURE		
				4	GLOBAL			
P 0000				5	main	PROCEDURE		
				6		ENTRY		
P 0000	8F			7		di		!disable interrupts!
P 0001	56	FB	77	8		and	IMR,#%77	!IRQ3 polled mode!
P 0004	56	FA	F7	9		and	IRQ,#%F7	!clear IRQ3!
P 0007	E6	F7	40	10		ld	P3M,#%40	!enable serial I/O!
P 000A	E6	F4	01	11		ld	T0,#1	
P 000D	E6	F5	0D	12		ld	PREO,#(3	!bit rate = 19,200;
				13			SHL 2)+1	continuous count mode!
P 0010	B0	E0		14		clr	R0	!init. zero byte counter!
P 0012	E6	F1	03	15		ld	TMR,#3	!load and enable
				16				T0!

```
17  !collect input bytes by counting the number of null
18  characters received. Stop when non-zero byte received!
19  collect:
```

LOC	OBJ	CODE		STMT	SOURCE STATEMENT			
P 0015	76	FA	08	20		TM	IRQ,#%08	!character received?!
P 0018	6B	FB		21		jr	z,collect	!not yet!
P 001A	18	F0		22		ld	R1,SIO	!get the character!
P 001C	56	FA	F7	23		and	IRQ,#%F7	!clear interrupt request!
P 001F	1E			24		inc	R1	!compare to 0 . . . !
P 0020	1A	05		25		djnz	R1,bitloop	! . . . (in 3 bytes of code)!
P 0022	06	E0	08	26		add	R0,#8	!update count of 0 bits!
P 0025	8B	EE		27		jr	collect	!add in zero bits
				28	bitloop:			from low end of 1st
				29				non-zero byte!
P 0027	E0	E1		30		RR	R1	
P 0029	7B	03		31		jr	c,count_done	
P 002B	0E			32		inc	R0	
P 002C	8B	F9		33		jr	bitloop	

```
34
35  !R0 has number of zero bits collected!
36  !translate R0 to the appropriate T0 counter value!
37  count_done:                                    !R0 has count of
                                                    zero bits!
```

LOC	OBJ	CODE		STMT	SOURCE STATEMENT			
P 002E	1C	07		38		ld	R1,#7	
P 0030	2C	80		39		ld	R2,#%80	!R2 will have T0 counter value!
P 0032	90	E0		40		RL	R0	
				41				
P 0034	90	E0		42	loop:	RL	R0	
P 0036	7B	04		43		jr	c,done	
P 0038	E0	E2		44		RR	R2	
P 003A	1A	F8		45		djnz	r1,loop	
				46				
P 003C	29	F4		47	done:	ld	T0,R2	!load value for
				48				detected bit rate!

```
49  !Delay long enough to clear serial line of bit stream!
```

LOC	OBJ	CODE		STMT	SOURCE STATEMENT			
P 003E	D6	0000 *		50		call	DELAY	

```
51  !clear receive interrupt request!
```

LOC	OBJ	CODE		STMT	SOURCE STATEMENT			
P 0041	56	FA	F7	52		and	IRQ,#%F7	
				53				
P 0044				54	END	main		
				55	END	bit_rate		

```
0 ERRORS
ASSEMBLY COMPLETE
```

Fig. 4.32 Baud rate routine.

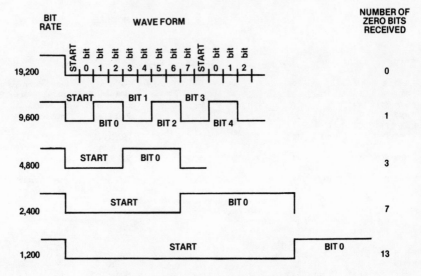

Fig. 4.33 Waveforms into Z8601 UART.

Bit Rate	Number of Bits Received Per Bit Transmitted	Number of 0 Bits Collected as Data Bits		T_0 Counter	
		dec	binary	dec	binary
19200	1	0	00000000	1	00000001
9600	2	1	00000001	2	00000010
4800	4	3	00000011	4	00000100
2400	8	7	00000111	8	00001000
1200	16	13	00001101	16	00010000
600	32	25	00011001	32	00100000
300	64	49	00110001	64	01000000
150	128	97	01100001	128	10000000

Fig. 4.34 Bit rate information.

The subroutine TOD is activated every 10 milliseconds by the T1 timer interrupt. The subroutine checks if one second has elapsed, by testing to see if 100 of the 10 millisecond interrupts have occurred. If a second has elapsed, the second counter is incremented and tested to see if a minute has elapsed. If 60 seconds have elapsed, the minute counter is incremented. The hour counter is adjusted in the same way.

4.9.5.4 SCANNER ROUTINE
The fourth software module is the scanner routine, which is a foreground process. This means that the routine is continually being executed, except when interrupts occur. The purpose of the scanner is to detect a positive-to-zero transition on one of the ten switch inputs in the Z8601. When such a transition is detected, the computer checks whether enough memory is available in which to store the switch closure time. If there is

```
LOC  OBJ  CODE  STMT SOURCE STATEMENT
                  1   TIMER1        MODULE
                  2   CONSTANT
                  3   HOUR          :=              R12
                  4   MINUTE        :=              R13
                  5   SECOND        :=              R14
                  6   HUND          :=              R15
                  7                 $SECTION PROGRAM
                  8   GLOBAL
                  9   !IRQ5 interrupt vector!
                 10                 $ABS            10
P 0000 000F'     11   IRQ_5         ARRAY           [1WORD]       :=      [TOD]
                 12
                 13                 $REL
P 000C           14   TOD_INIT                      PROCEDURE
                 15   ENTRY
P 0000 E6  F3  93  16               LD              PRE1,#%(2)10010011
                 17                                 !bit 2-7: prescaler =
                                                    36,
                 18                                 bit 1: internal clock;
                 19                                 bit 0: continuous
                                                    mode!
P 0003 E6  F2  00  20               LD              T1,#0          !(256) time-out =
                 21                                                1/100 second!
P 0006 46  F1  OC  22               OR              TMR,#%OC       !load enable T1!
P 0009 8F        23                 DI
P 000A 46  FB  20  24               OR              IMR,#%20       !enable T1 inter-
                                                                   rupt!
P 000D 9F        25                 EI
P 000E AF        26                 RET
P 000F           27   END           TOD_INIT
                 28
P 000F           29   TOD           PROCEDURE
                 30   ENTRY
P 000F 70  FD    31                 PUSH            RP
                 32   !Working register file %10 to %1F contains
                 33   the time of day clock!
P 0011 31  10    34                 SRP             #%10
P 0013 FE        35                 INC             HUND           !1 more .01 sec!
P 0014 A6  EF  64  36               CP              HUND,#100      !full second
                                                                   yet?!
P 0017 EB  13    37                 JR              NE,TOD_EXIT    !jump if no!
P 0019 BO  EF    38                 CLR             HUND
P 001B EE        39                 INC             SECOND         !1 more
                                                                   second!
P 001C A6  EE  3C  40               CP              SECOND,#60     !full minute
                                                                   yet?!
P 001F EB  OB    41                 JR              NE,TOD_EXIT    !jump if no!
P 0021 BO  EE    42                 CLR             SECOND
P 0023 DE        43                 INC             MINUTE         !1 more
                                                                   minute!
P 0024 A6  ED  3C  44               CP              MINUTE,#60     !full hour yet?!
P 0027 EB  03    45                 JR              NE,TOD_EXIT    !jump if no! |
P 0029 BO  ED    46                 CLR             MINUTE
P 002B CE        47                 INC             HOUR
                 48   TOD_EXIT:
P 002C 50  FD    49                 POP             RP             !restore entry
                                                                   RP!
P 002E BF        50                 IRET
P 002F           51   END           TOD
                 52   END           TIMER1
     0 ERRORS
ASSEMBLY COMPLETE
```

Fig. 4.35 Real-time clock routine.

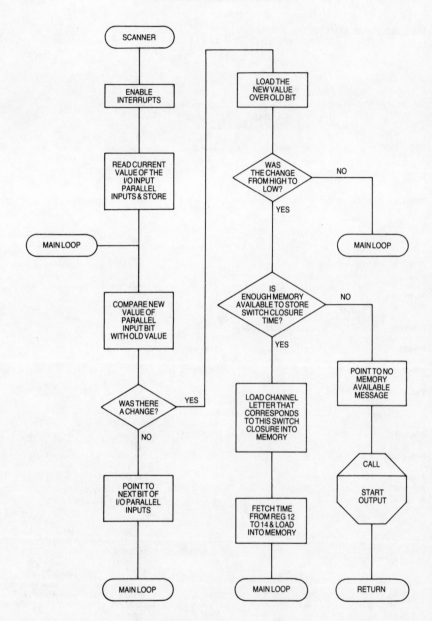

Fig. 4.36 Scanner routine flowchart.

not enough memory, a message is printed on the terminal saying, 'NO MEMORY'. If there is enough memory, the letter identifying the channel that the switch closure occurred on is stored into external RAM memory, along with the time of day. Fig. 4.36 shows a general flowchart for this routine.

4.9.5.5 RECEIVE CHARACTER ROUTINE

The fifth software module is the receive character routine; the flowchart is given in Fig. 4.37. This routine is activated via a UART from the terminal or computer. The first action taken in the routine is to enable interrupts so that the T1 time-of-day interrupt can occur, keeping the time of day

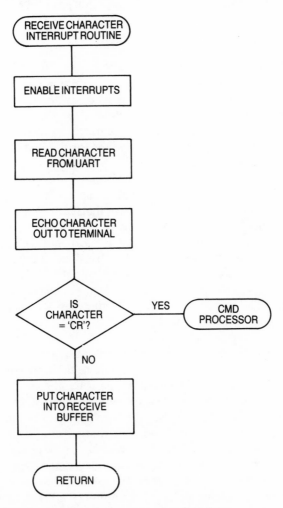

Fig. 4.37 Receive character routine flowchart.

accurate. Next, the routine reads the character from the UART and stores it into a receive character buffer. The routine then tests whether this received character is a carriage return. If it is not a carriage return, the routine returns to the code that was interrupted. If the received character is a carriage return, it indicates that a whole command has been entered and the command processing routine (Fig. 4.38) determines what command has been entered and then takes the requested action. All the commands have some sort of printed response, so a start output routine is executed after a command is finished, which starts the output by loading the first character of the response into the UART. When this first character is shifted out of the UART, an interrupt occurs and the transmit character routine is activated and prints the remainder of the response.

4.9.5.6 TRANSMIT CHARACTER ROUTINE

The sixth and last software module is the transmit character routine (Fig. 4.39) and is used to output a series of characters to the UART under interrupt control. This routine is activated by the interrupt that occurs when the UART has transmitted a character. The routine will first test whether it has encountered the delimiter for the end-of-message (FF_{16}). If it has encountered the delimiter, it will return directly to the routine that was interrupted without loading another character.

Because of this, further interrupts cannot occur until the command processor initiates the sending of another message via start character output. If the delimiter has not been encountered, the transmit character routine tests whether the DUMP flag is set. If the DUMP flag is not set, the characters being output are all ASCII values. If the DUMP flag is set, the data in the external RAM is being output, which consists of binary numbers intermixed with the ASCII values identifying the channels. Therefore, the transmit character routine has to recognise the binary numbers and translate them to ASCII. The transmit next character routine uses a pointer as the address from which to fetch the next character to be output. This point is initially loaded by the command processor with a value that is appropriate to the response necessary. The point is then incremented to the next character after the UART is loaded.

After the data logger is reset, the initialisation routine is executed and the Z8601 is configured into the appropriate operating mode. The program then idles in the baud rate routine until a carriage return is received. The baud rate of the terminal (or computer) that sent the carriage return is calculated by the data logger, the data logger baud rate then is set to the same value, the READY is typed on to the terminal (or sent back to the computer). The time-of-day timer is now running, and T1 interrupts are occurring every 10 milliseconds to keep the clock

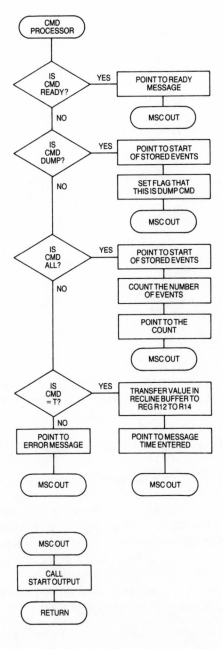

Fig. 4.38 Command processor flowchart.

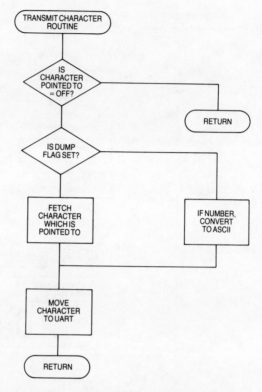

Fig. 4.39 Transmit character routine flowchart.

running on time. An operator then must load the initial time of day, using the T command.

The program now begins looping through the scanner routine, watching each switch input for a positive-to-zero transition. If a switch closure occurs on one of the channels, the letter identifying that channel is loaded into memory with the time of day. If a command is typed on the terminal as each individual character is received, it causes an interrupt to the scanner routine; the character is stored in the receive buffer by the receive character routine. When a carriage return is typed, the command processor is executed, the command is acted upon, printing started, and a return made to the scanning program that was interrupted.

4.10 FUTURE DEVICES

Future variants of the Z8 will include devices which work at higher clock speeds, customised additions to the basic architecture, with the likely appearance of on-chip gate arrays for specialised interfaces, and the development of an enhanced Z8 known as the Super 8. This device, which will appear in the early part of 1984, will offer considerable improvements over the memory and I/O features in existing Z8s.

The main peripheral features of this device will include a UART and a USART, four counter/timers, a DMA channel and five I/O ports. Hardware Multiply/Divide is supported as well as all the possible bit test instructions, PUSH and POP instructions for upward or downward growing user stacks and instructions for writing 'Threaded Code' (ENTER, NEXT AND EXIT) such as found in languages like 'FORTH'.

The register file has been increased from 144 registers in the Z8 to 352 registers. Of these, 192 are available as general registers while the remainder are only accessible via DA, ID or IX modes. This is so that stacks and other data structures can be protected from invalid register accesses. For storage of internal program memory, different versions of the device will be provided with on-chip ROM of 4 K, 8 K or 16 K bytes.

Versions of the Super 8 will have imbedded software in the form of Basic or Forth interpreters similar to that seen today in the Z8671. In the late 1980s, enhancements of this device are likely to appear which will be optimised to process 16- and 32-bit data types.

Summary

This chapter is a comprehensive introduction to many of the sophisticated features of the Z8 family. It shows that not only does the Z8601 reduce device count by including all the components on one chip, but it also gives great flexibility in its use. It is possible to trade I/O for memory, a baud rate generator for a timer or trade a UART for two or more external pins, etc.

The design example presented in the case study was chosen to illustrate several important features of the Z8; however, it did not fully exercise the capacity of the device. There are certainly many problems to which the designer can fully apply the power of the Z8 family devices.

REFERENCES AND BIBLIOGRAPHY

4.1.   Zilog Data Book 1982/83.
4.2.   Zilog Z8 Technical Manual.
4.3.   Zilog UPC Technical Manual.

CHAPTER 5

The COPS 400 Microcontrollers from National Semiconductor

By Reinhold M. Hohol

5.1 HISTORY AND OVERVIEW

COPS is an acronym which stands for Control-Orientated-Processor-System. In essence this acronym describes COPS devices quite well, as the entire capability of these processors is not one of clever computing in the common sense: COPS are plainly control orientated. The COPS family provides flexible yet cost effective system solutions in a variety of applications requiring timing, counting, monitoring and other control functions. COPS devices are used to replace discrete logic functions in high volume consumer products such as car radio and cassette players, electronic games (e.g., TIC TAC TOE and MASTER MIND) on the one hand, and much more sophisticated automotive and white good products such as washing machines and car injection systems on the other. But even in lower volume industrial products, a COPS based system allows one to add features, miniaturise and reduce the overall electronic component count.

The history of COPS can best be described as evolutionary rather than revolutionary in nature. The main roots of this microcontroller family date back to the years 1970 to 1975, to the boom in pocket calculators. And indeed, certain elements of the calculator-type architecture are still to be found in every COPS processor. The first and the most obvious remainder is the 4-bit wide datapath, which came about as a result of the BCD arithmetic notation used in common handheld calculators. Other related features include LED (Light-Emitting-Diode) drive capability on some output lines and provisions in the I/O (Input/Output) structure to support time multiplexed LED displays directly. Even today, some of these functionalities are found in COPS and related devices as, for example, in the TMS1000 family from Texas Instruments.

Based on a 'low level' of functionality, such as counting, addition, subtraction, and display, the first 4-bit COPS microcontroller devices were built, using PMOS (P-channel-Metal-Oxide-Semiconductor) technology. During this time quite a number of different COPS devices emerged, i.e. the MM57140, a single-chip system with direct LED display and keyboard interface, and the more versatile and expandable MM5782, a multichip solution. However, all these devices lacked one or several attributes necessary for easy manufacturing and testing. From a user point of view, prohibitive factors included too great a spread in the product family, i.e. an existence of too many and too different parts. Inconsistencies between COPS family members in regard to compatibility, transparency – and, worst of all, the absence of one instruction set common to all family devices.

Nevertheless, the most severe inconsistency later turned out to be instrumental in creating one of the largest advantages in terms of the definition and orientation of the next generation of the COPS microcontroller family. Due to the non-existence of a generally available software debugging and development system for the actual engineer wishing to use COPS, a large in-house engineering group at National Semiconductor developed most of the programs for various customers. In this way, knowledge and expertise in regard to those early devices was concentrated in this group, which naturally influenced the further evolution and development of the COPS family. One result was that every COPS microcontroller now makes use of the same ROM efficient instruction set, which often results in significantly less program space requirement than with other contemporary 4-bit and even 8-bit single-chip microcomputers.

Also realised through the activity and backed by the main purpose of this group was the need for a dedicated development system for the creation, as well as the verification of software and hardware. This system was designed, and became known as the COPS PDS (Product-Development-System): an easy to learn and use system, featuring a PDP-8 like line orientated editor, one assembler for all the different microcontrollers, and a disk operating system supporting one floppy disk for bulk storage. Above all, the PDS was not marketed as yet another development system. Rather, it is cheap when compared to its functionality, and supports the entire COPS family. Without hardware upgrades, users can easily start a development and have a clear picture of the costs involved.

Thus, a streamlined family approach, plus a dedicated development system set the pace for the current COPS microcontroller family. Further, a change in semiconductor technology away from PMOS to more advanced NMOS (N-channel) and CMOS (Complementary P- and N-channel) processes allowed for smaller, more economical chips. To the end user this meant cheaper, faster devices with lower power consumption thus allowing battery operation.

5.2   THE COPS MICROCONTROLLER FAMILY

5.2.1   General Concepts

The historical development of COPS, with its calculator-type predecessors, already indicates the necessity of distinguishing between a COPS microcontroller and the more 'classic' microprocessors. COPS devices are 'microcontrollers'; they are not typical microprocessors nor a variation of 'classic' microprocessors. The COPS architecture is certainly not one normally associated with most popular microcomputers. A microcomputer has been defined in Chapter 1 as a processing unit comprising all system elements, such as ALU, program store, data storage and I/O on a single-chip. In comparison a microprocesor lacks program, data storage and I/O, and facilitates only the addressing or access to these off-chip elements. Therefore, a COPS microcontroller is a microcomputer (Fig. 5.1). However, such terminology is still too general in regard to the potential use and functionality of the device, and the term 'microcontroller' is perhaps more appropriate to COPS.

The COP400 family is now comprised of a large number of devices which enable the engineer/user to select the devices best suited to a specific application. The software is upwardly compatible; programs written on one device may be transferred to the next larger device (larger in terms of memory capacity) with little or no change. The package pin configurations have also been selected so that movement up or down (again using memory size as the variable parameter) within the family can easily be accomplished. All COPS microcontrollers – from the COP411L,

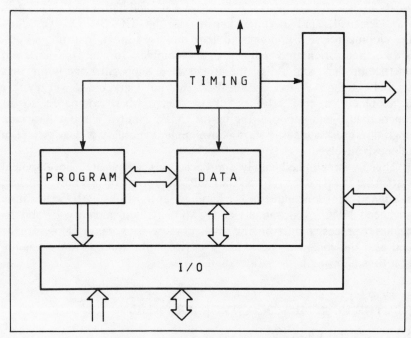

Fig. 5.1 A COPS microcontroller.

the smallest device, to the COP2440, the most sophisticated device, to the COP484, the device with the largest memory – have the same basic architectural structure. In addition to the large number and wide range of devices, all the COPS microcontrollers have a number of I/O options – mask programmable and specified at the same time as the program – which allows the user to tailor, within limits, the I/O characteristics of the microcontroller to the system. Thus, the user can optimise the microcontroller to the application, thereby achieving maximum capability and minimum cost.

The COP400 series and the COP300 series, which is the nomenclature for the extended temperature range versions, are general purpose single-chip devices. These devices are complete microcomputers, containing all system timing, internal logic, ROM (Read Only Memory), RAM (Random Access Memory) and I/O necessary to implement dedicated control function to a wide variety of applications.

The COPS family is comprised of:

ROM-less devices.	Dual CPU devices.
Single-chip devices.	Dedicated peripherals.

5.2.2 COPS ROM-less Devices

Several COPS microcontrollers require external program memory. Basically, the ROM on these devices has been removed from their single-chip counterparts. These ROM-less devices are primarily intended for use in program development, debug, device emulation, prototyping and low volume production. Table 5.1 provides a list of COP400 ROM-less devices currently available or in design. As can be seen, quite a number of devices are presently available. The devices have been selected so that each COPS microcontroller, in NMOS or CMOS technology, has at least one complementary ROM-less device that can be used for accurate emulation.

5.2.3 COPS Single-Chip Devices

Table 5.2 provides a list of COPS single-chip microcontrollers currently available or in design. The list is extensive and shows one of the largest selections in any given family available on the market. Many of the variations are simply different packagings of the same die or device: e.g. the COP441 is actually a COP440 in a 28-lead pack, the COP442 is the COP440 in a 24-lead pack, whereby the COP440 is a 40-lead device. Another important characteristic of this family is the common ground in regard to the pinout on all single-chip devices: all 28-pin devices have the same pinout, all 24-pin devices have the same pinout, the COP411L and

Table 5.1 National semiconductor COPS microcontroller family guide – ROM-less devices.

COP	401L	402	402M	404C	404L	404	2404	408	409
ext. ROM x 8	– 512	– 1024			– 2048			– 4096	– 32768
RAM x 4	32	64		128		160		256	512
Inputs	0	4		4		4		8	
Bidirectional TRISTATE I/O	8	8		8		16		8	
Standart I/O	4	4		4		8		4	
Outputs	4	4		4		4		4	
Serial I/O & Event counter	yes	yes		yes		yes		yes	
Internal time base counter	no	yes		yes		yes		yes	
Time Base counter programmable	no	no		yes	no	yes		yes	
Interrupt	no	yes	no	yes		yes 4 sources		yes	
Stack Levels	2	3		3		4	4 per CPU	4	8
MICROBUS Opt	no	no	yes	yes	no	yes		yes	
Instr. Cycle	15-40	4-10		4-DC	15-40	4-10		4-25	
Package size	40	40		40/48	40	48		40	

COP411C have the same pinout, the COP422 and COP422L have the same pinout, and so on.

Architectural details of both the ROM-less and single-chip devices are described later in the discussions on architecture and instruction set.

5.2.4 COPS DUAL CPU Devices

Probably one of the most unusual architectural variations of any microcomputer family is the DUAL CPU concept found in the COPS family. Increasing the internal processing power by paralleling central processing units was, until recently, found only in the architecture of large mainframe or supermicroprocessor units, as DEC's VAX11/780, Intel's iAPX432 and National Semiconductor's NS32132.

The COP244x devices contain almost every system element or register twice, e.g. one program counter, accumulator, etc. is available to each of the two CPUs (X and Y); RAM, ROM and I/O, however, are shared and accessible by both CPUs. The only system element common to both CPUs is the ALU. Interference between the two processing units is resolved by alternately executing their instructions, thereby avoiding access conflicts. This allows parallel execution of the same piece of code by CPU X and CPU Y and, if applicable, branching off to different program locations where the individual execution continues. Such code sharing greatly reduces the amount of ROM space needed to perform

Table 5.2 National semiconductor COPS microcontroller family guide – single-chip devices.

COP	41O	41OC	411L	411C	.42O	42OL	42OC	421	421L	421C	422	42L	.44L	44C	44L	445C	44O	441	442	2440	2441	2442	.464	464	465	.484	485
ROM × 8	512				1024								2048				2048						3072			4096	
RAM × 4	32				64								128				160						192			256	
Inputs		0				4				0		4		0		4		0		4		0		4		0	
Bidirectional TRISTATE I/O	4		8			8			8				8		16	8	16	8	8	8	8			8		8	
Standard I/O	4		3			4			4				4		8	4	8	4	4	4	4			4		4	
Outputs	4		2			4			4		2	2	4		4	4		4						4		4	
Serial I/O & Event counter			yes			yes			yes				yes		yes	yes		yes	yes					yes		yes	
Internal time base counter			no			yes			yes				yes		yes	yes		yes	yes					yes		yes	
Time Base counter programmable			no			no		yes		yes		no	no	yes	no	yes	yes		yes	yes				no		no	
Interrupt			no			yes			yes				yes	yes	no	yes	yes		yes	yes	yes			yes		no	
Stack Levels			2			3			3				3	3		4	4		4 per CPU					4		4	
MICROBUS Opt			no	yes		no	yes		no				no	yes		no	yes		no	yes				no	yes		no
Instr. Cycle	15-40 4-DC		15-40 4-DC			15-40 4-DC	4-10 4-DC		4-10 4-DC		15-40	15-40	15-40 4-DC	15-40 4-DC	15-40 4-DC		4-10	4-10						4-25		2-25	
Package size	24	20			28			24		20			28	24		40	28	24		40	28	24		28		28	24

functions. Parameter passing between the two processors preferably takes place in RAM. The power of the dual processors becomes apparent when two or more tasks must be performed and where one task is continuous and cannot be disturbed or interrupted.

Consider the following example application: the microcontroller must monitor two switches and two pulse train inputs. It must also output a continuous square wave which is a function of all the inputs (Fig. 5.2). The tasks are partitioned such that processor Y will read a value in RAM and count it down to toggle an output. This is a constant process which gives a continuous output stream. Processor X counts pulses on one input, measures the period of another, and reads the switches. Processor X will be interrupted to do a complex calculation based on the input values.

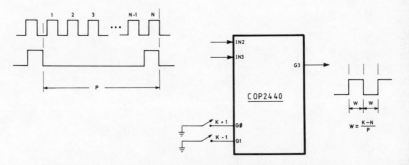

Fig. 5.2 Application example for the COP2440.

This execution is exceedingly difficult to do using a single processor, since the one output must be constantly updated. Therefore, the programmer of a single processor trying to do this task would have to interleave the code to update the output with all of the other codes (i.e. multiply, divide, add, counting, etc.).

Using a DUAL CPU device like the COP2440, the program would be split between the two internal processors. Processor Y reads data register W and counts it down in a fixed loop. Processor X counts the pulses on IN2 in the T counter and measures the period of the pulse on IN3 by a software loop that counts the instruction cycles in memory register C. When a negative edge arrives on IN3, the calculation of the pulse width is performed and the two keys are read. The program then branches back to the main loop to repeat again.

5.2.5 MICROWIRE – COPS Peripheral Devices

The range of COPS microcontrollers is supported by a number of compatible, standard peripheral devices (Table 5.3). These devices add distributed processing and other capabilities to a COPS system. For the communication between CPU and peripheral, a serial link, the so-called MICROWIRE, is used and supported by all members of the COP400 family. This serial data exchange makes efficient use of the available I/O lines, as only three pins are necessary on each device to hook onto the serial bus. The lines required are: Serial-Data-IN (SI), Serial-Data-Out (SO) and the synchronising clock (SK). MICROWIRE differs from the serial Inter IC bus from Philips-Valvo (with which it is compatible), in that it does not treat the exchange of data as a background process in the CPU. The data exchange on a MICROWIRE bus is fully under software control and must be created by the programmer.

Figure 5.3 shows a COPS system making use of several MICROWIRE peripherals, i.e. analog input (COP432), timer and event counter (COP452), a vacuum fluorescent display driven by a COP470 and data storage and system control using the COP498. Among the peripheral functionalities provided are several analog to digital converters, data memory extensions, multi-function timer and counter elements display drivers for LED, VF (vacuum fluorescent) and LCD (liquid crystal) type display units, and specialists such as digital phase-locked loop synthesisers and non-volatile EEPROM memories.

Two major benefits are created by this peripheral approach. One enables the function to be placed in close proximity to, say, the source of the analog signal, thus reducing a number of problems associated with the transmission of analog signals over large distances. This is also valid for

Table 5.3 National semiconductor COPS – microwire peripheral devices.

Periperal	Function	Features	Package Size
COP431	A/D Converter	1/0 differential/single inputs	8 Pin
COP432		2/1 differential/single inputs	8 Pin
COP434		2/4 differential/single inputs	14 Pin
COP438		4/8 differential/single inputs	20 Pin
COP452	Frequency Counter and Generator	2 independent Counter/Timers	14 Pin
COP470	VF Driver	8 Segments, 4 Digits, Brightness control	20 Pin
COP472	LCD Driver	12 Segments, 3 Backplanes	20 Pin
COP498	CMOS RAM and Timer	64 x 4 Bit RAM, 1 Timer	8 Pin
COP499	CMOS RAM	64 x 4 Bit	8 Pin
COP494	EEPROM	16 x 16 Bit, Single supply voltage nonvolatile Memory	8 Pin
DS8906	PLL, Digital Phase Locked Loop	PLL with 6 open collector outputs	20 Pin
DS8907		with 7 open collector outputs	20 Pin
DS8908		with 8 open collector outputs	20 Pin
MM5/xxx	VF, LCD, LED Drivers	This family of display drivers are not actual COP peripherals, but are compatible to the MICROWIRE interface.	40 Pin

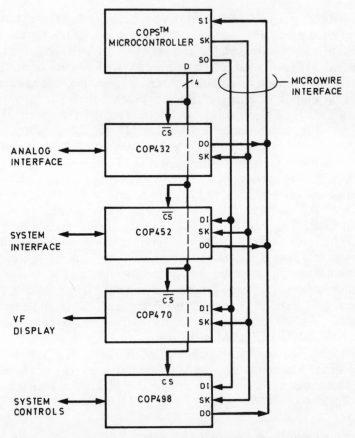

Fig. 5.3 A COPS system with MICROWIRE peripherals.

cases when an LCD display driver is mounted on the reverse side of an LCD glass substrate. Here the only wiring is the three MICROWIRE signals. This eases mounting and interconnection of the several system modules. The second major benefit is the possibility of combining the most efficient and best suited semiconductor technologies to achieve the best cost/performance ratio. For example, for analog functions, low-power data memory and LCD drivers, the best semiconductor technology is CMOS; for VF display drivers it is PMOS or one of the newer high voltage PMOS/CMOS mixtures; for processing speed and small chip size it is NMOS. It becomes apparent that implementing all this on one chip would create technological problems and move the cost of such a device into prohibitive regions. Thus, in order to satisfy the different needs of most applications in the consumer and automotive fields, the MICRO-WIRE peripheral concept provides an alternative to many design problems.

5.3   ARCHITECTURE OF COPS MICROCONTROLLERS

The following section deals with the internal architecture of COPS microcontrollers. Figure 5.4 is the generic COPS microcontroller block diagram, showing the various registers, latches, datapaths and system control elements of the device. The diagram is basic to most COPS devices and the deletion or addition of certain elements then determines the different microcontrollers of the family.

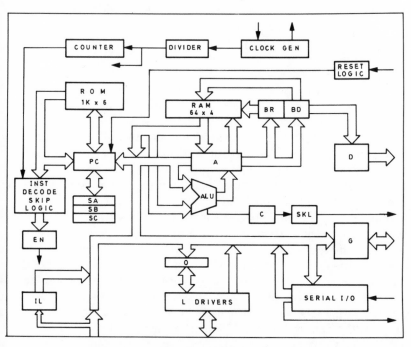

Fig. 5.4 COPS microcontroller block diagram.

5.3.1   COPS Memory Structure

Program Memory – ROM. The program memory in a COPS microcontroller is a Read-Only-Memory (ROM). This ROM is organised as a number of 8-bit words. COPS microcontrollers with ROM capacities of 512, 1024, 2048, 3072, and 4096 8-bit words are found in the family. The ROM words are addressed sequentially by a linear, binary program counter. In ROM-less devices this program counter is brought outside the device to address external memory. The program counter starts at zero and if there are no jumps or subroutines or table look-ups, it will increment to the maximum value possible with a binary counter of that length (i.e. 9, 10 or 12 bits long), then roll over to zero and begin again. For the purpose of properly initialising the device, the instruction at the first ROM location must be a clear accumulator command.

Internally, the COPS microcontroller's ROM imposes a transparent page, block, chapter structure, where a page consists of sixty-four consecutive ROM words. The lower six bits of the program counter are zeros at the beginning of a page and are ones at the end of any page. A block in ROM is composed of four consecutive pages (256 ROM words). Thus, the first address of a block becomes the first address of a page, and the last address of a block is also the last address of a page.

The chapter division is only relevant to those COPS devices with more than 2048 ROM words, or ROM-less devices capable of addressing a similar range. Fig. 5.5 illustrates the page/block/chapter divisions and the addresses related to them.

The semi-transparency of this internal structure has some effect on program transfer and control instructions. Some jumps, subroutine calls, and also table look-ups are affected by this structure. The block divisions are significant in the table look-up and indirect jump operations. For subroutine calls and direct jumps, only the page and chapter organisations are relevant. The page/block/chapter structure has no effect on the normal operation of the program counter.

Complete, operational programs may be written without any consideration of this internal structure. Such programs, however, will use more code, and therefore require a larger ROM capacity than a program written bearing this ROM organisation in mind.

Data Memory – RAM. The data memory in COPS microcontrollers is organised as a number of registers whose elements are selected using an X-Y addressing scheme. Each register or row is sixteen digits long. Each digit (BCD) consists of four bits. The smallest COPS devices, the COP410 and COP411 versions, are exceptions to this rule, as they contain only eight digits. However, their internal RAM addressing is transparent to the larger devices without program modification. Depending on the type of microcontroller, the data memory of a COPS can utilise the following organisations:

128 bits (4 registers × 8 digits)
256 bits (4 registers × 16 digits)
512 bits (8 registers × 16 digits)
640 bits (10 registers × 16 digits)
768 bits (12 registers × 16 digits)
1024 bits (16 registers × 16 digits)

In order to address any of the individual RAM digits, COPS microcontrollers contain a dedicated RAM address register: the B

Hex	Address	Page	Block	Chapter
000	– 03F	0		
040	– 07F	1	0	
080	– 0BF	2		
0C0	– 0FF	3		
100	– 13F	4		
140	– 17F	5	1	
180	– 1BF	6		
1C0	– 1FF	7		
200	– 23F	8		
.				
.			2	0
.				
2C0	– 2FF	11		
.				
.				
.				

Fig. 5.5 Page/block/chapter division.

register. This register can be loaded directly or through the accumulator and is divided into two distinct parts: BR – the register address (equal to the Y co-ordinate) and BD – the digit address (the X co-ordinate). BD is four bits wide in all devices whereas BR is two three or four bits wide, depending on the particular device (Fig. 5.6). The existence of this dedicated register for data memory addressing causes most COPS instructions not to hold any RAM address field. This saves overhead in code (which would normally add to the instruction) and in turn increases the ROM code efficiency of the instructions set.

The data memory digit addressed by the B register is normally accessed through the A register. The value stored in the RAM digit may be either loaded from the Q register, or the L port, to the G port, or

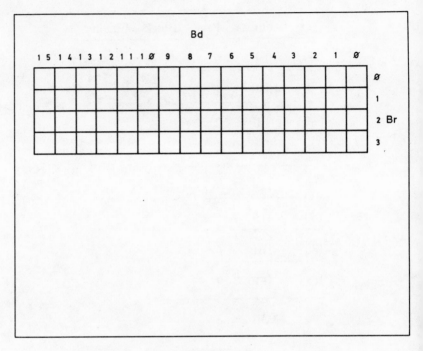

Fig. 5.6 RAM addressing with the B register.

directly by the program. On those devices which have H and R ports, the specified RAM digit may be loaded to those ports or loaded from the R port. Two instructions, LDD and XAD, specify a RAM location within the instructions. These operations allow a RAM digit to be loaded to, or exchanged with, the accumulator, without altering the B register. This is useful when a RAM value has to be updated on occurrence of, say, an interrupt, while the current B register value should not be affected.

In addition, the BD portion serves as source register for the D output register. On software command, the contents of the BD can be transferred to the D port. This direct path from BD to D can be quite useful when keyboard scan routines are implemented. In this case BD acts as an output value, selecting a row of keys, while at the same time it can be used as a RAM address to store the input value from the keyrow.

Subroutine Stack – COPS microcontrollers have a separate subroutine stack composed of two, three or four save registers. These registers are independent of the data memory and therefore do not, in the case of subroutine nesting, interfere with, or reduce the size of, the data memory. The user cannot access the subroutine stack and read or write to the stack and make alterations. There are programming restrictions imposed by this. That is, only a limited number of stack operations are

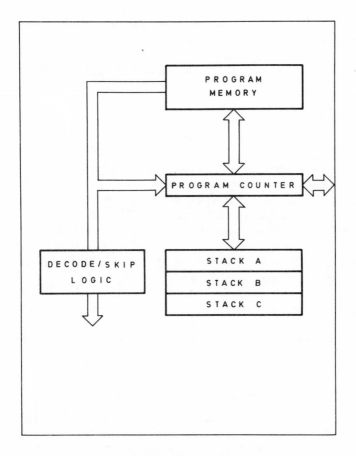

Fig. 5.7 COPS stack arrangement.

possible, if the stack is used up, or subroutines nested too deep, the program cannot return properly to the highest level.

On all COPS microcontrollers with two or three stack levels the stack is merely a last-in-first-out type of buffer for the current program counter (Fig. 5.7). A physical transfer of stack contents on all operations affecting the stack takes place.

On devices with four or more levels of subroutine stack, there is no comparable data movement. Instead, these devices have a stack pointer which increments or decrements on operations affecting the stack. The program counter of these devices is loaded to or from the stack location addressed by the stack pointer.

The programmer does not have access to the stack in most COPS microcontrollers. There are, however, some devices which do give the programmer stack access. These are the COP44x and all DUAL CPU devices. On these the programmer may read or write the entire stack or any portion thereof. The user may also read or write the stack pointer in these devices. This naturally gives increased flexibility. However, care must be exercised when writing programs that exploit this.

5.3.2 The ALU

The ALU is a four-bit wide unit (Fig. 5.8). It performs all the arithmetic and logic functions in a COPS device. The destination of all such operations is the four-bit accumulator A. One input to the ALU is always the accumulator. The other input is either an immediate operand specified by the instruction itself or, most commonly, the RAM digit currently addressed by the B register. The ALU also outputs a carry flag on arithmetic overflow. Depending on the instruction being executed, this carry bit may be loaded into the one-bit C register. The C register also acts as input to the ALU. In this way the value of the C register may also be included in additions, or it can be tested to perform a branch in the program.

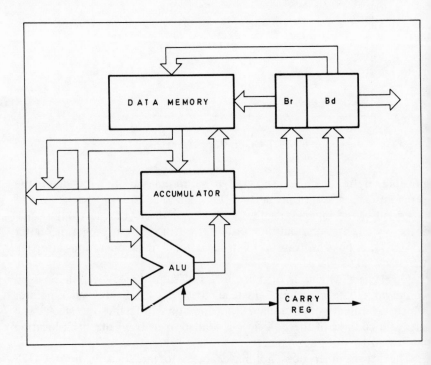

Fig. 5.8 The ALU and associated units.

5.3.3 Input And Output

5.3.3.1 PARALLEL I/O

There is one input only port: the IN port available on some COPS microcontrollers (Fig. 5.9). This port is available only on devices with twenty-eight or more pins. On software command, the four IN lines are read into the accumulator as a group of four bits. In addition, the direct inputs, IN0 and IN3, have latches associated with them. These latches capture a high to low transition on either line. The status of these latches is read into the accumulator on software command. Thus, the program can read the present status of the IN lines directly, or it can read the status of the latches associated with IN0 and IN3. The latter is quite useful in checking asynchronous external events which run in parallel with the normal processing cycle of the program.

IN1 is also the interrupt input on all devices. The decision on whether or not to use interrupts or to enable or disable interrupts is merely a software decision, and depends largely on the application and its requirements. As such, in a given program flow, interrupts may always be enabled, never enabled, or sometimes enabled.

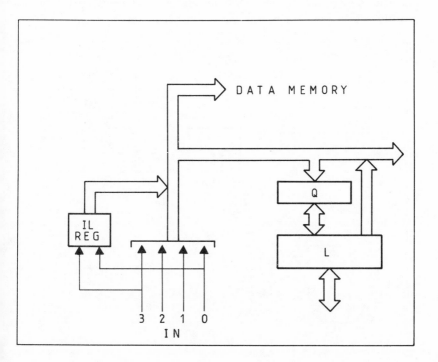

Fig. 5.9 The In port.

The CMOS devices and those with large ROM and more I/O, use the lines IN0 to IN3 to resolve additional functional attributes, such as counter input and input to a zero crossing detector. On the COP 420C and COP444C, IN2 may be masked programmed to be an input to the time base counter. This is a hardware selection on these devices and is not software alterable. The COP440/COP441 and COP2440/COP2441 may also use IN2 as an input to the timebase counter. On these devices, however, the choice is controlled in software by the programmer.

Bi-directional TRI-STATE I/O – All COPS microcontrollers have at least one 8-bit bi-directional I/O port. In an output operation, the L lines output the contents of the 8-bit Q register (Fig. 5.10). The input path is from the pins to the RAM and accumulator. Note, the L lines are drivers only; they do not retain any data. For this port, output data is stored in the Q register. The L drivers can be TRI-STATED for ease of interfacing to a system bus. TRI-STATE is a term used to describe the high impedance state on bi-directional input and output lines. This avoids data contention in a bus-orientated system, i.e. two output drivers working against each other.

The COP440 and COP2440 have an additional 8-bit bi-directional I/O port: the R port. The R port contains latches and drivers. The input path is from the pins to the accumulator and to RAM. Data at the R pins

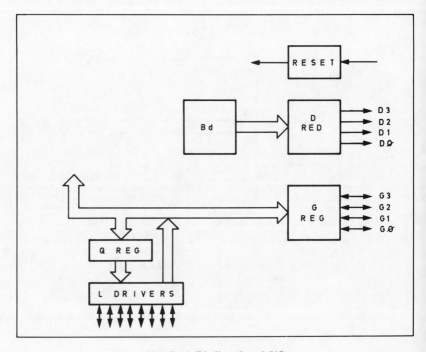

Fig. 5.10 Bi-directional I/O.

cannot be latched into the R register by any external signal. The internal program must do this gathering, by reading the input on the fly, thereby bringing the current input values on to the internal data path. Like the L port, the R port can also be TRI-STATED for simple bus interface.

Bi-directional I/O – The G port is a 4-bit bi-directional I/O port. The G outputs are latches with associated drivers at their output lines. Thus data can be written to the G port and appear immediately at the pin. The input path for G is from the pins directly to the accumulator. In addition to reading the port, the G lines can be tested by the programmer, individually or as a total of four bits. The input signals at the G inputs are not held, as the latches present on this port are for outputs only. Another critical point arising when using the G port is that, because of the hardware implementation of the drivers and latches of this port, a logical '1' has to be written to the individual pin on G in order to configure it as an input.

The COP440 and COP2440 feature an additional bidirectional I/O: the H port. This H port is essentially a duplicate of the G port, except that H cannot be checked directly using test instructions. There is no restriction on H or G as to which lines may be inputs or outputs. All the G lines may be inputs; all the G lines may be outputs; any G line or group of G lines may be outputs with the remaining lines being inputs. The same is true of the H lines.

Outputs – The D port is an output only port. The outputs are latched. On software command, the content of BD – the lower four bits of the RAM address register B – are copied to D. These outputs will remain in that state until the next write to D. The D port can be loaded only via the BD register.

5.3.3.2 THE SIO REGISTER

This register is a dual-purpose 4-bit register. Depending on the state of the EN register – whose contents are alterable by the program – this register can be configured as a 4-bit binary down counter or as a 4-bit serial shift register. When SIO is selected as a down counter, SI is the counter input – the counter decrements on the high to low transition of the signal at the SI input – provided the input remains low for at least two instruction cycles. In this case, SK and SO are simple logic level outputs which are controlled directly by the program (Fig. 5.11).

When SIO is a shift register, SI is the input to the 4-bit shift register, and SO is the shift register output. Essentially this turns the SIO register of any COPS microcontroller into its serial port. SK is a synchronising serial clock running at the instruction cycle rate. Important for the system designer is that when SIO is enabled as a shift register and SO enabled as a shift register output, whatever is at SI will appear at SO four instruction

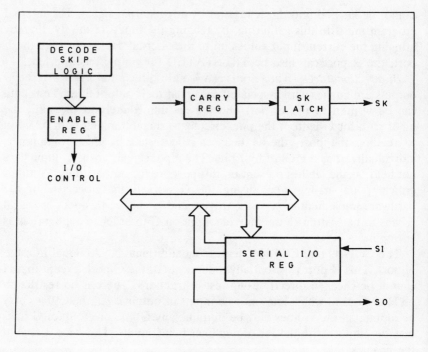

Fig. 5.11 The SIO register.

cycles later. When enabled as a shift register, SIO is always shifting at the instruction cycle rate regardless of the status of SO or SK.

5.3.3.3   THE EN REGISTER

The enable (EN) register is an internal 4- or 8-bit register loaded under program control. The state of the individual bits of this register selects or deselects features configuring I/O in the microcontroller.

EN0-EN3

These bits of the EN register are present on all COPS microcontrollers. Their function is to configure the SIO portion of the devices.

   EN0, the least significant bit of the enable register, controls the status of the SIO register. A logic '1' configures the SIO register to a 4-bit asynchronous binary down counter decrementing its value by one on each low-going pulse at the SI input. This pulse must be low for at least two instruction cycles. With EN0 reset to a logic '0', the SIO register turns into a 4-bit serial shift register which shifts left, from SI toward SO, one bit during each instruction cycle. Data is shifted into the least significant bit of SIO from the SI input. With EN0 reset, SK becomes a logic-controlled clock, the period of which is the instruction cycle time.

EN1 controls the interrupt. With EN1 set, the interrupt is enabled. If a signal which meets the timing requirements appears at the interrupt input, IN1, and EN1 is set, then the interrupt will be recognised and processed. If the EN1 bit is reset, the interrupt will be ignored. Obviously, the status of EN1 is significant only in those COPS microcontrollers which have interrupt capability. In addition, it is good practice to keep this bit reset even on devices with no pin available for interrupt input.

EN2 controls the L drivers. With EN2 set, the L drivers output the data contained in the Q register to the L I/O port. With EN2 reset, the L drivers are disabled, thereby placing the L I/O port into a high impedance condition.

EN3, in conjunction with EN0, controls the SO and SK outputs and their function when the SIO register is used. Setting this bit to '1', if the shift register is enabled, configures SO and SK for serial output and synchronisation. With the binary counter enabled this bit controls the logic state of SO and SK.

EN4-EN7

These 'extra' four bits of the enable register are present only in the following devices: COP440, COP441, COP442, COP2440, COP2441, and COP2442.

EN4, EN5 are two bits which select the interrupt source:

EN4	EN5	Interrupt Source
0	0	IN1 – low going pulse.
0	1	CKO input (if mask option selected).
1	0	Zero crossing on IN1 (or level transition).
1	1	T Counter overflows.

EN6: With EN6 set, the input pin IN2 becomes the input source of the internal 8-bit T counter common to those devices. With EN6 reset, the input to the T counter is the output of a divide-by-4 prescaler whose input is the instruction cycle frequency. This provides a 10-bit timebase counter. On the COP442 and COP2442 – two devices where IN2 is not available – the EN6 bit functions as an enable or disable bit to the T counter; setting EN6 disables further counting. With EN6 reset, the above 10-bit timebase counter is produced.

EN7 is similar in its effects to those results obtained of EN2, since it controls the R I/O port. With EN7 set, the contents of the R register are output to the R I/O port. With EN7 reset the R I/O port is placed into a high impedance condition. The contents of the R register are thereby not affected.

Loading the EN register can take place at any time during program execution. There are no restrictions of any nature. However, one drawback of EN is that it is a write only register, except on the larger COP440 type devices where it can be accessed for reading. This makes independent code generation or segmentation difficult, as each program segment must take care of its own I/O configuration. A common way of overcoming this situation is to maintain a copy of the current EN register configuration in data memory for reference by other system routines.

5.4 THE COPS INSTRUCTION SET

5.4.1 Basic Characteristics

As mentioned in the section on architecture, the instruction set of a COPS microcontroller is not typical compared to a conventional microprocessor. The COPS programming language has been described as bizarre by those infatuated with more popular microprocessors, and by so-called 'microprocessor purists'. From this perspective the COPS instruction set is, indeed, bizarre. It is, however, this 'bizarre' nature that gives all COPS microcontroller devices their power, efficiency and versatility. The COPS instruction set is both cause and effect of the COPS architecture. The reason which led to the current COPS silicon implementation is the previously mentioned joint influence of an existing processor and calculator architecture, plus the experience gathered by the in-house system designers' group. Thus, the combination of COPS instruction set and architecture are intended to help achieve, in a specific application, a maximum function and capability with minimum memory.

Because of the small, but nevertheless very significant, difference in price between a half and a one kilobyte ROM device, the effective use of memory is the key in high-volume consumer applications. In addition many unrealised single-chip microcomputer programs or applications exist simply because the program was 1,025 or 1,026 bytes long, and did not fit into the fixed amount of memory on the targeted microcontroller.

As is evident from the previous section on the basic architectural elements and the COPS block diagram in Fig. 5.4, COPS micro-controllers do not have memory mapped input/output. The input and output facilities are separate and independent elements of the architecture and not linked to the memory. The data memory – RAM – has a dedicated address register independent of program memory or I/O section. Hence COPS instructions are generally relieved of the burden of having to carry some form of address along with them. Naturally, this tends to increase the program memory efficiency, since this results in shorter instruction object code.

It is also quite common for a COPS instruction to contain a multiplicity of functions, a fact which obviously creates program efficiency by performing, in a single instruction, a number of functions that would otherwise need several instructions. This 'feature' was initially one of the greatest problems with which the COPS programming novice was confronted. Users are generally accustomed to instructions, such as those on the Intel 8048, which do only one thing, for example, move a byte from RAM to the accumulator. During the initial phases of working with COPS, this seems to create a barrier to users who do not use the second order effects contained in COPS instructions. (But, once the user sees the tremendous effects of some instructions, and how these help to produce more efficient programs, he will start 'to miss' COPS instructions on other machines.)

The test instructions, like most COPS instructions, do not contain an address. The reason for this unconventional fact is that COPS devices cannot test-and-branch. COPS, in opposition to this standard microprocessor philosophy, use skips rather than test-and-branch to control the program flow. Therefore, a successful test causes the next instruction to be skipped and the second instruction after the test will be executed. It is, however, quite common for one or both of the instructions following the test to be jumps or subroutine calls. More importantly, this skipping characteristic allows the programmer to do a number of 'unusual' things. Tests without subsequent jumps are common as well. In this case, either the B register, or the accumulator A, or other parameters, can be altered in line, without jumping, by judicious use of the test instructions. Furthermore, the skip feature has also been built into a number of arithmetic functions as a secondary function, thereby eliminating the need to make separate tests. This again yields improvements in memory efficiency.

Although the basic COPS instruction set comprises only fifty-four instructions, not every instruction will be discussed in the following paragraph. Instead, a few characteristic instructions will be examined, taken from the various groups, which will demonstrate special effects common to COPS. For a detailed description of each individual instruction, the reader is referred to the individual datasheets, and Ref. 5.1 (see end of this chapter).

5.4.2 Instructions

5.4.2.1 ARITHMETIC AND LOGIC INSTRUCTIONS
The arithmetic and logic instructions affect the following registers:

* A – The 4-bit accumulator.
* C – The 1-bit carry register.
* RAM (B) – One digit out of the data memory addressed by the B register.

The operands for mathematical operations are the above three registers, In addition, the use of direct data contained in the instructions is possible. Operations allow 4-bit wide addition, complement, complement and add, set and reset, clear and the only logic function, exclusive-or. The absence of other logical functions, apart from XOR, is probably the most severe drawback in the COPS instruction set. The source operands for all instructions are the data memory, the accumulator, and the carry register. The only destination possible for a result of an arithmetic or logic function is the accumulator. Tests and resulting skips are triggered only by the state of the carry flag. Here a distinction between the actual carry register, the carry out of the ALU and the mere arithmetic overflow is necessary. For example, the instructions ASC and CASC use the C register in the addition and test for C = 1 to determine the skip:

$$\text{ASC} \qquad A + C + RAM\,(B) = A; \text{Carry} = C$$
$$\text{CASC} \qquad \bar{A} + C + RAM\,(B) = A; \text{Carry} = C$$

Whereas the instruction AISC Y adds the variable Y to the accumulator and skips on an arithmetic carry out from the addition. However, this does not alter the C register.

$$\text{AISC Y} \qquad A + Y = A$$

There are no subtract, multiply, rotate or shift instructions as these functions can be built using the available instructions. A left-bit-shift can easily be implemented by incorporating binary doubling approaches, by merely adding in a binary fashion.

```
; EXAMPLE:
;                     bitwise left-shift using binary addition.
LBSHIFT:   LD         ; load RAM (B) to A.
           ADD        ; A + RAM (B), this doubles A.
           X          ; put doubled/shifted digit back to RAM (B).
           RET        ; exit/return this program.
```

5.4.2.2 TRANSFER OF CONTROL INSTRUCTIONS
This group consists of seven instructions. Their purpose is to alter the otherwise linear flow of the program. The jumps do not perform any tests

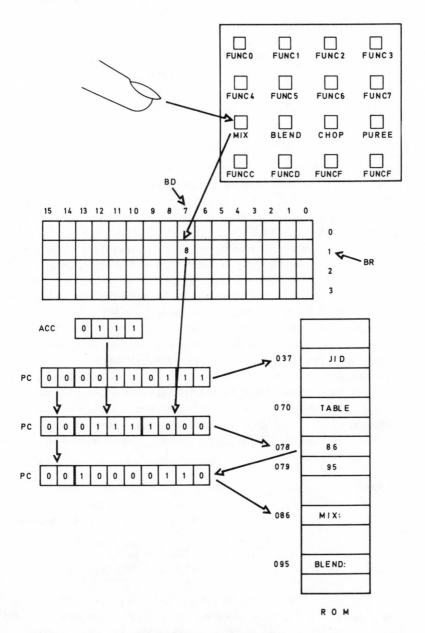

Fig. 5.12 Jump Indirect – JID.

on registers, as this is handled by either implied or explicit forms of test-and-skip instructions. Four variations of a jump exist: JP – the short jump within a 64-word range or the so called page jump; JMP – the long jump which contains the full destination address in its object code and covers the full program memory; JSRP – the jump to the dedicated subroutine area in pages two and three of memory; JSR – the global call of a subroutine any place in memory. The latter two jumps are comparable to other micros' call instructions. As the jumps to subroutines store the program counter on the stack, the return instructions – RET, RETSK – properly manage the stack when transferring program control back to the next higher level of program nesting.

In addition to these direct addressing instructions there is the instruction JID for indirect jumps. Figure 5.12 shows the data and address moves associated with an indirect jump. As shown, this function can be used to immediately translate the push of a button on the function keyboard to a jump to the related service routine. On the keyboard matrix the decoded key 'MIX' translates to the binary number '8' which is stored in data memory. The value in the accumulator serves as sort of bank select and controls the memory range for the following JID instruction. When the JID is executed the current program counter is discarded, the PC is loaded both with the values of the accumulator and with the currently addressed data memory digit. This forms an intermediate pointer to the program memory. The value found under this address in the program memory is then loaded into the program counter and the execution continues at this 'calculated' address.

Test Instructions – Closely related to the program control instructions are the test instructions. These instructions perform a test on a hardware register or on an input port. According to the result, the program counter is incremented by two to skip the next instruction if the test yields a true condition. Alternatively, the program counter is incremented by one to execute the next instruction.

```
; EXAMPLE
;                                    Test the G1 pin for low to
;                                    synchronise with an external event.
TEST:     SKGBZ    1            ; G1 = 0 ?
          JP       TEST         ; No, test again.
SYNC:     JSRP     ACT          ; Yes, call subroutine ACT.
```

The testable registers or inputs are: the carry register C, the timebase counter, the G input port as a whole or an individual pin on G, equality between accumulator, and the data memory and any bit in the current RAM digit.

As an example, the following BCD add routine illustrates the use of multi-function instructions:

```
; EXAMPLE
;                             BCD addition – 4 digits in register 0.
;                             add to register 3, result in register 0.
BCADD:    LBI    3,12         ; start, set RAM pointer to R3 digit £12.
LOOP:     LD     3            ; fetch data and point to RO.
          AISC   6            ; decimal adjust for carry if A = 9.
          ASC                 ; A + RAM (BR, BD) + C = A, add.
          ADT                 ; decimal adjust result.
          XIS    3            ; result to RO, increment BD, point to
                                R3.
          JP     LOOP         ; XIS will skip over this if BD past 15.
DONE:                         ; ready.
```

The second instruction LD first loads the accumulator with the one of the operands and then changes the BR part of the data memory pointer B, thereby pointing to the second operand and preparing everything for the following addition. The XIS instruction serves for storing the result in RAM. It checks if all four BCD digits have been added by incrementing BD and checking for 'end of register'. If this is the case then it skips and terminates the routine. Otherwise it points back to the register row where the first operand is found and continues the addition. The presence of 'boundary checks' and data pointer changes in the load-and-exchange instructions frees the programmer from the need to implement this function by separate code.

5.4.2.3 MEMORY AND REGISTER REFERENCE INSTRUCTIONS

In terms of size, the group of instructions dealing with transfers of data to and from registers and memory is the largest. Seventeen basic functions are available. The prime functions are those of copying and exchanging data. This can occur between data memory, hardware registers and direct data contained in either the instruction or the program memory. Setting or resetting of individual bits in data memory is also possible.

The unique instructions in this group for exchanges between accumulator and data memory are very interesting in regard to the single-chip goal of maximum instruction effectiveness versus length of program memory. The XIS (exchange increment and skip) and XDS (exchange decrement and skip) are typical of the multiple functionality found in some COPS instructions.

```
XIS    R    RAM(B) <—> A, BD + 1 => BD, BR xor R => BR
XDS    R    RAM (B) <—> A, BD – 1 => BD, BR xor R => BR
```

They not only exchange data, they also generate a skip when incrementing or decrementing BD 'off the end' on a RAM register. The

BD portion of the B register decrements from 15 to 0 and increments from 0 to 15. This becomes very useful in loop operations as the need for testing the completion of the loop is often eliminated. A third effect is caused by the R argument of these instructions. R is exclusively-ored with the second half of the B register, the BR part. Thus, a change in the currently selected data memory row or register can be facilitated.

The effectiveness of instructions such as LD, X, XDS and XIS, which affect BD or BR is even greater when they are used in conjunction with an optimised data memory layout. The careful allocation of RAM is essential in single-chip environments. Careful placement of data in RAM can have a large impact on the amount of program memory required. The use of a RAM map such as the one shown in Fig. 5.6 (a visualisation of the data placement in RAM) is an invaluable aid. This facilitates the use of instructions which terminate by 'falling off the end' of a register.

The first instruction, LBI 3,12, in the above example, has yet another useful 'special' effect. An LBI instruction, if placed in consecutive order with other LBIs, will produce a skip over of all following code until it encounters an instruction which is not an LBI. This greatly reduces code as it allows one to write multi-function or purpose subroutines by creating routines with several entry points.

```
; EXAMPLE
;                        use of LBI to create multiple entries.
RSH0:   LBI     0,15     ; shift register row 0.
RSH1:   LBI     1,15     ;       register row 1.
RSH2:   LBI     2,15     ;       register row 2.
RSH3:   LB      3,15     ;       register row 3.
        CLRA             ; clear accumulator.
LOOP:   XDS              ; shift digit, point to next, done?
        JP      LOOP     ; no, not passed BD = 15 yet.
        RET              ; yes, done, return.
```

Depending on the entry point, this routine will right shift the data memory register 0, 1, 2, or 3 one digit. The successive LBI skip feature is thus ideal for use in the programming problems above, in arithmetic routines where the same routine can be used several times regardless of the data location, in tests, and in not so obvious situations such as outputting a RAM value to a port. It may even be used to create a value rather than pointing to one.

One of the most powerful instructions is LQID. This COPS instruction performs a direct table look-up in one go. A 4-bit value contained in RAM is translated to an 8-bit value. Figure 5.13 shows the use of this instruction to realise a seven-segment LED display connected to the L output drivers. The value to be displayed, 2, is placed in RAM and,

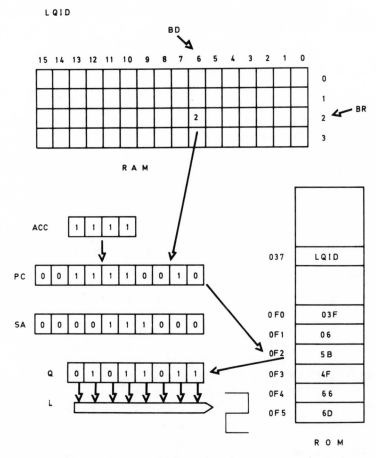

Fig. 5.13 Seven-segment display driving with LQID.

similar to JID, the accumulator serves as a pointer to the actual translation table. Upon execution of LQID, these two values are substituted in place of the program counter. The old PC is saved on the stack and the memory value found under the newly formed address is then loaded into the Q register. By enabling the L drivers, the decoded RAM value becomes visible on the LED display. In general, table look-ups using LQID provide an effective and fast way of translating values by passing unnecessary and bulky codings of algorithms. Here the applications range from simple BCD-to-seven-segment display transformations, calculating the firing angle controlling a triac, compensating torque on a motor controller, fast multiply (A x RAM (B) = Q), finding compensation values for thermocouples and other sensors, selecting the correct station number or intermediate frequency on a receiver, and determining the correct coding for data scramblers. In short, the possibilities for this instruction are endless.

5.4.2.4 INPUT AND OUTPUT INSTRUCTIONS

The last group of instructions deals with getting data in and out of the microcontroller. For every portion of the input/output system there is at least one instruction transferring data to or from the outside world. All instructions in this group are unidirectional, i.e. working from a hardware register such as BD towards an output such as the D-lines, with the exception of XAS, the instruction for simultaneous loading and reading the SI0 register. There are no special effects linked to the I/O instruction group. The following small program once again merely shows the use and effect of multiple entries into a program:

```
; EXAMPLE
;                          Multiple entry output routine.
ENTRY1:   LBI     0.15     ; point to digit (0,15) in RAM.
ENTRY2:   LD               ; load accu from RAM.
ENTRY3:   CAB              ; copy accu to BD register.
ENTRY4:   OBD              ; output BD to D port.
ENTRY5:   RET              ; return to mainprogram.
```

It is entirely conceivable, and good practice not only in COPS programming, that every instruction in this example be made an entry to the subroutine. Assume this code is placed in page 2 of program memory. A single byte JSRP call to ENTRY1 will output the value in RAM (0,15) to the D port. A JSRP to ENTRY2 will take the currently addressed digit to the D output. Calling on ENTRY3 outputs the accumulator to the D-lines. ENTRY4 just copies BD to D and ENTRY5 is, effectively, a NOP – no operation – which is useful as a delay in timing loops.

The general rule for every microcomputer, microprocessor and especially for COPS microcontroller programming: regardless of what the instruction set implies at first sight, as long as it serves the purpose, do it. There is, in many cases, only 512 bytes of program memory to do the job!

5.5 CASE STUDY – DIGITAL TV TUNING SYSTEM

The following section shows a practical application of a COP micro-controller in a TV tuning system. To fulfil the requirements of the application, two COP devices are working together in a master-slave configuration. Because of the rather large number of I/O lines needed for a TV tuning system, additional peripheral devices are used. Communication to those devices uses the MICROWIRE serial interfacing which is common to all CPUs and peripheral members of the COP family. The peripherals specifically required in this tuning system are:

MM5439   A digital phase-looked-loop circuit with serial control input. This device allows digital tuning by change of frequency bands, in addition analogue outputs are provided to adjust for volume, brightness, etc.

MM5450   LED driver chip.

COP494   Non-volatile memory (EEPROM), this device is used for storage of tuning and other system information.

The two COPS microcontrollers used are COP420s, each with one Kbyte of program and sixty-four digits (4-bits) of data memory, twenty I/O lines and a serial interface. The MICROWIRE interface allows the connection of a variety of peripherals such as A/D converters, timers and memory to tailor the system to the application requirements.

5.5.1 Hardware Configuration

To avoid relinquishing later changes to hard- and software, several initial precautions in respect to the final system configuration have to be considered. For a digital tuning system the following conditions obtain:

On one hand, general functions exist, such as: receiving control information from the remote control handset, reading the EEPROM or program memory, calculating the divider ratio sent to the PLL and scanning the keyboard; and on the other, features affecting performance, the human interface, and comfort of the overall system. Important in this respect is the way of entering information, actions activated by control commands and the display of information.

Taking these functions into consideration, an optimised task partitioning between master and slave is to be found. A possible solution to this partitioning is: the slave will act as 'intelligent peripheral controller' which takes care of all basic I/O functions, whereas the master will coordinate the overall system functions present, as well as future 'feature' additions to the system. Figure 5.14 illustrates the TV tuning system which consists of the slave processor controlling the PLL circuit, keyboard and the non-volatile memory chip. The master processor is driving the LED display device and the serial MICROWIRE bus. Similarly to the hardware, the software tasks are partitioned as well, thereby keeping redundant communication exchanges to a minimum.

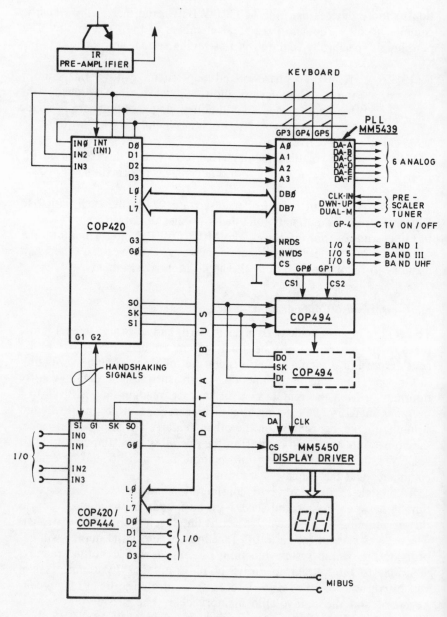

Fig. 5.14 Digital TV tuning system – block diagram.

5.5.2 Master/Slave Handshaking

Handshaking between master and slave happens with only two control lines, 'master ready' and 'slave ready'. The exchange of data is facilitated over the bi-directional data bus constructed by connecting the L ports of both COPS devices together. The protocol for data exchange is shown in Fig. 5.15. Any data transfer is always initiated by the master. It sets the 'master ready' line to high and places data in the common bus. This request is answered by the slave dropping the 'slave ready' line after reading the information. To ensure correct synchronisation between the two devices, the state of the 'slave ready' or 'master ready' line is tested by either device before any action on the bus takes place. The master releases the L bus after the slave dropped the ready line, thus the slave can use the bus for data transfers to the PLL or the master. When the slave is done with its tasks it pulls the 'slave ready' line high, to signal the master that it is done and ready to do another task. Using this communications protocol, data is transferred in both directions. To secure the data itself, additional precautions can be taken, such as:

● Inserting a parity bit to easily detect data errors.
● The slave decodes the command before it signals 'slave ready'. Meanwhile, the master starts a 'slave time out' routine and performs a system diagnosis and error logging if the test yields negative.
● The slave reacts always with 'slave ready' but in the returned data error information is contained.
● Dedicated master and slave protocol procedures.

By defining logic levels for the handshaking in the protocol procedure it is necessary to have the inactive level equal to the reset or idle condition on the I/O line used. Otherwise, it might happen that during

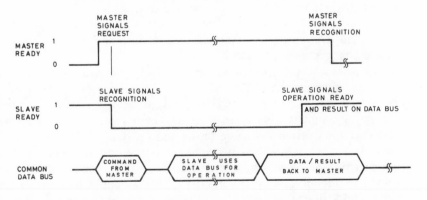

Fig. 5.15 Digital TV tuning system – handshaking protocol.

reset of the processors or during power-up, the handshaking starts with an error condition right away, or data is transferred but both devices are not interpreting the information the correct way.

5.5.3 Partition of Software Tasks

When dividing the software into individual actions or tasks, one can always follow a general rule which is applicable to all microcomputer algorithm problems. The software for the TV tuning system will be used for explaining this approach. Figure 5.16 shows a generalised schema of the program flow.

Each loop is entered after a validated input from either the keyboard or the remote control unit. If the entry is valid is must be decoded and acted upon, using for example, JID instructions. In executing these commands, the controller will write or read from the peripheral devices, data memory or its partner CPU.

The complete task should first be partitioned into small, independent units. For each of these units the necessary amount of program and data memory is evaluated. Additionally, the required data communication and receiving peripherals are determined. Thus, by gathering an overview on the complete system software needed, the individual tasks are assigned to either master or slave.

As a first step, software tasks dealing with the same peripheral controller or device are combined, coded and linked to master or slave. By performing all this partitioning and precoding, a picture of program and data memory usage is gained. In particular, a more sound basis for assessing the amount of program memory required is obtained and some insight into communication issues.

When partitioning tasks, the large amounts of code and the time which communication between devices generally takes should always be considered. By a trial and error exchanging of tasks between master and slave it is possible to try and optimise the organisation of program memory and RAM usage. But possible effects on communication created by these changes must be assessed.

Later, the software for master and slave can be written and tested completely independently. Test programs simulating the other micro-controller are short, and quick to produce. Integrating the master and the slave into a complete system becomes a rather simple task, as only the communication portion has to be tested and verified.

The above system has actually been built and is presently being used in the production of TV sets by a large European electronic manufacturing group. The principles of design and development applied here are useful in any COPS design and they are also valid for other microcomputer devices and applications.

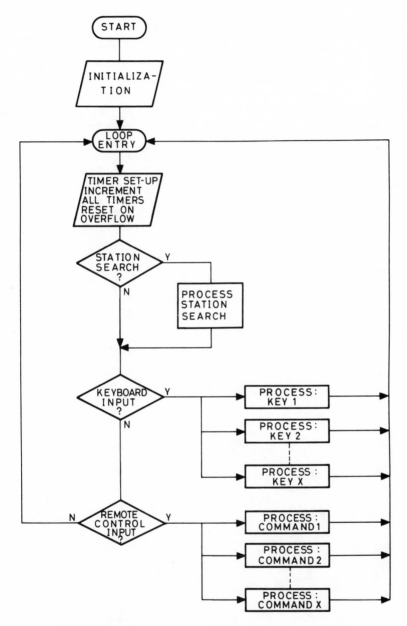

Fig. 5.16 Digitial TV tuning system – program organisation.

Summary

In this chapter many of the interesting and novel features of the COPS family are discussed. This family has developed from calculator chip origins and has been adapted to provide many useful features for low-cost systems. The case study gives an insight into how some of these features can be exploited in a real application emphasising the approach taken. This approach, of course, is widely applicable to other microcomputer design problems.

REFERENCES
5.1. COPS Microcontroller Handbook, National Semiconductor.

CHAPTER 6

The MK68200 – a 16-bit Microcomputer from Mostek

By Alan Gant, PhD, Patrick McGehearty, PhD, and
Denise Burrows, PhD

6.1 INTRODUCTION

The MK68200, a new single-chip microcomputer from Mostek, utilises the latest in MOS/VLSI semiconductor technology to provide high levels of function and performance. With this device, designers of high performance microcomputer systems can implement their entire system on a single silicon chip.

It has become apparent that such a high performance single-chip microcomputer architecture is needed in the industry, because of the nature of many cost sensitive applications which require the features inherent in the 68200's design. Such applications include control and instrumentation, especially robotics, engine controls, and intelligent peripheral controllers. These high technology applications require computational power above and beyond that provided by the 8-bit single-chip devices currently available.

Since many of these applications are I/O intensive, extensive bit manipulation capability must be provided along with fast accessing of I/O ports. The instruction set must be powerful, but must also be optimised in order to save code space to meet the constraints of on-chip ROM. Further, instruction execution time must be kept to a minimum so that high speed control loops may be coded with ample time available for numerical calculations. Rapid interrupt response as well as provisions for multiple interrupt sources must be incorporated for efficient processing of external signals. The MK68200 addresses these many requirements and provides the designer with the flexibility to develop control and instrumentation applications. The MK68200 is a complete computer with a high performance 16-bit processor, RAM, ROM, timers, interrupt control, parallel input/output, and serial USART – all on a single silicon chip. The block diagram in Fig. 6.1 illustrates the main features offered by the MK68200.

If these on-chip resources are not sufficient for some applications, a portion of the parallel interface may be replaced with a fully-functional external address and data bus. This bus has a very generalised interface, enabling the MK68200 to connect easily to the buses of many existing microprocessors as an intelligent DMA or peripheral controller. As a

207

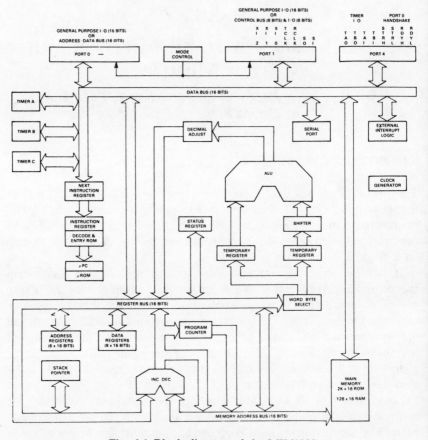

Fig. 6.1 Block diagram of the MK68200.

mask option, the control bus for the MK68200 can be made to interface directly to the MK68000.

With all of these features, the MK68200 provides a cost-effective solution as a stand-alone controller for industrial equipment, as an intelligent peripheral controller in multi-chip microprocessor systems, or as a high performance attached processor in multiprocessor systems. As with current single-chip microcomputers, the MK68200 is the first of a family of devices, each addressing a particular segment of the high-performance microcomputer market with a special complement of on-chip RAM, ROM, and I/O facilities.

Using the easy-to-program MK68000 architecture as a guide, the MK68200's instruction set was optimised for single-chip operations. The primary design goals included code space efficiency, high throughput, extensive I/O features, and flexibility of use. (Obviously, all features had to fit on a single chip.)

The MK68200's major features, then, include the powerful instruction set and extensive I/O capabilities, both of which have been optimised for a single-chip microcomputer. The decision to utilise a 16-bit microcomputer architecture for the 68200 came after much careful consideration, and reflects the attention paid to market demand. Whereas low end applications are served by such 8-bit machines as the MK3870, most high end applications like those mentioned above exceed the computational capacity of 8-bit single-chip devices. As with all single-chip microcomputers, the goal of minimising cost requires that the silicon area be fully optimised. The need for higher levels of performance in computational capacity dictated the development of a new architecture; hence the 16-bit machine was adopted. An advanced architecture, where the goal of optimal register usage is critical, should have the capability to treat data registers as either 8- or 16-bits wide. Furthermore, like the 68000 and other 16-bit machines, the MK68200 incorporates features such as regularity, multiple addressing modes, and a modern instruction set. However, while these other machines were intended primarily to support data processing applications, the MK68200 was optimised for control and I/O intensive operations.

6.2   REGISTERS AND MEMORY

The internal register set is composed of three main groups of 16-bit registers: eight data registers, six address registers, and three system registers. Each group of registers has unique properties. The data registers may each be referenced as either a word register or as two byte registers. The address registers may only be referenced as words, but they may be used either for data or as addresses into memory. The system registers are comprised of a program counter, a stack pointer for interrupts and subroutine calls, and a status register to hold condition codes and user status information. In addition, the stack pointer may be used anywhere the other address registers are valid, so accesses relative to the system stack pointer can be made. Fig. 6.2 shows the register set and memory map for the MK68200.

The arrangement of stack pointer, address registers, and data registers allows the user to allocate up to fourteen word registers for data purposes, or sixteen byte registers and six word registers for data purposes, or as few as eight for data with a maximum of six registers for addressing. Many of the addressing modes of the MK68200 utilise the address registers as stack pointers, which means that multiple user stacks can be created.

The memory space of the MK68200 can be expanded to a full 64 K bytes. The complement of on-chip memory consists of 4 K (4096) bytes of

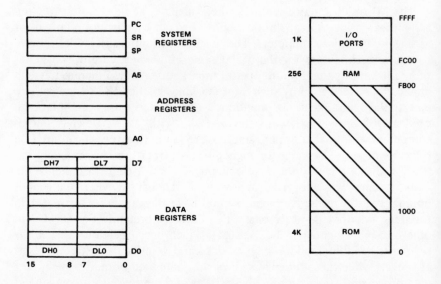

Fig. 6.2 Register set and memory map for the MK68200.

user-defined ROM and 256 bytes of RAM. Of course, these values will change for future members of the family.

6.3 I/O FEATURES

The I/O capabilities of the MK68200 are extensive and include three timers, a serial channel, an interrupt controller, and parallel I/O and external buses. Forty out of the forty-eight pins on the device are used for I/O and their functions are highly programmable by the user. The three 16-bit timers included in the MK68200 architecture provide the designer with a remarkable degree of power and flexibility in the organisation of real time control. The Serial I/O channel (SIO) is a powerful USART with full and half-duplex communication capability and a variety of operating modes. Word length, parity, and start and stop bits are fully programmable; moreover the MK68200's SIO has a full capability wake-up option with automatic address match, an option which allows the SIO – and therefore the MK68200 – to generate and be the origin of addressed messages. Such a feature ensures that a large number of MK68200's can share a single serial channel for applications such as distributed control. The interrupt controller of the MK68200 is so extensive that it allows for up to nine external and seven internal interrupt sources to be used (see Fig. 6.3).

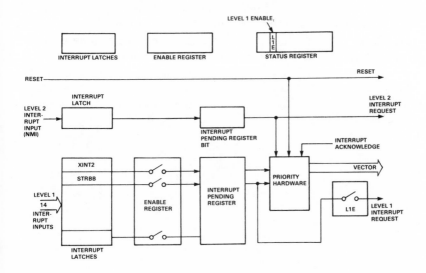

Fig. 6.3 Interrupt controller.

Among the external interrupt sources, Reset and Non-Maskable Interrupt (NMI) take priority over all other interrupts. The remaining interrupts, having a well-defined default priority order, can be reordered in any manner the system designer desires with a small software overhead. The parallel I/O port with handshaking control and external bus options ensure easy external bus interface and allow the MK68200 to act as either a bus master or as a bus slave. As a bus master, the chip serves as the central processing unit of a system, while as a bus slave, the MK68200 becomes a highly intelligent versatile DMA or peripheral controller.

6.3.1 Timers

The three timers on the 68200 provide wide flexibility in their use. They can be used as generators internal events or to measure the external world. Each timer has the ability to notify the processors via interrupts, a function which is highly programmable. Specifically, five of the interrupt vectors are dedicated to timer functions. Numerous combinations of timers and modes are available, and when one of the timers is not required in a particular application, the external pins associated with it are released for use as general purpose I/O or as interrupt sources.

All of the timers are capable of operating at the internal clock rate of the 68200, which initially is up to 6 MHz. Thus, the timers can resolve events to within about 167 microseconds. In addition, all timers employ full 16-bit counters. The use of 16-bit counters provides distinct advantages over 8-bit timers. No prescaler is needed to time moderately long events; even at 6 MHz, a 16-bit timer only overflows once every 11 milliseconds, and the resolution of the timer remains 167 microseconds. Moreover, prescaling can drastically reduce the resolution time for 8-bit timers. Another advantage of the long time to overflow is the reduction in processor overhead when very long intervals are desired.

Table 6.1 Timer modes.

Timer	Modes
A	Interval
A	Event
A	Pulse Width and Period Measurement
B	Interval
B	Retriggerable One-shot
B	Non-retriggerable One-shot
C	Interval
C	Baud Rate Generation

Each of the timers is capable of a different set of operating modes. The particular modes available with each timer are shown in Table 6.1. Timer A is the most powerful of the three. Associated with it are two separate latches and one counter. When Timer A is programmed for Interval mode, its counter will increment at the internal clock rate of the 68200. The counter value is initially compared continuously to the value stored in the Timer A High Latch. When the two values are equal, Timer A generates an interrupt to the processor, resets its counter, and immediately begins to increment again, this time comparing to the Timer A Low Latch. The comparison process continues to alternate between the High Latch and the Low Latch as long as Timer A is enabled. The use of two latches has several advantages. The timer may be used directly to alternate between two time intervals. If an application needs to time very short intervals which must be changed, then the program can be altering the value in the High Latch while the counter is utilising the Low Latch, and vice versa. This procedure can greatly increase the allowable delay when servicing a timer interrupt. Also, if desired, the Timer A Output pin (TAO) may be enabled in this mode, and it will generate a pulse train which tracks the operation of the timer. TAO will be high when the timer is being compared to the High Latch and low for the Low Latch. Thus, both the period and duty cycle of the pulse train are fully selectable. One potential use of such a pulse train is the generation of appropriate frequencies for the transmitter section of an FSK modem. A simple low-pass filter is all that must be added externally.

When Timer A is placed in Event mode, its internal counter counts edges on the Timer A Input pin. The user may select either the rising or falling edge as the active edge. As the counter increments on each active edge, it is compared to the value stored in the Timer B Latch. A match causes the counter to reset and start over and also generates an interrupt to the processor. Additionally, another independent interrupt may be generated by each active edge of the input pin.

The third mode for Timer A is Pulse/Period Mode. Rather than simply counting edges on the input pin, the actual times that the pin stays high and low are measured. When the timer is enabled in Pulse/Period Mode, the counter begins incrementing at the internal clock rate of the processor. When an edge occurs on the input pin, TAI, the current value of the counter is stored in one of the two latches, and the counter resets and resumes incrementing. If the edge which just occurred was a high-to-low transition, the input pin has just completed a time interval at a high level and the counter value is stored in the High Latch. Similarly, a low-to-high transition will cause the counter to be saved in the Low Latch. Thus, the last high and low intervals reside in the High and Low latches, respectively. With this information, the pulse width for either an active high or active low pulse may be ascertained, as well as the total period of the waveform. In order to provide this information to the processor at convenient times, interrupts from Timer A may be programmed to occur on every edge of the input or only on the rising or the falling edge. The measurement of the period of a signal can be used to implement the receiver section of an FSK modem, assuming the incoming sine wave is squared up with external circuitry.

Timer B can be operated in one of three modes. First, it can be used in an Interval mode similar to Timer A's. In this case, however, only one latch is available. Timer B's counter increments at the internal clock rate of the processor, continuously being compared to the Timer B Latch. In addition to the features available on Timer A's Interval Mode, Timer B will release its output pin, TBO, for use as a general I/O pin when it is not needed by the timer.

The other two modes of Timer B are unique and allow the timer to function as a one-shot generator. The one-shot may be programmed for either retriggerable or non-retriggerable operation. When the timer is inactive, an active edge on the Timer B input starts the counter. Further edges on the input are ignored in non-retriggerable mode, but they restart the counter in retriggerable mode. In either case, if the counter ever matches the Timer B Latch, an interrupt to the processor is generated. When operated in retriggerable one-shot mode, Timer B can serve as a watch-dog timer which alerts the processor if an edge does not occur on the Timer B input often enough.

Timer C is a relatively simple timer, although it retains the full 16-bit resolution of the other timers. Timer C runs freely as an interval timer, and can interrupt the processor on each completion of its time interval. Its most useful function is its ability to serve as a baud rate generator for the serial port (USART) of the MK68200.

6.3.2 Serial Port (USART)

The MK68200 includes a very powerful synchronous/asynchronous serial channel. This serial port has full duplex capability with double-buffered transmit and receive. Maximum operating rates exceed 250 Kbits/second in asynchronous mode, and 1 Mbits/second synchronous. Word length, start and stop bits, parity, and sync search are fully programmable. Either internal or external clocks may be selected, and separate rates may be used with external clocks. The registers associated with the serial port are depicted in Fig. 6.4. The Mode and Sync Registers are used to configure the port, while the transmit and receive Control and Status Registers deal with the independent functions of the two sections. The transmit and

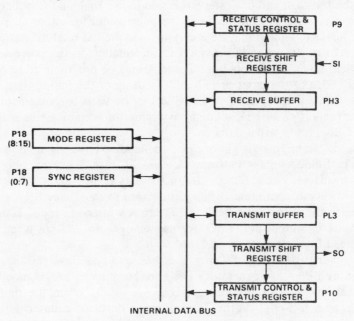

Fig. 6.4 Serial port registers.

receive Buffers provide fast program access to data for the serial port. The serial port directly supports virtually any known asynchronous character format, allowing from five to eight data bits and four types of parity: odd, even, fixed '1', and fixed '0'. For synchronous communication byte synchronous modes are supported. The serial port does not directly compute and check CRC or other error codes, because the user can use the MK68200 processor to customise these functions without paying the additional cost for special hardware on the chip.

The interrupt capability of the serial port is designed for rapid service. The transmitter section interrupts the processor whenever its data buffer becomes empty, allowing the processor an entire word transmission time to reload the buffer before underrun will occur. The receiver section employs two interrupts to simplify and speed up processing. A Receive Normal Interrupt occurs whenever a word is received and no errors have occurred. A separate Receive Special Condition Interrupt occurs whenever any of the following conditions happen: framing error, parity error, overrun, or sync/address match. With these two interrupts, the user can use a very short service routine for the Receive Normal Interrupt, which only needs to move the Receive Data Buffer to a memory buffer and return. Such a service routine requires only two one-word instructions on the MK68200. A more complicated service routine can be written to handle the cases for the Receive Special Condition Interrupt.

The serial port has a unique ability to communicate with other MK68200s sharing a single serial link. A Wake-up Bit can be appended to each word transmitted, to signal the difference between a conventional data word and a special-purpose address word. A word frame with wake-up is shown in Fig. 6.5. The receiver section can then be programmed into one of three wake-up modes: Wake-up on Any Character, Wake-up on Any Address, or Wake-up on Address Match. In all of these modes, the receiver assumes that a Wake-up Bit is included in the frame format. The three modes differ only in the conditions which must be met before the receiver acknowledges the receipt of a word.

For Wake-up on Any Character, each character received is loaded into the buffer, status is loaded, and an interrupt is generated to the processor. This mode may be used whenever all traffic on the serial link is to be monitored. Wake-up on Any Address causes the receiver to load only words whose Wake-up Bit signifies an address. Finally, Wake-up on Address Match ignores all received words except those whose Wake-up Bit signifies an address and whose data is exactly equal to the word stored in the Sync Register. In this way, a receiver will ignore all traffic except its own particular address. After it receives its address, it can change its mode to Wake-up on Any Character in order to capture the remainder of the message. The operation of the serial port with Wake-up will be detailed further later in this chapter.

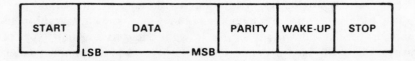

Fig. 6.5 Word frame with wake-up.

6.3.3 External Bus

For applications in which the on-chip RAM, ROM, or I/O resources are not sufficient, a portion of the external pins can be reconfigured into a complete External Bus with address, data, and control. The address and data information are multiplexed onto sixteen shared lines, while bus control signals occupy another eight pins. Depending on the application, two different control signal sets are available: the UPC (Universal Peripheral Controller) bus is ideal for connection into a system using a 68000 as its CPU, and the GP (General Purpose) bus is intended to be easily connected to several existing 16-bit microprocessor buses. The pinout of the MK68200 with External Bus is shown in Fig. 6.6. Note that even with the External Bus, the pins associated with the serial port, timers and external interrupts are retained.

The capabilities of the External Bus bear more similarity to the buses of 16-bit microprocessors than to the limited external referencing capabilities of current single-chip mirocomputers. The MK68200 can address up to 64 K bytes of external space, which may include any combination of ROM, RAM, or I/O devices. In addition, the External Bus can be shared among several bus masters by utilising the bus request and grant facilities provided on-chip. In the case of the UPC bus, the MK68200 functions as a bus slave and makes requests for the External Bus using the standard 68000 bus arbitration protocols. The capabilities of the UPC bus are extended by the GP bus, which allows the user to configure the MK68200 as either a bus slave or as the bus master. The pins labelled BUSIN and BUSOUT are defined as either request or grant when the chip is reset. Also, the GP bus has the added ability to accept 256 external interrupt vectors.

Automatic Bus Arbitration makes the MK68200 especially attractive in systems with multiple processors or multiple bus masters. Since a microcomputer has internal resources of ROM, RAM, and I/O, it may only need to access the External Bus rarely. During these internal accesses, the MK68200 does not affect the External Bus. However, when a reference occurs which exists externally, the bus controller automatically requests the External Bus and causes the processor to wait until the bus has been granted. If the very next bus cycle is not an external reference, the controller relinquishes the bus immediately. In this way,

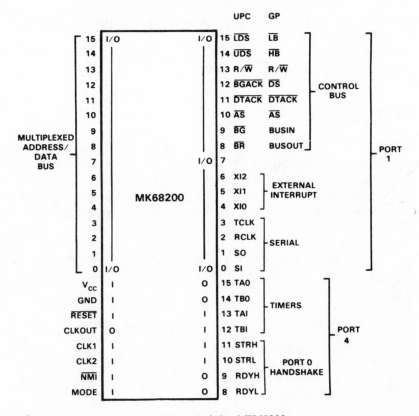

Fig. 6.6 Pinout of the MK68200.

External Bus cycles are only used when the MK68200 is actually transferring data for the outside world. When successive bus cycles refer to the External Bus, the bus controller will continuously hold the bus once it is acquired. Thus, the programmer has the ability to determine in what fashion the MK68200 will access the External Bus: cycle stealing, burst mode transfers, or block mode transfers.

An application area in which most of the features of the External Bus are used is intelligent peripheral controllers. The MK68200 can interface with a wide variety of peripherals owing to its extensive I/O capabilities. With the addition of the External Bus, it also has the ability to perform Direct Memory Access (DMA) operations directly into system memory. Also, the added facility of Automatic Bus Arbitration guarantees that the MK68200 will use as few system bus cycles as is necessary to perform its data transfers. The internal resources coupled with the high performance of the processor allow the user to place a large portion of the peripheral control software into the controller itself. One potential application of such a peripheral controller is for Local Area Networks, such as

Ethernet. The GP bus is directly compatible with the bus used by the
MK68590 LANCE, or Local Area Network Controller for Ethernet,
which is currently in design at Mostek. Planned to be completed in
October, 1983, and 'on sale' in April, 1984.

6.4 INSTRUCTION SET

The MK68200 has fifty-six generalised instructions that handle both 8-bit
and 16-bit data, combining the space advantages of 8-bit architectures
with the speed advantages of 16-bit architectures. These instructions
utilise nine addressing modes to ease the programmer's task and reduce
the number of instructions required to implement a specific function. See
Table 6.2.

Table 6.2 Addressing modes of the MK68200.

NAME	EXAMPLE
REGISTER DIRECT	MOVE DO, D1
REGISTER INDIRECT	MOVE (A3), DO
REGISTER INDIRECT WITH POST-INCREMENT	MOVE.B DLO, (AO)+
REGISTER INDIRECT WITH PRE-DECREMENT	MOVE D2,−(AO)
REGISTER INDIRECT WITH DISPLACEMENT	MOVE DO,246(AO)
MEMORY ABSOLUTE	MOVE $FBOO, DO
IMMEDIATE	MOVE #4,DO
PROGRAM COUNTER RELATIVE	JMPR NEXTCODE
INPUT/OUTPUT PORT	MOVE PO,DO

The register indirect addressing modes support re-entrant procedures
and interrupt routines. Re-entrant procedures are very helpful in
implementing well structured programs. The pre-decrement and post-
increment modes simplify and speed the saving and restoring of registers
on interrupt entry and return. The register indirect with displacement
addressing mode supports stack relative parameter access and table look-
ups. A special I/O port addressing mode optimises the interface to the
I/O devices both on- and off-chip by allowing single word instructions to
access the I/O ports.

The fifty-six instructions are summarised in Table 6.3. All add,
subtract, and negate instructions support byte (8-bit) and word (16-bit)
modes of operation. Further, either binary or decimal (packed BCD)
arithmetic may be used in either byte or word mode. Short instructions
are available for arithmetic with small constants, such as loop counters, to
save code space and increase execution speed. Fast 16-bit multiply and

Table 6.3 MK68200 instruction summary.

Inst.	Description	Inst.	Description
ADD	Add	HALT	Halt
ADD.B	Add Byte	JMPA	Jump Absolute
ADDC	Add with Carry	JMPR	Jump Relative
ADDC.B	Add with Carry Byte	LIBA	Load Indexed Byte Address
AND	Logical And	LIWA	Load Indexed Word Address
AND.B	Logical And Byte	LSR	Logical Shift Right
ASL	Arithmetic Shift Left	LSR.B	Logical Shift Right Byte
ASL.B	Arithmetic Shift Left Byte	MOVE	Move
ASR	Arithmetic Shift Right	MOVE.B	Move Byte
ASR.B	Arithmetic Shift Right Byte	MOVEM	Move Multiple Registers
BCHG	Bit Change	MOVEM.B	Move Multiple Registers
BCLR	Bit Clear		Byte
BEXG	Bit Exchange	MULS	Multiply Signed
BSET	Bit Set	MULU	Multiply Unsigned
BTST	Bit Test	NEG	Negate
CALLA	Call Absolute	NEG.B	Negate Byte
CALLR	Call Relative	NEGC	Negate with Carry
CLR	Clear	NEGC.B	Negate with Carry Byte
CLR.B	Clear Byte	NOP	No Operation
CMP	Compare	NOT	One's Complement
CMP.B	Compare Byte	NOT.B	One's Complement Byte
DADD	Decimal Add	OR	Logical Or
DADD.B	Decimal Add Byte	OR.B	Logical Or Byte
DADDC	Decimal Add with Carry	POP	Pop
DADDC.B	Decimal Add with Carry	POPM	Pop Multiple Registers
	Byte	PUSH	Push
DI	Disable Interrupts	PUSHM	Push Multiple Registers
DIVU	Divide Unsigned	RET	Return from Subroutine
DJNZ	Decrement Count and Jump	RETI	Return from Interrupt
	if Non-zero	ROL	Rotate Left
DJNZ.B	Decrement Count Byte and	ROL.B	Rotate Left Byte
	Jump if Non-zero	ROLC	Rotate Left Through Carry
DNEG	Decimal Negate	ROLC.B	Rotate Left Through Carry
DNEG.B	Decimal Negate Byte		Byte
DNEGC	Decimal Negate with Carry	ROR	Rotate Right
DNEGC.B	Decimal Negate with Carry	ROR.B	Rotate Right Byte
	Byte	RORC	Rotate Right through Carry
DSUB	Decimal Subtract	RORC.B	Rotate Right through Carry
DSUB.B	Decimal Subtract Byte		Byte
DSUBC	Decimal Subtract with Carry	SUB	Subtract
DSUBC.B	Decimal Subtract with Carry	SUB.B	Subtract Byte
	Byte	SUBC	Subtract with Carry
EI	Enable Interrupts	SUBC.B	Subtract with Carry Byte
EOR	Exclusive Or	TEST	Test
EOR.B	Exclusive Or Byte	TEST.B	Test Byte
EXG	Exchange	TESTN	Test Not
EXG.B	Exchange Byte	TESTN.B	Test Not Byte
EXT	Extend Sign		

divide instructions support those applications which require rapid numerical calculations. Sample instruction execution times are shown in

Table 6.4 as well as execution times for several 16-bit microprocessors.

For applications which perform a large number of operations on bits, several powerful bit manipulation instructions are provided. These instructions include test, set, clear, change, and exchange functions. Similar to the 68000, each bit operation tests the destination bit before it performs the stated function. The 68000 bit operations are extended by the MK68200 to include a bit exchange operation. This feature aids in the manipulation and construction of arbitrary bit patterns. An important function of the bit operations is the efficient control of I/O lines. In addition, the carry bit is used as the destination for the bit operations to allow fast serial-to-parallel and parallel-to-serial conversions. A serial-to-parallel conversion can be made by a series of bit tests on the serial source of data, alternated with a series of rotates with carry on the parallel destination. In this way, a conversion can be made at a cost of two instructions per bit to be converted. Also, the use of the carry bit allows the result to be used in add with carry operations.

All values in the following table are internal clock cycle counts. For most microprocessors, different clock rates are available at different prices. To calculate execution time, divide the clock cycle count by the clock rate for the processor.

Table 6.4 Performance comparison.

Instruction	MK68200	68000	Z8000	8086
Add #1 to Register	3	4	4	2
Add Register to Register	3	4	4	3
Add Indirect to Register	6	8	7	14
16 × 16 Multiply	21	70*	70*	124
Typical clock rate	6MHz	8MHz	6MHz	8MHz

*Indicates maximum value

Since a large percentage of most programs are 'assignment' type instructions, the MK68200 provides a flexible complement of move instructions. The simple move instruction is available with every addressing mode. As the most common immediate value for move instructions is a zero, the Clear instruction is provided for the most common addressing modes. In addition, an exchange instruction is provided to speed exchange of blocks of data. The bit exchange instruction allows move instructions to operate on bits, bytes and words. Further, a move multiple instruction is provided to allow several registers to be saved or restored with a single instruction. This instruction reduces procedure call and interrupt entry and return overhead. A byte version is also available to allow quick transfer of blocks of byte data.

The MK68200 supports an extensive complement of logical and shift instructions. The logical instructions include And, Or, Exclusive Or and Not instructions on both byte and word data. Arithmetic and logical shifts are provided as well as rotates, all with or without the carry bit. All shifts may be for either byte or word data. Single bit and multiple bit shifts are available.

A powerful set of compare and program control instructions is provided. In addition to the normal compare instruction, a test of a masked portion of a word or a byte is possible. The Jump and Call instructions may be absolute or Program Counter relative. They may also be conditional for any condition code, and the same set of condition codes that the 68000 provides is available on the MK68000. (See Table 6.5). A short form of relative Jumps and Calls is available to reduce code space and speed execution. A loop instruction, DJNZ, Decrement and Jump if Non-Zero, is also provided to speed execution of inner loop code.

Several miscellaneous instructions round out the MK68200 instruction set. These include Halt, Address calculation, Sign Extension, Interrupt

Table 6.5 Condition codes.

CONDITION CODE TABLE

Condition	Condition Code	Status Register Flag
zero	Z	Z
minus	MI	N
carry set	CS	C
overflow set	VS	V
equal	EQ	Z
less than	LT	N.XOR.V
less than or equal	LE	Z.OR.(N.XOR.V)
lower	LO	C
lower or same	LS	C.OR.Z
not zero	NZ	$\overline{Z}$
plus	PL	$\overline{N}$
carry clear	CC	$\overline{C}$
overflow clear	VC	$\overline{V}$
not equal	NE	$\overline{Z}$
greater than	GT	$\overline{Z}.AND.(\overline{N.XOR.V})$
greater than or equal	GE	$\overline{N.XOR.V}$
higher	HI	$\overline{C}.AND.\overline{Z}$
higher or same	HS	$\overline{C}$

Control and Null Operation instructions. This total instruction set gives the programmer great flexibility and ease of use.

Since the MK68200 is a pipelined processor with instruction look-ahead and a high performance ALU, its performance is comparable to the leading 16-bit microprocessors. (See Table 6.3).

The Condition Codes Table (Table 6.5) shows the relationship between condition codes and the corresponding Status Register flags utilised to derive the condition.

The following examples have been written to emphasise the ease with which the MK68200 may be programmed. The first example, Fig. 6.7, demonstrates the use of the MK68200 code for a simple multiplication of two 32-bit signed numbers. A more comprehensive program to perform floating point multiplication for a 32-bit number is shown in Fig. 6.8. It should be noted that both examples will also perform multiplication on unsigned numbers by simply replacing MULS by MULU.

Both examples demonstrate some of the added features found only in the MK68200, in particular the bit exchange command (BEXG).

Clock periods	Instructions		Comments
			;D0,D1 contain first 32-bit operand
			;D2,D3 contain second 32-bit operand
			;D0,D1,D2,D3 will contain 64-bit result
			;D4,D5,D6,D7 used as temporaries
3	MOVE	D0,D4	;Copy operands
3	MOVE	D1,D6	;to temporary destinations
21	MULS	D3,D4	;D4,D5 contain result
21	MULS	D3,D6	;D6,D7 contain result
3	MOVE	D1,D3	;Copy operand to prevent destruction
21	MULS	D2,D0	;D0,D1 contain result
21	MULS	D3,D2	;D2,D3 contain result
3	ADD	D3,D6	;Combine intermediate results
3	ADDC	D2,D1	;
3	ADDC	#0,D0	;include high bit carry
3	MOVE	D6,D2	;Prepare low 32 bits
3	MOVE	D7,D3	;
3	ADD	D5,D2	;Add intermediate result
3	ADDC	D4,D1	;
3	ADDC	#0,D0	;including high bit carry
			;Operation complete

117 clock period = 19.5 microseconds

Fig. 6.7 MK68200 code for 32 × 32 multiply with 64-bit result.

Fig. 6.8 MK68200 code for 32-bit floating point multiply.

Clock periods	Instructions		Comments
			;D0,D1 contain first Floating Point operand
			;D2,D3 contain second Floating Point operand
			;D0,D1 to contain Floating Point result
			;D4,D6,D7,A0,A1, SR bit #5 used as
			temporaries
			;Representation is IEEE standard
			;Bit 31 = sign bit
			;Bit 30-23 = Exponent in excess 128 notation
			;Bit 22-0 = Fraction (includes hidden bit at
			bit 23)
	FMUL:		;Entry Point
	; Check for zero operands		
3	SUB	#0,D0	;Test high word of first operand for zero
4 or 7	JMPR	Z,FMZ1	;If yes, check low word
	FMZ3:		
3	SUB	#0,D2	;Test high word of second operand for zero
4 or 7	JMPR	Z,FMZ2	;If yes, check low word
	FMZ4:		
	; Check operands for sign, store sign of result in bit #5 of SR		
	; Obtain exponent of result		
	; Compute result		
	; Split up first operand		
3	ROL	DO	;Move first exponent to byte boundary
			;Move sign to C-bit
3	BEXG	#5,SR	;Move sign of first operand to temporary
			;for sign of result
3	MOVE	DH0,DL4	;Move exponent part to exponent location
3	CLR	DH4	;Clear high byte
3	MOVE.B	#1,DH0	;Put hidden bit in fraction part
3	ASR	D0	;Restore fraction to byte boundary
	; Split up second operand		
3	ROL	D2	;Move second exponent to byte boundary
			;Move sign to C-bit
4 or 7	JMPR	CC,FMPOS	;No change to result sign if second
			;operand is positive
3	BCHG	#5,SR	;Otherwise, change sign of result
	FMPOS:		
3	ADD	DH2,DL4	;Compute new result exponent
3	ADDC.B	#0,DH4	;Place carry (if any) in high byte
6	SUB	#$80,D4	;Adjust exponent for excess 128 representation
3	MOVE.B	#1,DH2	;Put hidden bit in fraction of second operand
3	ASR	D2	;Restore fraction to byte boundary
	;At this point:		
	; SR,#5 = Sign of result		
	; D4 = Exponent of result (plus normalisation)		
	; DL0,D1 = First operand fraction		

Clock periods	Instructions		Comments
	; DL2,D3	= Second operand fraction	
	;Multiply fractions		
3	MOVE	D1,A0	;Copy low part of first operand
21	MULS	D2,A0	;Multiply high part of second operand
			;with low part of first operand
			;24 bit result placed in A0,A1
3	MOVE	D3,D6	;Copy low part of second operand
21	MULS	D0,D6	;Multiply high part of first operand
			;with low part of second operand
			;24 bit result placed in D6,D7
3	ADD	D7,A1	;Add products
3	ADDC	D6,A0	;25 bit result in A0,A1
3	MOVE	D3,D6	;Copy low part of second operand
21	MULS	D1,DS6	;Muliply low part of second operand
			;with low part of first operand
			;32 bit result in D6,D7
21	MULS	D2,D0	;Multiply high part of second operand
			;with high part of first operand
			;16 bit result in D1, zero in D0
3	ADD	A1,D6	;Combine results
3	ADDC	A0,D1	;Final 48 bit answer in D1,D6,D7
			;Low 16 bits in D7 are discarded
3	BTST	#15,D1	;Check for possible normalisation
4 or 7	JMPR	CS,FMNO	;If high bit is set, no normalisation needed
3	ASL	D6	;Shift low 16 bits
3	ROLC	D1	;Shift high 16 bits.
3	SUB	#1,D4	;Adjust exponent
	FMNO:		
3	MOVE.B	DH1,DL0	;Put result
3	MOVE.B	DL1,DH1	; in final
3	MOVE.B	DH6,DL1	; position
3	SUB	#0,DH4	;Check for over or underflow on exponent
4 or 7	JMPR	NZ,FMBOUNDS	;if so, jump to error handler
	;Place sign and exponent in result		
3	ASL	D0	;Match byte boundaries for exponent
3	MOVE.B	DL4,DH0	;Store exponent
3	BTST	#5,SR	;Place sign in C-bit
3	RORC	D0	;Reverse previous shift, place sign in high bit
	FMEND:		
	;;End of floating point multiply		
	;;The following code is out of the main flow of code		
	FMBOUNDS:		
6	MOVE	#ERRORCODE,D6	;Set error code
9	CALLA	FLOATERROR	;Call the floating point error handler
7	JMPR	FMEND	;Leave routine
	;continue check for zero values		
	FMZ1:		
3	SUB	#0,D1	;Check low word of first operand for zero
4 or 7	JMPR	NZ,FMZ3	;If not, return to mainline code
7	JMPR	FMEXIT	;If so, result is zero

Clock periods	Instructions		Comments
	FMZ2:		
3	SUB	#0,D3	;Check low word of second operand for zero
4 or 7	JMPR	NZ,FMZ4	;If not, return to mainline code
3	CLR	D0	;If so, set result
3	CLR	D1	;to zero
7	JMPR	FMEXIT	;Leave multiply routine

203 clock periods for typical Floating Point Multiply
  = 33.83 microseconds

6.5 CASE STUDY – DISTRIBUTED CONTROL

Distributed control is becoming a major application area with the ever-decreasing cost of both processing power and communications. Serial networking using single-chip microcomputers is becoming an increasingly popular design approach for implementation of such distributed control systems. Applications such as robotics, factory automation, engine control, and energy management are representative of such systems.

One application area which merits closer attention is robotics. Consider, for instance, a robot arm with six independent joints. In the past, a fairly powerful minicomputer would have been required to perform the control of the arm. Feedback of each joint's position (and perhaps even velocity) would have been provided to the minicomputer as inputs, which would then have computed the actual trajectory of the arm and compared it with the desired value. Next, the appropriate drive signals would be calculated and sent to each joint. This problem of robotic control can be solved using several MK68200's which communicate over a single shared serial link in place of a single high performance minicomputer.

A single MK68200 could be assigned the control of each joint, and another MK68200 could be used as the central co-ordinating controller. A block diagram of such a system is shown in Fig. 6.9. Because of the processor's high performance, complex control algorithms for each joint's motion can be computed in real time by that joint's local processor. The communication along the serial link consists only of high-level commands to the joints and status information from the joints. The central controller is free to spend its time plotting trajectories or interfacing with a human operator.

In order for each processor to be able to spend as much time as possible on its specific task, the link traffic intended for other processors

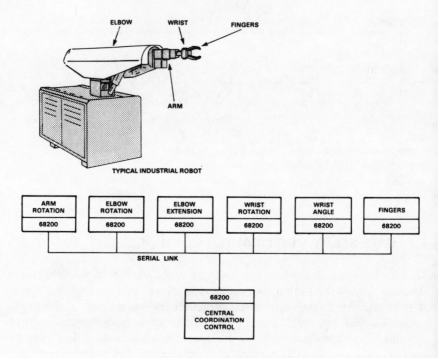

Fig. 6.9 Serial network robot arm controller.

needs to be ignored. The Wake-up feature of the MK68200 is uniquely suited for this task. Each processor is assigned an address on the link, and all messages are prefixed with a one-character address. If each of the receivers is programmed in Wake-up on Address Match mode and each processor's Sync Register is loaded with its unique address, then each will ignore all traffic on the link except when its own address is received. Since addresses are differentiated from normal data by the Wake-up Bit appended to each character, no data values need be reserved for addressing purposes in the protocol. This ability allows the transmission of binary data instead of other less efficient encodings such as ASCII hexadecimal data.

The transmission of a single command message along the link could operate as follows. The central controller determines and builds the message in its internal RAM. Before transmitting the actual data of the message, the controller first sends the address of the destination joint's processor. The transmission of addresses is accomplished with a two instruction sequence. First, a special control bit is set in the serial transmitter's control register stating that the next character to be sent is an address. This bit is automatically reset as the address is sent, and no action is necessary to transmit data characters. Second, the address of the destination processor is loaded into the transmit buffer. Now the central controller can wait for an interrupt signalling that the transmit buffer is empty and can then send the successive data characters in the message.

In this example, the receiver section of each possible destination processor will be in Wake-up on Address Match mode. As the destination address is received in each serial port, only the joint processor whose Sync Register matched the word transmitted by the central controller with a Wake-up Bit signifying address, will interrupt its processor. That processor can then proceed to change its mode to Wake-up on Any Character. It can then wait for an interrupt for each new data character as it is received. When the message is complete, the joint processor can return its receiver mode to Wake-up on Address Match, and it will not be interrupted until the next message is sent with its address. If the command which was received required that information be returned to the central controller, the joint processor can follow the same procedure detailed above by sending the unique address of the central controller.

This example can be extended to include a complete automated factory assembly line. For each machine on the line, a system similar to that detailed above could be constructed. In order to co-ordinate all of the

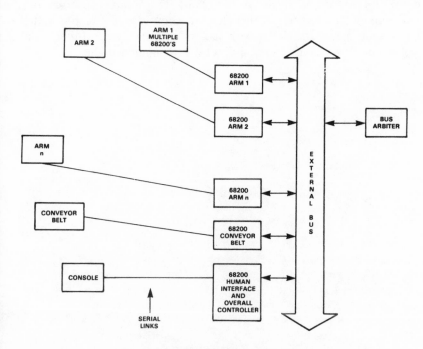

Fig. 6.10 Assembly line controller.

machines, the central controllers of the machines must be interconnected. A straightforward, high performance interconnection can be obtained by placing all of the central controllers on a shared External Bus. This total assembly line system is pictured in Fig. 6.10. The machines to be controlled – such as robot arms and conveyor belts – are connected to their central controllers via low-cost serial links which can be quite long. The collection of central controllers which share a single External Bus can be implemented on a single printed-circuit board. In addition to the 68200 controllers, only a simple bus arbitration circuit and line drivers for the serial links are needed. If a more elaborate central system is desired, a general purpose microprocessor such as the 68000 can be substituted as the overall controller.

This brief discussion of a factory automation application illustrates the MK68200's capabilities for distributed control.

Summary

Mostek's 16-bit single-chip microcomputer, the MK68200, offers the designer the versatility, function, and performance levels usually associated with 16-bit microprocessors. By using the MK68200, designers of high performance microcomputer systems can now implement their entire system on a single silicon chip. The unique features of the microcomputer, detailed in this chapter, show how the chip is suited to application areas associated with factory automation, real-time control, intelligent DMA controllers, and network communications.

Index